More praise fo

"*Cascade Summer* puts you on the trail. Welch's humility is striking and his tales entice you. It's a rich journey into Oregon's past and the sublime of the Cascades. A must read for anyone who loves Oregon."

—*James Meacham,*
Co-editor, The Atlas of Oregon *and* The Atlas of Yellowstone

"Combines a brisk and readable style with well-researched looks into Oregon's history, especially through the lens of Judge John Waldo's journals. *Cascade Summer* is a welcome addition to the library of anyone who has hiked the PCT, intends to do so, or simply shares a love of wild places."

—*Jay Bowerman,*
Principal researcher, Sunriver Nature Center

"*Cascade Summer* confirms Welch's place among Oregon's finest storytellers. No other author twines his love for the state with such a unique blend of humor, history, passion, and profundity. This is no travelogue of a trail, but a human adventure that brings into play unexpected challenges, unexpected heroes, and an unexpected ending. A gold-star read."

— *Dean Rea,*
UO School of Journalism & Communication Hall of Achievement inductee

"Welch tells a great story of planning and then making an epic adventure reality, reconnecting with the pleasures of one's youth, and exploring the history of his beloved home state of Oregon through relating Waldo's nineteenth century travels and efforts to preserve the Cascades. Welch captures perfectly the spirit of the trail: its beauty, the interesting characters one encounters along the way, the fears and disappointments, and especially the excitement and joy."

—*Laura Buhl,*
Solo finisher of the 2,650-mile Pacific Crest Trail, 1999

"In *Cascade Summer*, Bob Welch masterfully captures the PCT I remember from my hiking and mountain climbing days. A marvelous story for outdoor novices, enthusiasts and aficionados!"

—*Lewis L. McArthur,*
Editor, Oregon Geographic Names

"I loved *Cascade Summer*. Couldn't put it down. Welch sets out on a bold adventure and, in so doing, inspires others to do likewise."

—David Imus,
Creator of national award-winning maps of Oregon and the United States

"A beautiful story. Part Oregon environmental history, part trail narrative, and part can't-put-down inspirational—*Cascade Summer* reminds us that life is about unknowns and we all have our own trail that runs through it."

— Eric Blehm,
Author of Fearless *and* The Last Season,
one of Outside *magazine's Top 10 great adventure biographies*

Also by Bob Welch

The Wizard of Foz: Dick Fosbury's One-Man High-Jump Revolution
Lessons on the Way to Heaven (with Michael Fechner Jr.)
The Keyboard Kitten Gets Oregonized (with artist Tom Penix)
The Keyboard Kitten (with artist Tom Penix)
Resolve: The Epic Story of a Soldier, a Flag, and a Promise Kept
52 Little Lessons from A Christmas Carol
52 Little Lessons from Les Miserable
52 Little Lessons from It's a Wonderful Life
My Oregon III
My Oregon II
My Oregon
Easy Company Soldier (with Don Malarkey)
Pebble in the Water
My Seasons
American Nightingale
The Things That Matter Most
Stories from the Game of Life
Where Roots Grow Deep
A Father for All Seasons
More to Life Than Having It All

Cascade Summer

My Adventure on Oregon's Pacific Crest Trail

Bob Welch

Copyright © 2012 by Bob Welch

P.O. Box 70785
Springfield, OR 97475

All rights reserved.

No part of this book may be reproduced in any form without written permission from the author, except by a reviewer who may quote brief passages.

Author information:

www.bobwelch.net
bobwelch23@gmail.com

Cover photo of Bob Welch by Glenn Petersen.
Taken on the PCT from near Three Fingered Jack, looking southwest with Mount Washington rising above the clouds.

Back photo of Bob Welch by Glenn Petersen.
Taken on the PCT at the Brown Shelter junction in Southern Oregon.

Front and back cover designs, and interior maps, by Tom Penix.
tompenix@gmail.com

Waldo photo opposite page from the Salem Public Library Collections, Ben Maxwell Collection 1285.

*In memory of Judge John Breckenridge Waldo,
whose love and protection
of the Cascade Range
remind us that we matter
to those who follow us on the trail.*

Contents

Prologue   9

PART 1   The lure of the trail
Chapter 1   Seeds   13
Chapter 2   The decision   19
Chapter 3   Thinking small (and light)   27
Chapter 4   The waterfall   33

Part II   Breaking trail
Chapter 5   First steps   43
Chapter 6   Left behind   50
Chapter 7   In Waldo's footsteps   58
Chapter 8   From whimsy to worry   66
Chapter 9   Calm before the storm   72
Chapter 10   Going to meet the devil   77

Part III   The disappearing trail
Chapter 11   Enlightenment   87
Chapter 12   Adoption   99
Chapter 13   'Mt. Sielsen'   107
Chapter 14   Reunion   114
Chapter 15   Waldo's vision   130
Chapter 16   Farewell to friends   137

Part IV	**Back on the trail**	
Chapter 17	The return	147
Chapter 18	Above the clouds	157
Chapter 19	Waldo's triumph	171
Chapter 20	The perfect day	183

Part V	**The foreboding trail**	
Chapter 21	Dreams deferred	197
Chapter 22	The dilemma	208
Chapter 23	'Evacuate'	215
Chapter 24	The one-handed clap	221

Epilogue	230
Author's note	234
Afterword (Glenn Petersen)	236
Appendix	
1. Waldo's 26 summers in the Cascades	238
2. My Oregon PCT, day by day	240
3. What I took with me	241
4. By the numbers	242
5. The best, worst, least, and most	243
6. *The Register-Guard's* "Base Camp" Web site URL	243
Bibliography	244
Acknowledgments	246
Book club guide	249
Welch's books, speaking, and writers workshop info	252

Memorial Weekend 1974: Left to right, Glenn Petersen, Ann Youngberg, Sally Youngberg, and Bob Welch before backpacking up Eagle Creek on the Columbia Gorge.

In the woods, too, a man casts off his years, as the snake his slough, and at what period soever of life, is always a child. In the woods, is perpetual youth.

— Ralph Waldo Emerson,
quoted by Judge John Waldo in a journal entry
from Mount Jefferson, August 20, 1905

Prologue

IT WAS THE sixth day since my brother-in-law and I had left the Oregon-California border in an attempt to hike the 452-mile Oregon portion of the Pacific Crest Trail. We had already put in nineteen miles and had four uphill miles to Freye Lake. We had just taken a break beside Cascade Canal near Highway 140, which twisted through the southern Cascades between Medford and Klamath Falls. And I was dying.

OK, not literally dying, but *laterally* dying, having propped my fresh-from-the-creek feet over a log while lying on my back to ease the swelling. I didn't want to move again. Ever. But the first lesson of long-distance hiking was to go even when your body said no. After saying hello to a California couple who had spent the previous night in the same meadow as us—a couple who now walked past looking no more rumpled than two L.L. Bean models—we returned to the trail.

For a year Glenn Petersen and I had trained, planned, and envisioned our ultimate triumph. We would be standing on the Bridge of the Gods over the Columbia River, celebrating the trip of a lifetime. Fatigue would not stop us. Blisters would not stop us. Mountains would not—

SHE CAME OUT of nowhere: The Messenger of Doom, a backpacker walking toward me, obviously whipped. Her presence startled me because we'd seen only a handful of hikers, none going the opposite direction. Until now.

She had on a ULA Ohm ultra-light pack, just like mine. She was a little younger than me. And she was walking slightly ahead of a man of similar age—her husband, I later learned.

"Hey, samer packs," I said, stopping to chat.

"Yeah," she said, "where you headed?"

"The Columbia River," I said. "My brother-in-law and I are doing just Oregon."

"Do you have ice axes and crampons?"

The question furrowed my mental brow. I shook my head no; this, after all, was Oregon, the most benign of the three PCT states.

"We didn't either," she said. "Wish we had. We turned around at Devils Peak. Too much snow."

"Really?" I said.

"It was scary. We nearly died."

If the ice axes and crampon references were sucker punches to my gut, the "we-nearly-died" line froze me like a stun gun. In those three words, a year's worth of preparation, planning, and training seemed suddenly in jeopardy. Sure, we knew this had been a near-record snow year, but this was late July, not early June. We expected snow, but not snow that could kill a trip. Or us.

OK, relax, I told myself. *Maybe she's overstating the danger.*

"We were going to do Oregon, too," she said. "We'd planned this for a year."

This, I realized, wasn't some willy-nilly decision; she and her husband had found the stretch so scary that they'd given up their entire trip and walked twenty-six miles back rather than risk pushing ahead. I couldn't dismiss her warning.

We traded "good lucks." I headed my way, she hers. I turned to see Glenn talking to her. I waited to compare notes.

"Doesn't look good, Bob," he said.

I didn't want to hear that. I wanted to hear something optimistic, some flaw he'd sensed in their decision, some reason why it made sense for them to turn back but not us. Instead, Glenn did what he always did when indecision arrived: He pulled out his maps. He pointed to brown-on-white contour lines tightly bunched at Shale Butte, Lucifer, and Devils Peak, the red-marked PCT trail running far higher—nearly 7,000 feet—than I'd imagined.

"The challenge is the north face of Devils Peak," he said. "It falls off steeply."

I knew the PCT wouldn't be a pine-needled Interstate 5 and knew we were going to encounter lots of snow, but danger had never figured into my pre-hike equation. We'd talked about what-if-we-get-separated scenarios. Storms. Injuries. That kind of stuff. But this was not California's Sierra Nevada portion of the PCT, where ice axes and crampons were standard operating gear.

"So, why do we have to stay high like this?" I said. "We have maps, GPS, compasses. Why not leave the trail and pick it up here?" I pointed to a spot northeast of Devils Peak. "Stay low. Skirt around the mountain. Stay out of the snow."

"Bad idea to leave the trail," said Glenn.

Glenn was an Eagle Scout, the son of a Scout leader. I had been kicked out of a Cub Scouts meeting by Kenny Clark's mom for getting too "rambunctious." And later dropped out of Webelos, a transition program from Cub to Boy Scouts.

"We're just going to have to check it out for ourselves," said Glenn.

So, that was that. We were going to walk twenty-six miles, mostly uphill, knowing that we might need to turn around and walk twenty-six miles back. In defeat.

Welcome to the Pacific Crest Trail. Sometimes it was your friend, sometimes your adversary, but always it was a mystery. I planted my trekking poles and, along with Glenn, headed up the hill, into the fading light, for Freye Lake. And for whatever lay beyond.

Part I
The lure of the trail

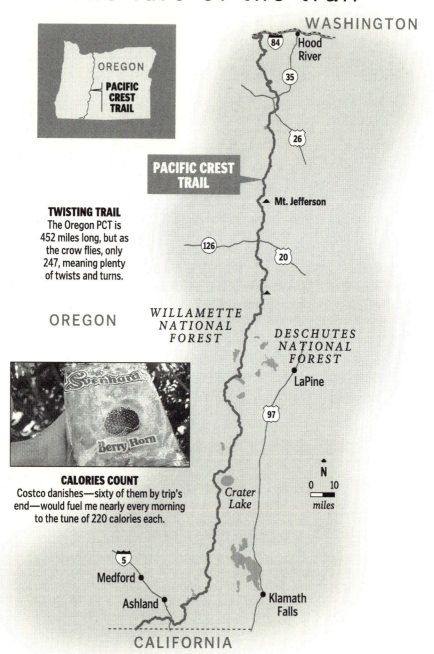

TWISTING TRAIL
The Oregon PCT is 452 miles long, but as the crow flies, only 247, meaning plenty of twists and turns.

CALORIES COUNT
Costco danishes—sixty of them by trip's end—would fuel me nearly every morning to the tune of 220 calories each.

I have discovered that even the mediocre can have adventures and even the fearful can achieve.

—Edmund Hillary,
the first person to summit Mount Everest

1. Seeds

MY FATHER Warren, in his trail-dusted soul, was a fly fisherman. It began in his Portland boyhood when he and his buddies biked from their Fremont neighborhood to the Sandy River. Or hitchhiked east up the Columbia River Gorge to hike in and fish Wahtum Lake or Eagle Creek.

He attended then-Oregon State College but left school to join the Navy, only the bombing of Hiroshima and Nagasaki precluding him from heading to Japan as a landing-craft coxswain for a planned invasion of the mainland. After marrying my mother in 1946, the two honeymooned at Three Creeks Lake, in the shadows of the Three Sisters mountains, so he could fish. A photographer by trade, he made a movie, *Trout in the High Country,* about fly-fishing the lakes tucked high into the Cascades. He designed and built a waterproof housing for his movie camera so he could better film trout under water. He designed and built boats.

For him, backpacking was not only about enjoying nature, but also about getting deeper into the back country so he could catch more and bigger fish. I still have 1960s footage of him and a friend bouncing up a trail with an aluminum cart they'd designed and built. Picture a two-ended wheelbarrow, only with a single bicycle tire in the middle;

one man pulled from the front, the other pushed from the back. That way, they could bring in dad's heavy 35mm movie camera.

My father loved the wilderness. In the late 1960s, at a time when car bumpers were first sporting "Ecology Now" stickers, he was writing impassioned letters to Oregon's congressional delegation in Washington, D.C., pleading with them to vote against a proposed dam on the South Santiam River.

Decades later, with tongue only slightly in cheek, he said that when it was his time to die, he wanted to hike into one of his favorite high Cascade lakes one last time and let winter take him home.

I WAS NEVER the fisherman he was, but I grew to love the art of working a fly rod and the smell of the sandy trails in Central Oregon and the way water from a high lake smelled when you splashed it in your face.

I remember my first pair of "Tuffy" hiking boots and movies of my sister, Linda, and me—perhaps ten and seven years old—hiking along the Breitenbush River north of Mount Jefferson. I remember how my father ended *Trout in the High Country* with a shot of me walking down a trail as he—the narrator—said his hope for the future was this: that his son, when grown, would be able to enjoy the same unspoiled wilderness he had. And I remember, as a teenager on warm August evenings, traipsing with him through the blow-down near Cultus Lake in an attempt to find—unsuccessfully, as it turned out—the on-the-map but elusive Comma Lake.

Amid it all, I absorbed from him the idea that what made the wilderness special was that your destinations did not come easily. You had to earn your way to fish a high-mountain lake. And, in so doing, you were granted a privilege enjoyed by few others, and certainly not one that should be available to on-trail motorcyclists. My dad deterred them by dragging logs across the trails behind us.

For my high school graduation present, he gave me a used Nikkormat camera. Symbolically, he was, I believe, giving me permission to see the world though my own eyes. And I did. In the next four years, I backpacked more than at any other time in my life, chronicling my journeys with that camera. The week before my wedding in 1975, two buddies and I climbed the South Sister, then hiked forty-five miles from Elk Lake to Cultus Lake over three days, returned home to Corvallis, and ran the mile in an all-comers meet that night, our feet aflame as we wobbled down homestretch.

I didn't marry the girl next door; she actually lived four houses away. Her name: Sally Jean Youngberg. In 1976, after I earned a journalism degree at the University of Oregon in Eugene, we moved to Bend in Central Oregon, where I worked at *The Bulletin*. Our two sons were born in a hospital from whose windows the Three Sisters were etched sharply against the western sky. We followed newspaper jobs to Bellevue, Washington, then back to Eugene. Camping, with few exceptions, gave way to kids' baseball on summer weekends. Our two sons played, Sally kept score, and I coached—without regret. They were wonderful years. But they were years without mountains. Years without camping.

Early one August morning in 1996, I got the phone call from my sister. My father was dying. A few minutes later, another call. My father was dead. He was seventy-two. He died at Black Butte Ranch, a golf resort nestled in the ponderosa pines just east of the Cascade crest. It was a place where anglers with $1,000 Orvis rods cast their lines into spring-fed lakes while restaurant diners watched from above $30 plates of Applewood Smoked Halibut. Given his death near a high-mountain lake, my mother said, my father had gotten his wish. "He just decided to take the deluxe route."

In the years since his death, I grew closer than ever to my mother, Marolyn, inspired by her unwillingness to quit—she took more than a year to battle back from near-death in a car accident and survived a Galapagos Island tour boat's sinking that left four dead—and by her zest to live life fully. In her eighties, she still sailed with me regularly. Meanwhile, when I thought of my father, it was often in context of the wilderness that he had introduced to me and that, amid a busy life, I had almost forgotten existed.

With my two sons, Ryan and Jason, now grown and starting families, I found myself musing about a return to the trails.

I HEARD HER footsteps before I saw her. It was August 1999 and, amid the hardened lava on Oregon's Old McKenzie Pass, I had just reached the main north-south trail after a short trip to the top of 6,872-foot Little Belknap Crater. I was waiting for my brother-in-law, Glenn Petersen, who wasn't far behind me on this short day hike. In all directions, a spread of black lava stretched beyond, fronting a handful of mountain peaks seemingly tired from summer's heat and anxious for new coats of winter white.

"Morning," I said after she reached the two trails' cinder-rock intersection. She was bronzed by the sun, wearing a good-sized pack, and not breathing particularly heavily. I pegged her to be in her mid-twenties, a little more than half my age of forty-five.

"Hello," she said.

"Where did you start from?" I asked.

"You mean today or in the beginning?"

"The beginning, I guess."

She nodded to the south. "Mexico."

I nearly fell off the rock. "And, uh, where are you finishing?"

She looked to the north. "Canada."

Obviously, this wasn't time for me to brag about bagging Little Belknap, a nub that, despite the rocky trail, I'd seen kids summit in tennis shoes. I got off the rock and reached for my pen and Post-It pad in my pocket. She was, I learned, Laura Buhl, a twenty-six-year-old University of Oregon student in Eugene, where I was the features editor of *The Register-Guard* newspaper but would start soon as a general columnist.

Ironic. She was on a 2,650-mile north-south trail and, at the point I met her, was essentially as close to her home base as she ever would be; Eugene was only sixty miles west, in Oregon's lush Willamette Valley. On this day, Buhl would hit the 2,000-mile mark. Her plan, she said, was to arrive at the Canadian border on Saturday, September 25, celebrate with friends in Seattle on Sunday, and begin fall term classes at UO Monday morning. She said it all matter-of-factly, as if telling a roommate that she was headed out for bagels and would be back by noon.

She did exactly what she set out to do, I learned a month later. Buhl was on time for her 8 A.M. Monday class, "Jogging," appropriate for a university in Eugene, known as "Track Town USA." Her feat—averaging twenty-one miles per day for 148 days—seemed no less incredible to me than the Eagle landing in the moon's Sea of Tranquility after a 238,000-mile journey from Earth. My fourth piece as a *Register-Guard* columnist was about Laura Buhl.

I was enthralled with the logistics of it all, how she had food mailed to pickup points along the way, such as Elk Lake Lodge. How, with thirty to thirty-five pounds on her back, she'd crossed part of the Mojave Desert, over 13,153-foot Forester Pass in California, and through remnants of one of the heaviest snowfalls in Northwest history. How she had encountered two bears, seven rattlesnakes, and about seven trillion mosquitoes. Endured temperatures from thirty to ninety-five degrees and waterless stretches of thirty-five miles. And not only survived rain, snow, cold, and a desert windstorm that left her sun-screened face looking like sandpaper, but made it to class on time that first morning.

As an adjunct professor of journalism at the University of Oregon, I had students who couldn't make an 8:30 A.M. class on time from their apartment three blocks away. "Let me tell you," I'd begin the subsequent lecture, "about Laura Buhl."

In 1999, 270 hikers had attempted the same journey, according to the Pacific Crest Trail Association. Fewer than sixty had made it. "I've always been intrigued by the romance of the border-to-border trip," Buhl told me. "Two borders. One trail. It's perfect."

Perfect, yes. But perfect for folks such as Buhl who had the time; the unencumbered lives; and the bones, tissue, and muscles of youth. Not perfect, however, for folks like me with full-time jobs, a handful of freelance pursuits, too much body fat, and a couple of medical challenges.

Still, I began wondering. *Could I?*

A FEW YEARS LATER, I met Judge John Waldo. Sort of. I was perusing *The Register-Guard's* library in search of a book on former Oregon Governor Tom McCall. Along the way I found a tattered, three-ring binder named simply "John Breckenridge Waldo."

Was this the same Waldo for whom Waldo Lake in the Cascades east of Eugene was named? I opened it. Yes it was. Waldo, the notebook said, was "a mountain lover who spent his summers exploring the mountains and lakes in the Cascades. Each year he would leave the valley in early summer, and head for the wildest and remotest parts of the Cascades either alone or with such friends as John Minto, the state horticulturist, or William Gilbert, the federal court justice." The notebook, compiled by a U.S. Forest Service sociologist, Gerald Williams, in 1986, was a collection of letters Waldo had sent home to his wife in Salem from 1880 to 1907.

Waldo, I realized as I read on, was more than a part-time mountain man. He was a Thoreau-inspired poet and a politician who, amid the late-century land grab, saw the vulnerability of the Cascade Range and stepped up to protect it from miners, "sheep men," and others out to exploit it.

"The still woods," he wrote from the banks of Pamelia Lake in the shadow of Mount Jefferson, "surely they are not all made merely to be cut down. Let wide stretches still grow for the spiritual welfare of men. How good they seem here today—the untrammeled, the unhandseled wilderness, untouched by men. ... Cannot wide expanses still be preserved?"

In part because of the mountain air's health benefits, Waldo headed for the high country from Mount Hood in northern Oregon to Mount Shasta in northern California. He and his buddies cleared trails ("one way of paying my share of the moral tax for the privilege of coming to the mountains"), stocked lakes and streams with trout, fished, hunted, and hiked.

As I considered a long hike on the PCT, it was as if three voices from the past were calling me: my father's, Buhl's, and Waldo's. It was as if my father had gathered the tinder and Buhl had lit the match. Now, Waldo's ghost was blowing on the smoldering possibilities. As if my father were a conduit to my personal past, Buhl to the PCT itself, and Waldo to my native Oregon, collectively, the three urging me to return to a place I'd known but forgotten.

2. The decision

MY DECISION TO hike the Oregon portion of the Pacific Crest Trail had nothing to do with escape. I loved my family, liked my job, enjoyed my friends. Though I failed with great regularity, my life was rooted in the grace of God. I wasn't responding to a mid-life crisis and wasn't trying to "find myself" on the trail; if I was still "missing" this deep into life, chances are I was going to need more than a two-foot-wide trail to discover where I'd been and where I needed to go. Finally, I wasn't trying to prove anything, not even to myself. Eleven-year-olds had completed the entire Mexico-to-Canada PCT. In 2010, a 74-year-old man and his 69-year-old wife hiked the 2,650 miles. The Oregon portion was roughly one-sixth of that and was the trail's most benign section; I had no illusions that I was doing the equivalent of swimming the English channel, climbing Everest, or sailing around the world.

Waldo spent twenty-six summers in the Cascades. As I read his words, as I breathed the pine-scented air of which he wrote, as I imagined the wilderness I'd once known, all I longed for was one such summer. Just one. My own Cascade summer, as it were.

I'd done some short-term forays into the mountains in recent years. Glenn, in earlier years, had summited a handful of Oregon's highest: Jefferson, Mount Washington, the North Sister, and Three Fingered

Jack. In 2008, the two of us hiked to the top of Oregon's third-highest mountain, the South Sister. That same year, with the U.S. Olympic Track & Field Trials in Eugene, while trying to explain to out-of-town readers how amazingly diverse Lane County was, I wrote: "If you really hustle, you can walk the beach at sunrise, stop at the back-to-the-sixties Glenwood Restaurant in Eugene for granola, yogurt and fruit, catch the last of the morning rise with your fly rod on the McKenzie River, play a quick nine at Tokatee Golf Course and climb to the top of the South Sister—elevation 10,358 feet—by dark. Where else can you build a day like that in a single county?"

The next year I decided to find out if we could actually do it. Glenn was game to join me; so was my eldest son, Ryan, then a 30-year-old self-employed videographer. We left Florence on the central Oregon coast at 6:11 A.M. and stood atop the South Sister at 6:26 P.M.—and, in the meantime, had eaten at the Glenwood, fly-fished the McKenzie, and played nine holes of golf.

Meanwhile, Buhl's trip continued to tug at me. In 2010, I read some books on the PCT, my favorite of which was Dan White's *The Cactus Eaters: How I Lost My Mind—And Almost Found Myself—on the Pacific Crest Trail*. White and his girlfriend, East Coasters at the time, had decided to go for it on a whim, their lack of preparedness telling along the way. The book was hilarious, the insight helpful, the lessons profound. Among them, from a fellow hiker named Kirk: "If you ever get the urge to quit, I want you to think about this: Never quit on a down moment. Never make your resolution to quit in town. Never decide to quit during an eight-day stretch of hard rain. Make the decision when you're feeling great."

I also re-read a book by Eugene author and Oregon hiking expert Bill Sullivan: *Listening for Coyote: A Walk Across Oregon's Wilderness*. Sullivan, with far more wanderlust than I, decided to blaze a new southwest-to-northeast trail across Oregon. And did so, lugging a sixty-pound pack 1,361 miles from Cape Blanco to Hells Canyon over sixty-five days.

I had long had a fascination with odd challenges; for example, I had once created, and cajoled son Ryan into playing, a seven-mile-long golf hole on the sandy beach north of our family's cabin on the central Oregon coast. (It was a par 72. We both shot four-under-par 68s.) In 1989, I backpacked forty miles through Seattle's suburbs for a series of columns for the Bellevue, Washington, newspaper I worked for at the time. I had run two marathons and been part of two Hood-to-Coast Relay teams. (Mount Hood to Seaside while hopscotching through Portland.) In other words, I'd long had the "crazy" gene when it came to physical challenges.

Still, I realized, the entire PCT was out of the question. I couldn't get five months off. And even if I could, I wasn't keen on spending five months away from my family; by now, Sally and I had three grandchildren, all of whom lived within fifteen minutes of us. Who wanted to give up the privilege of seeing them for nearly half a year?

That said, every second the biological clock ticked was a second that, given my age, would only make the trip more difficult and only shove me closer to not committing. As a Neil Young fan, I kept hearing lyrics from his song "Hey Hey, My My (Into the Black)" that tugged at my soul: "It's better to burn out than to fade away." I agreed. As, apparently, did John Waldo, based on an 1896 journal entry in which he wrote: "Better to wear out than rust out."

Finally, the idea hit: Why not hike only the Oregon portion of the trail? That was doable. Four hundred and fifty-two miles. Maybe a month on the trail. I crunched the numbers: thirty days at roughly fifteen miles per day, which might be all that I could handle after my orthopedic surgeon told me my age-worn second metatarsal joint on my right foot was basically toast.

I liked this plan. Sally liked this plan. But if I had the "why" and "what" down, the next question was "who?" Plenty of long-distance hikers go it alone, but solo wasn't my, or Sally's, preference. (Fine most of the time, deadly, perhaps, in an emergency.) I needed someone with a passion for hiking and for the outdoors. Someone who could get the time off. Someone who, like me, was just a tad nutty. Most of all, I needed someone who I could not only stand for thirty days amid all sorts of challenging situations—and long stretches of repetitive hiking—but someone who could stand *me*. As a sailor, I knew the maritime rule: Each day you spend on a boat with someone is a day your boat shrinks by a foot. I expected the PCT would be no different.

I could be high-strung, moody, impetuous, emotional, pouty, whiny, and overly sarcastic—all before breakfast. I could hold family and friends to unrealistically high standards, demanding that everyone be as obsessively driven as I was about a particular outing. (See wedding-rehearsal planner Jack Byrnes, played by Robert DeNiro, in *Meet the Parents.*) I could be so single-mindedly committed to something that the details of life—say, leaky roofs and life-insurance payments—might go easily overlooked.

Groucho Marx once famously said: "I don't want to belong to any club that will accept me as a member." I could relate. So, who could I get to round out a two-person club whose sole purpose would be to hike the tree-thick backbone of my beloved Oregon?

SALLY DIDN'T need to mull the question at all. "Glenn," said *She Who Knows All*.

When I first heard the suggestion of my brother-in-law, my reaction was a little like an NFL fan hearing his favorite team's No. 1 draft pick was not a quarterback, running back, or wide receiver but a right guard. A guy who just blocks. I mean, was Glenn Petersen *exciting* enough? *Interesting* enough to sustain my mood for a month? Some might suggest he, like Waldo, had a "retiring disposition, bordering on shy." I'd suggest he was flat-out dull.

This, after all, was a family doctor who gave his wife Pyrex for Valentine's Day. Walked to work. Did a triathlon using a bicycle that still had the plastic child seat on back. And, after going to Hawaii for a medical conference, said, "I don't *get* that place."

Given as much, I affectionately referred to him as "Dr. Dull." For Christmas, in fact, I once gave him a copy of a book called *Dare to Be Dull,* personally autographed to him by its author, Joseph L. Troise, whom I had interviewed in Seattle for a newspaper story. For another Christmas, I gave him the "Glenn Petersen 12-Month-a-Year Sleep Calendar," each month showing him in various napping poses—at our beach house, at Black Butte Ranch, the list went on.

And this was the guy who I was going to try to carry on a month-long conversation with?

"Don't you see?" said *She Who*. "He's just what you need. He's not someone who's going to drive you crazy by talking all the time. Plus, he's a doctor. That could come in handy."

My mind flashed to that motel scene in *Planes, Trains & Automobiles* when Steve Martin tells John Candy he's a human "Chatty Cathy" doll who never shuts up. "I could tolerate any insurance seminar. For days, I could sit there and listen to them go on and on with a big smile on my face! And they'd say, how can you stand it? And I'd say, because I've been with Del Griffith, I can take anything!"

She Who was absolutely right. I didn't want Del Griffith; heck, in some ways, I *was* Del Griffith. I wanted Glenn Petersen, the human embodiment of the Hippocratic Oath: "At first do no harm." Not likely to get on my nerves. Like me, a native Oregonian who loved this state. But, blessedly, unlike me: steady, even-keeled, savvy. An Eagle Scout. And, yes, a medical doctor.

In many ways, Glenn was similar to Judge John Waldo: honorable, competent, and on the quiet side. Waldo, on a few prominent trips to the mountains, had been accompanied by *his* brother-in-law, Edward J. Humason. According to Felix W. Isherwood, who often went with Waldo on his summer sojourns, Humason was "the humorist of the party." Sounded a bit like Glenn's brother-in-law. Me.

Ironically, Glenn and I first got to know each other while backpacking on Eagle Creek—the same Eagle Creek that served as an alternative ending for the Oregon portion of the PCT. It was Memorial Day weekend 1974 and my most vivid memory is of Glenn and me wrestling in a creek. It had begun as all-in-fun splash revenge, but in our quests to impress our respective girlfriends, we'd wound up wrestling in the water like a couple of drunk cowboys.

Back then, he looked a little like a young John Denver: slim with round-rimmed glasses and brownish-blond hair, slightly curly. He drove a blue Volkswagen bus—an upgrade from a '52 Chevrolet he'd had—and was a zoology major at OSU with aspirations of becoming a doctor.

In many ways, we were opposites. He had grown up in Eugene, home of the more liberal University of Oregon, and attended Oregon State University, for whom he now rooted. I had grown up in Corvallis, home of the more conservative OSU, and attended UO, for whom I now rooted. I was a writer, he wrote little more than prescriptions at his family practice clinic in Albany, forty miles north of Eugene. I loved used-book stores; he bought new. My tools were somewhere amid Christmas decorations, unsold boxes of books I'd written, and four decades worth of writing files; he could find a half-inch socket wrench in a split second. I was more socially outgoing; he, at best, let others dominate a conversation, at worst, fell asleep on a couch at family gatherings. I wore my emotions on my sleeve; he could be in emotional turmoil and his expression would change less than a face on Mount Rushmore.

In many ways, however, we were similar. Same ages, essentially; he just eighteen months older. Married to two best-friend sisters. And though we didn't agree on everything, we shared a similar Christian faith. We enjoyed sports, had played lots of golf together, and were bound by a birthday card we'd recycled back-and-forth for thirty years.

But here's what may have made us most compatible: beneath all the joking, we respected each other deeply. Though he was a prime target for my comedy—something, I think, he genuinely enjoyed, at least most of the time—he knew, deep down, that I held him in high esteem. He was all those Boy Scout things—brave, honest, loyal, etc., as if he'd just walked out of the organization's 1964 handbook—but more: A loyal husband. A caring father. A committed believer whose faith—unlike that of so many modern-day, self-righteous Pharisees—played out in the real world with no hypocrisy.

I remember exactly when I realized his true character. By his mid-thirties, Glenn and his wife Ann, Sally's sister, were deeply involved with a Christian medical organization in Haiti, the poorest country in the Western Hemisphere. In 1988, he talked me into joining the team for a fifteen-day trip. The incident happened at the end of a long day in the rural clinic, a cinder-block church that we modified for evening worship with the Haitians: a *tap tap,* a Haitian bus that carried about three times as many people as it's designed for, had flipped. Half a dozen people had been injured, some seriously.

From a distance, I watched as Glenn and the medical staff calmly stopped what they were doing and patched up the injured. As I watched him tend to those in need, his gloved hands covered in blood, I saw my brother-in-law more clearly than I'd ever seen him before. In our decades of friendship, we'd spent most of our time together at family gatherings and on golf courses. Fun stuff. But conflict reveals character in a way that good times do not, and I saw it in Glenn that day. Later, after the clinic had closed, people gathered for dinner, but Glenn wasn't there. I wandered over to the church. There he was, quietly setting up the two-bit sound system for the evening service.

In 2009, Sally and I returned to Haiti with Ann and Glenn and their eldest daughter, Carrie. He hadn't changed a bit. Solid. Consistent. A quiet hero. He didn't rub it in when his Beavers beat my Ducks, nor did I when my Ducks beat his Beavers. He could beat me at golf and not gloat. I could beat him at Scrabble and only gloat for a short time—and then only if it was a decisive win in which further humiliation seemed justified. All in all, I realized, if he weren't the "let's-talk-life" guy who I'd go to if my world were crumbling, he would make a great long-distance hiking partner.

BUT WAS he even mildly interested? I popped the question in July 2010.

Yes, he told me, that sounded fun. (I can't picture him saying "cool.") But that wasn't good enough for me. I remembered that advice from *The Cactus Eaters* about never quitting when conditions were at their worst. If you really think you must quit, the guy suggested, then quit when conditions are at their very *best*. That will be proof positive that your "wanna-quit" decision was not just a phase you're passing through. You really want to quit.

Conversely, I decided, if Glenn really wanted to go, he had to be willing to say yes even when considering this trip at its very *worst*; there's nothing more disheartening than inviting someone along for something and later finding they're not nearly as passionate about it as you are. (How many *Amazing Race* participants wind up wanting to strangle their partner for that very reason?) So, I teased Glenn with an e-mail list about why we should do the Oregon PCT soon:

1. We're not getting any younger. If we're going to do this, it'll be easier now than later.
2. It'd be a great way to see the backbone of Oregon.
3. It'd make two weeks' worth of columns.
4. I love a good cut-and-dry challenge. One state, bottom to top.
5. It gives me an excuse to get into, and stay in, good shape.
6. Gadgets. Maps. Planning. All fun.
7. You're the only person I think who could stand me for three-plus weeks.

But then I hit him with the hard stuff. "I don't think this is something we go into lightly," I wrote. "Why?"

1. It's 452 miles. That's 21 miles every day for three weeks or, more realistically, 16 miles per day for four weeks.
2. It's a long time to be away from our families. We need to make sure we're really up for that.
3. It entails at least a small amount of danger: dehydration, starvation, snake bites, mastocytosis attacks, Bigfoot attacks, etc.
4. If we're serious about doing this, I think we need to start at least foundational training this fall and serious training in January.
5. We need to decide on when we're going to go. (I'm thinking July 5-July 30.)
6. We need to determine whether our wives are up for this.

I ended the e-mail by telling him I just wanted to start the conversation. No need for a quick decision. "I'm leaning toward a yes but really want to talk this out and consider all things," I wrote.

The next day I got a short e-mail from him. It was comprised of three small words with one big implication:
"I am in."

3. Thinking small (and light)

I DOUBT THAT anyone who knew I was carrying an eleven-pound wrestling trophy in my pack to the top of Eugene's Mount Pisgah would have seen the method in my madness. Then again, people probably laughed at Rocky for pounding all that raw meat at the butcher's shop, too.

I'd received it as a white-elephant gift at a Christmas party and always wondered how I might use it. It now had a use—and, for all its levity, a touch of symbolic honor. At the top of Pisgah rested a monument in honor of author Ken Kesey's nineteen-year-old son, Jed, a University of Oregon wrestler who died in a van accident returning from a meet in Washington.

On July 13, 2010, I lugged that wrestling trophy to the top of 1,531-foot Pisgah just southeast of Eugene. It was my first official training session for the 2011 Welch-Petersen Oregon PCT trip.

With nearly six decades under our somewhat-strained belts, Glenn and I had few advantages over younger hikers going into our 452-mile trip, but what we did have was an equal amount of time to prepare. Specifically, we needed to get ready in terms of physical conditioning, equipment, and general logistics, like knowing how and where we were going to get food and water.

I became an instant sponge for anything and everything dealing with long-distance hiking. I read entire books devoted solely—no pun intended—to care of the feet for long-distance hiking and running. Began subscribing to *Backpacker* magazine. Met with a Eugene couple who kept three food dehydrators going 24/7 to prepare meals for their summer sojourns on the PCT. And spent entire evenings Internet surfing for PCT-related info.

When Waldo took to the mountains, he had little knowledge of places he was going other than what he'd learned on previous trips. Me? I found a Web site that graded cell-phone coverage on the PCT depending on your location and provider. Within weeks, I knew who the PCT cult leaders were, among them: Ray Jardine, the ultra-ultralight guru who recommended tarps, not tents, blankets not sleeping bags; "Erik the Black" Asorson, who could mesmerize me with a simple video showing nothing but how he packed his backpack; and a back-to-nature dude named Steve Gillman, who advised: "Need to leave a note for rescuers or other people in your party? White birch bark (*betula papyrifera*) can be easily peeled from the trunk and written on with pen, pencil or berry juice. I have even sent birch bark envelopes through the mail."

The least of my problems, I figured, would be what kind of bark I might need to write a rescue note on—though when joining a local FireMed plan that pays for ambulance transportation, I didn't hesitate to also add the Life Flight service.

I learned that the entire Mexico-to-California PCT required some six million steps, meaning we were going to need just over a million to get to the Bridge of the Gods. Learned that "a pound on your body is a pound in your pack"; in other words, I would need to whip myself into better shape than I was. Learned that selecting boots weighing 10½ ounces less than another pair could mean the equivalent of subtracting an additional three miles from a day's hike. (After considerable research, I settled on Merrell Moab Ventilators, extra wide and mid-, rather than low-cut, to lessen the chance of a sprained ankle: two pounds, two ounces per pair, exactly half the weight of a pair of Herman Munster boots I'd worn to the top of the South Sister two years earlier). And learned that the fastest known PCT crossing of Oregon was completed in ten days, fourteen hours, sixteen minutes, and twelve seconds.

It was a mark I did not believe would be in danger from the Welch-Petersen twosome. After ten days, we hoped to be somewhere north of Crater Lake, a third of our way to the Columbia River. Speed was not our concern. We had less lofty goals: Standing atop that bridge with a measurable pulse.

WHAT WE NEEDED, I decided early on, was a shakedown cruise. On August 13, 2010, we stuffed ourselves at the Vida Cafe just east of Eugene and headed an hour to the Willamette National Forest to hike on the PCT near the 10,085-foot North Sister. Lava lands. Obsidian cliffs. Beautiful country, where we might learn what, if any, of our equipment could be used. (Some, but not a lot.) What changes we might need to make regarding what we would bring. (Less of everything.) And what thirty to forty miles in a weekend actually felt like. (Ouch.)

I learned that I needed more than twice the amount of water Glenn did to keep going; I attributed that mainly to a handful of pills I had to take daily for a rare disorder I had called systemic mastocytosis, which causes an overproduction of mast cells in my body. What's more, I learned that if you don't absolutely need something, don't bring it. I learned, thanks to a thru-hiker heading for Canada, that we should "Hike our own hikes." And I learned something enlightening and frightening: I wasn't nearly as tough as I thought I was.

We hiked eight miles Friday night and fifteen Saturday, returning to the trailhead with plans to camp at nearby Scott Lake after a few more miles and a climb to the top of Scott Mountain Sunday morning. I was dehydrated. Listless. Mentally shot, sitting in the late-afternoon heat of a dusty parking lot with no desire to take another step. With whatever energy I had, I cast my verbal fly rod to see if Glenn would hit on my idea.

"Let's just grab a burger at the Vida Cafe," I said, "and call it good." It was a euphemistic smokescreen for what I was really saying: "Let's quit." I wasn't at all proud of the suggestion, but pride sometimes fades when you're nearly too tired to reach for your water bottle.

Glenn's response may have been the most critical line spoken before or during the next year's trip. He didn't scoff at me. He didn't berate me. He got up, got me a second bottle of water—the first had breathed a touch of new life into me—and said: "Hey, we can do this, Bob. Rest a little more, then we'll get going."

And he was right. Although a major blister erupted on my foot en route to the summit of Scott Mountain the next morning, we made it to the top and reached our goal: thirty-four miles between Friday night and noon Sunday. Had Glenn given in to my whim, quitting would have been that much easier the next time one of us got in a can't-go-on mindset. And if he'd ripped me for being a wimp—which I clearly deserved—it might have sent me wallowing in martyrdom; who knew the result with a reactionary like me?

The trip had been inspiring, not only for the beauty—the last thing I saw before nodding off Friday night was a shooting star—but for the people we met, notably Helen Chou. We saw her at 7:15 A.M. Saturday as we headed south on the PCT, just below Yapoah Crater. She was headed north. She couldn't have been five feet tall, though her refrigerator-like pack could have. She was hiking the entire 452-mile Oregon stretch, having done the 1,703-mile California section in three separate summers, years ago. She was eighty years old.

Chou was doing ten miles per day. And had twenty days' worth of food in her pack, about four to five times what the normal PCT hiker carries. Unless she were eating only popcorn and cotton candy, her pack had to have weighed at least forty to fifty pounds, nearly twice what most PCT hikers carry.

We chatted, said goodbye and watched her trudge ahead as if she were a slow-motion robot. Once home, I took a Post-It and stuck in on a shelf near where I was keeping all the PCT-related books, printouts, and maps that were morphing in my office like spring mushrooms. It said "Helen Chou." A reminder for next year, when I'd want to quit, about the resiliency of the human spirit.

AT *THE REGISTER-GUARD*, where I wrote a three-times-a-week column for the paper's City/Region section, I read an e-mail from a Eugene man, Craig Mayne. He had seen my column on our three-day hike and said that while on a weekend outing, he'd seen Chou near Elk Lake. "She was bending over to get water in a lake and I was afraid she was going to fall in and sink like an anchor," he said. "But what an inspiration."

Mayne, a tad younger than I, had done the Oregon section of the PCT the previous summer, ironically, with *his* brother-in-law—at least to start. His partner had gotten terrible blisters in the first few days—that would be my role in this PCT play, I figured—so Craig did the rest by himself. That would be Glenn, finishing at the Bridge of the Gods by himself, me back home.

Craig and I met for lunch at downtown's Sixth Street Grill. He already had a three-page list of suggestions prepared for me. Nonetheless, I peppered him with question after question. What kind of water filter did he take? How early did he hit the trail each day? What didn't he take that he wished he had?

From the outside, the trip suggested a simplifying of our lives, but the deeper Glenn and I got into planning, the more complex I realized this journey would be. Though our lives would need to fit into two thirty-pound packs, we still needed most of the same basic components of our non-trail lives: food, water, shelter, clothes, emergency supplies—only in miniature and as light as possible. My "to take" spreadsheet grew to seventy-eight items; only four weighed more than a pound each.

In long-distance hiking, thinking big meant thinking small. And light. A fellow PCT section hiker chided me for not planning to take the label off a water bottle I was taking.

Likewise, long-distance hiking meant preparing to live like a minimalist even as you maximized your credit card. The Eugene REI store became my second home. (Waldo's route into the Cascades sometimes included supply stops in Coburg and Eugene, so he, too, plunked down money in this area, though I doubt he got a yearly rebate as you do at REI.) I lay awake nights, wondering whether I could get by with a lighter plastic trash bag or I actually needed a poncho, later deciding *poncho* after reading a blog post from a guy who had done Oregon a few years before:

> August 7. 28 miles. Another day of Oregon liquid sunshine. A little too much liquid and not enough sunshine for my taste. It rained hard all last night but I survived warm and dry … . I traversed the Mount Thielsen Wilderness today. I never saw the mountain, the views back toward Crater Lake, or any of the surrounding lakes and forests. Between the rain, fog, and my flapping purple poncho I saw little except snowbanks and intermittent trail. It's too bad because I'm sure I missed out. I'm camped tonight on a saddle at 7,000 feet, about 4 miles north of Windigo Pass. There are huge snowbanks a few feet away but this spot is clear, albeit wet. It's cold, raining steadily, and the fog is pea-soup thick.

From our shakedown trip, I cut 5.14 pounds by upgrading only four items. I replaced a four-pound backpack with a 1.38-pound ULA Ohm like the one Mayne had used and allowed me to test; a 4.19-pound tent with a 1.71-pound Six Moon Designs Lunar Solo; a 2.25-pound sleeping bag with a 1.44-pound Mountain Hardwear Phantom 32; and a 2.5-pound blow-up sleeping pad with a .61-pound Therm-a-Rest Z-Lite sleeping mat. (Waldo, with horses, and sometimes wagons, packing his gear—including a portable table on which he could write—expressed no worry about weight, pointing out that "each horse carries two hundred, and most of them somewhat more." And he wasn't talking ounces.)

From Eugene to Albany and back, e-mails between Glenn and I ping-ponged back and forth. "What do you have for rain?" "You using gaiters?" I noodled nearly every aspect of the trip like a mad scientist, going so far as to make a detailed chart on how much water I needed per hour (twenty ounces in hot weather) and per mile (ten ounces).

On Christmas Eve 2010, I received an odd-looking and -feeling present from Glenn. It was, I soon discovered, a four-by-six-foot sheet of Tyvek house wrap, which he'd read made for a strong, lightweight ground cloth beneath a tent. My brother-in-law may have been reserved, but he clearly had a sentimental side.

4. The waterfall

TO DECIDE when to attempt our journey, we factored in a handful of variables: snow (we hoped to wait until August, to avoid as much covering the trail as possible), work schedules (neither of us could get a whole month off so we decided to do it in two, two-week stints) and football season (I was willing to miss one UO football game, September 3, but not two.) The result was this schedule: Part I, Friday, July 22, to Saturday, August 6, to get us 259 miles—57 percent of the entire distance—from the California border to Elk Lake in Central Oregon. And Part II, Saturday, August 27, to Thursday, September 8, from Elk Lake to the Washington border. En route, two of Glenn and Ann's three daughters—Carrie, thirty, and Molly, twenty-six—were going to join us at Crater Lake for a four-day stretch.

As the weeks slipped by, I quietly fretted about an intestinal flare-up of my mastocytosis that had once landed me in the emergency room—and about my feet, particularly my right foot. For three years, I'd been struggling with a form of plantar fasciitis, a painful inflammatory process of the plantar fascia, the connective tissue on the sole of the foot. It had forced me to give up running. And had led me to seeing a string of medical personnel: my primary-care doctor, James Buie, sent me to an orthopedic surgeon, Dr. Donald Jones, who recommended against surgery but referred me to an orthotics specialist, Kathy Sherwood, whom Jones said had done wonders for University of Oregon runners. She did the same for me, crafting a custom pair of orthotics and referring me to a physical therapist, Brian Gesik, who, each week, loosened up my foot to lessen the pain. The $64,000 question, of course, was one that couldn't be answered until we started hiking: On rugged terrain, how would the foot react to twenty miles a day for thirty straight days?

Glenn was the picture of health compared to me. Goodness, he was a doctor, the fixer not the "fixee." Over the years, I remembered him experiencing nothing beyond some occasional back problems and a spate of vertigo, an inner-ear disturbance that caused a loss of balance and vomiting. In short, I was the question, Glenn was the answer.

FOR SIX MONTHS my training wasn't much beyond a weekend hike of about six miles on two hills on Eugene's outskirts: Spencer Butte (2,055 feet) and the euphemistically named Mount Pisgah (1,531 feet). After the usual Christmas food overload, the weight was inching precariously close to the dreaded 200-pound mark, about ten-to-fifteen pounds beyond normal. I felt pathetically out of shape. But on January 24, I launched a ninety-day P90-X workout program: an hour a day, six days a week, of weights, push-ups, pull-ups, aerobic moves, and the granddaddy of them all, "Ab Ripper," to strengthen the core of my body. It worked. By the time I walked the Eugene Marathon on May 1—wearing a backpack, it took me six hours and thirty-six minutes and I beat only twenty-four of 2,291 people—I was down to 185 pounds and feeling strong. (Never mind that, because of too-small running shoes, I lost three toenails in that marathon.)

With the P90-X as a foundation, I began increasing my trail miles, treadmill miles, and stair-stepper miles—always with fifteen to twenty-five pounds of weight in my pack. Every few weeks, I went to a local high school stadium for a solid hour of up-and-down stadium steps, again, with a weighted pack.

I'd read accounts of young people doing absolutely nothing to get ready for the PCT—partying until daylight of their start date—and doing just fine. But at fifty-seven, I wasn't a young person. As the line from *Top Gun* suggests, I couldn't afford to be writing checks my body couldn't cash. I had one chance to make this trip work. I needed to be as ready as possible.

Exactly two months before our trip's start, I flew over the Three Sisters mountains en route to doing book research in Indiana. I mentally gulped. From the air, you see the ruggedness of terrain in a way no topography map can show. And the snow looked as thick as Arctic ice. After I arrived back at Eugene Airport, I had ten minutes to wait for a ride home. With bags in hand, I climbed up and down a twenty-three-step staircase eleven times. Author Rudyard Kipling, who had hiked the northern Cascades—and near Mount Hood—late in the nineteenth century once wrote: "If you can fill the unforgiving minute with sixty seconds' worth of distance run, yours is the Earth and everything that's in it." For me, filling such unforgiving minutes with exercises wasn't so much about inspiration. It was about desperation.

AT WORK, I took two steps at a time in getting upstairs to my second-floor cubicle. While waiting in post office lines I did calf-raises. I learned to balance training and the rest of my life, even if it got precarious at times; one Sunday morning, April 17, I began walking at 5:27 A.M., went 17.9 miles along the Willamette River that flows through Eugene, and still made the 11 A.M. service at Grace Community Fellowship. When my family walked a four-mile run/walk race, I happily did so—with a twenty-five-pound grandson, Keaton, on my back.

"I have decided to quit my job so I can devote full time to final preparations," wrote Glenn in a sarcastic e-mail. "I don't know how you have time to do all your training." Two weeks later, again with tongue in cheek, he wrote: "I have begun carbo loading. Is it too early?"

My worries were mainly physical: endurance, feet, mastocytosis. At times I found myself confident about reaching the Columbia; at times I'd be walking across a parking lot, notice my feet hurt, and think: *No way you can do this, pal.* And, I confess, I worried a bit about Glenn not getting enough trail miles in with weight on his back. When he went to Haiti in early June for a ten-day medical mission, I fretted about him getting out of condition.

"What are your three biggest concerns?" I asked Glenn during a phone call after his return.

"Easy," he said. "Snow, snow, and snow." Specifically, he worried about losing the trail in the snow—and about how his two daughters, Carrie and Molly, would fare. It had been an unusually heavy snowfall in Oregon's Cascades over the winter, and the compounding problem was a much cooler-than-normal spring and early summer. Snow that usually melted like an August ice cream cone wasn't going away as fast as usual.

Still, I thought Glenn was overreacting. "Face it, we're going to go through some snow," I said. "But it's not like we're going to be the first two guys on the PCT. We'll follow the foot tracks of others. And there'll be tree blazes all along the way. We'll be fine."

He wasn't so sure. And as the days passed, I couldn't ignore warnings we were seeing on the Web and in the newspapers. By mid-summer, some places in the Cascades had thirty percent more snow than normal years. Such talk underscored why I'd chosen not to tell *Register-Guard* readers about the trip—or invite them to follow us on a Web site for Part I. I wasn't sure we were going to make it. Instead, I decided to beta test a Web site on which I would post blog entries and photos for family and friends. If we were successful on Part I of the trip, we'd then invite readers to join us for Part II.

As I prepared, the irony, I found, was that nearly everything I would take to keep me alive—food, water, clothes, shelter—would make each step all that much harder. The take-or-leave tango was a complex one. Because of the drugs I took for my mastocytosis, my body absorbed water like a sponge. My initial plan was to carry 28.6 pounds, of which nearly a third—9.28 pounds—would need to be water. That stunned Glenn, who planned to carry less than half that weight in water. I wasn't thrilled by the reality either, but I'd done dozens of practice hikes and knew what my body required. Though my load would lighten as I sucked water from my 100-ounce CamelBak bladder, there was no way around the water weight.

My other "systems" and their weights looked like this: food (four days worth) 4.43 pounds, sleep (tent, bag, tarp, air pillow) 4.34 pounds, clothes 3.46 pounds, emergency 2.73 pounds, toiletries 1.56 pounds, pack 1.38 pounds, "kitchen" gear (collapsible rubber cup and plate, plus a fork and spoon) .89 pounds, communication (iPhone) .36 pounds, and miscellaneous .19 pounds.

When I looked at my plan, I immediately knew what the fallacy was: believing I could get by on only a pound of food per day. As with my personal finances, it was easy on a spreadsheet to make everything work out, much harder in real life. As our launch date neared, I realized I would probably need double the weight of food I'd originally planned to take.

I packed and weighed, repacked and reweighed, fretted and fretted some more. I replaced my regular toothbrush with a short-handle brush; jettisoned a pair of emergency gloves for unseasonable cold, realizing I could use my "sleep" socks if it got that bad; bagged a fleece top more because of its bulk than its weight; and got rid of electrolyte tablets I'd planned to put in my water for tasty energy boosts. Beyond the detachable-leg pants and dry-fit T-shirt I'd wear on the trail, I would bring a long-sleeve trail shirt, a down vest, a light rain top/bottom—and, to sleep in, long underwear and fresh socks.

Every long-distance hiker had to gamble. The only question was: *On what?* The Oregon Cascades in mid-summer were usually warm, not hot, during the day, and cool but not cold, at night. It rarely rained. Alas, depending on "usually" and "rarely" is dangerous stuff high in the mountains. Thundershowers happened. Cold snaps hit. For the same reason I bought life insurance hoping I would never have to use it, I knew I had to pack a poncho, emergency kit, and extra mastocytosis pills. Not to mention an EpiPen, in case the masto got triggered by, say, a bee sting. If something like that happened, and breathing got difficult, I was to jam it into my thigh and then seek medical treatment—uh, right, in the middle of a designated wilderness area, some points of which might be thirty miles from even the nearest Forest Service road. Oh, well … .

Dr. Kraig Jacobsen, my allergist and well-versed on mastocytosis, had given me his personal cell-phone number and a nine-day Prednisone supply, which, if necessary, would reduce inflammation, suppress the immune system, and, in so doing, ease the pain that, about once a year, hit my lower left intestinal area. It had worked at home. I didn't want to try it on the trail.

"Splurge on one item," my new trail guru, Craig Mayne, told me. His luxury item was a 3.4-ounce blow-up pillow. "Made all the difference. Slept like a baby." I was fine sleeping on a foam pad on hard ground—Waldo often used tree boughs for "mat" and pillow—but I did better with a head propped up by something softer than my boots and drier than sweat-soaked hiking clothes. I bought a pillow just like Mayne's.

Glenn would carry a solar battery pack that his daughters had given him for Christmas. It would power his GPS and my iPhone, though how effectively remained to be seen. Practice hikes had shown spotty results, largely because it didn't work much on shaded trails. My iPhone's priority was going to be, first, as a GPS; second, as a way to communicate home; and, third, as a way to send blog posts and photos.

Weirdly, one of the biggest take-or-leave issues for me was reading material. Waldo, sporting the neck-length beard of a mountain madman, often packed books into the mountains. He mentioned one October evening, in which, while a huge log kept the fire ablaze, he essentially read Marcus Aurelius all night. Most often, however, Waldo referred to reading Emerson and Thoreau, friends of one another in Concord, Massachusetts. (Whether there's any "Waldo" family connection between John *Waldo* and Ralph *Waldo* Emerson is doubtful. The "Waldo" surname, hardly uncommon, dates back to thirteenth-century Germany and shows up in Massachusetts as early as 1654.)

As a writer, I favored Thoreau, though his style could be the literary equivalent of slogging up high-mountain shale. Still, I counted it as one of my life's serendipitous moments when, while driving a rental car on back roads to a speaking assignment outside Boston, I accidentally came across his beloved Walden Pond. (While I found it ironic that there should be a gift shop in honor of the self-avowed anti-materialist, I nevertheless broke down and bought a "Simplify, Simplify" coffee mug.)

Initially, when planning the PCT trip, I had thought a lightweight book was the way to go; I ultimately bought a Pac-12 football preview magazine, ripped it in half—I would read Part II on the second leg of our journey—and, to save weight, cut out all advertising that didn't mean losing articles I wanted to read.

THE LAST month before our start date was hectic, the trip and the rest of our lives funneling into a fast-rushing river. I had a book deadline. Glenn was trying to recover from the Haiti trip and still find time to train. After work—he was doing double duty at an urgent care facility—he was running the streets of Albany as late as 11 P.M. every night. I kept telling him he needed less running, more stadium steps, more climbing, more hiking—and to do everything with weight on his back. But, then, he didn't have two buttes in his backyard as I did in Eugene, so I shut up, deciding I needed to take care of myself and let Glenn take care of himself.

Meanwhile, at *The Register-Guard,* colleague Bob Keefer pointed me toward a Web site showing Infrared Satellite Imagery of the Cascades with color-coded snow depths. Parts of our early goings showed six to twelve feet of snow in most places. In California, Keefer's twenty-five year-old son, Noah Strycker, had been on the trail for more than a month in an attempt to do the entire PCT; Bob wanted him to take a few weeks off to allow for snowmelt. Dozens of others had already done so. On the fringe of panic, I called Glenn at his office. "We're in trouble," I said. Days later, when I calmed down, Glenn and I traded places on the worry ledge. Now, he was the one fretting about the snow.

He was still fussing with a GPS he'd bought months before and had taken an REI class to better understand. Glenn embraced computers with the same enthusiasm that the Amish embraced cars, finding his GPS device more complicated than he'd imagined. As backup, I'd taken a refresher map-and-compass course at REI.

On a less important matter, we hadn't even decided on trail names, which were traditional on the PCT. In honor of my love for the Oregon Ducks, I'd toyed with QuackPacker, but Glenn wasn't hot on the whole trail-name idea, period. Some purists believed you had to earn your name on the trail. As the challenge before us grew closer, I came to realize that this trip wouldn't be about who I *said* I was. In the end, it would be about who I was, period.

TWO WEEKS before the big day, we gathered at my house in Eugene for a four-person summit: Glenn, Ann, me, and Sally. We needed to make sure everyone was coordinated in terms of our proposed schedule (we had mapped out our planned camping spots for all twenty-nine days) and resupply points (three for the trip's first half). In our backyard, we noodled over maps I'd tacked to the house. Glenn demonstrated his full-body mosquito suit. ("I would rather die of mosquito bites than be seen in that," I opined amid laughter.) And we discussed a topic we'd just as soon avoid but were wise not to: What to do if one of us, for any reason, couldn't stay on the trail.

An illness. A sprained ankle. A mastocytosis attack. Whatever. Was this "both in/both out?" Or should the other guy feel free to proceed—assuming, of course, that the person with the illness or ailment was safely en route home? Until such point in the trip, the healthy one was, of course, to stay with the one in trouble. But we agreed that if one person went down—as happened with Craig Mayne and his too-blistered-to-walk brother-in-law—the other should feel free to continue his way to the Columbia.

Amid the morning of checklists and charts, it dawned on me: A year had passed since we had committed to this journey. I had, my records showed, taken twenty-seven hikes—an average of 9.4 miles per hike—and climbed 22,500 vertical feet of buttes, hills, and coastal capes. We'd gathered reams of information, new equipment, and, soon, would head to Costco for bulk trail mix, thirty-count boxes of Svenhard's danishes, and enough high-calorie foods to make a health nut break out in hives.

I turned to Glenn. "We're really going to do this, aren't we?"

He pursed his lips slightly. "We're gonna try."

If it still didn't seem real, it did a few days later when I showed up at the UPS store to ship a box of food and fresh supplies to Hyatt Lake Resort. In a process that took nine hours, Sally and I had bought food and created sixteen one-gallon zip-lock bags full of it, one for each day. (Waldo wrote of, at times, wrapping a lunch for that day's "tramp" in an already-read *Oregonian* newspaper.) Somehow, knowing that box was en route to the southern Oregon lake resort and would be waiting for me to pick it up sealed my commitment.

In a twist that would have been laughable had we not been so concerned, our immediate dilemma was getting to the trail at the Oregon-California border to start the hike. A few days before we left, I spotted the following from the Pacific Crest Trail Association's Web site:

> From Windigo Pass to White Pass roughly two-thirds of the Oregon PCT and into southern Washington, the PCT is really holding snow this year. In general, snowmelt is about 3-4 weeks later than normal. As of mid-July there is still snow cover on well over half the trail. We expect snow cover to remain at the highest elevations and the northeast facing slopes until mid-August. If you venture out, please be prepared with the appropriate navigational tools. If you are looking for snow-free hiking we suggest the Columbia River area, or the Clackamas Lake/Warm Springs area.

When I spoke to a forest ranger about getting to the point where the PCT crossed the Oregon-California border, he scoffed. "You'll need to park your car near Mount Ashland Ski Area and walk twelve miles south"—backwards, in essence—"to get to your starting line." (Not that that was a problem for some adventurers in Waldo's time; in 1903, a climber named Sid Mohler hiked a hundred miles from his home in Oregon City, climbed Mount Jefferson, and walked back home.)

Glenn suggested that, a week before our start date, we drive four hours to the border and check out the snow situation for ourselves. The motion died for lack of a "second." We decided to just go—and to take our chances on a route to the Oregon-California border from west of the Siskiyou Mountains instead of east.

I said my goodbyes to my family: Ryan, daughter-in-law Susan, and their two kids, Cade, six, and Avin, soon to turn four; and youngest son Jason, daughter-in-law Deena, and their one-year-old son, Keaton.

A day before leaving, I sprayed my tent with a mosquito repellent and draped it over the grandkids' six-foot basketball hoop to dry. And I double checked my online communication system to make sure all was in order so I could not only track where we were but take notes.

"For an occurrence to become an adventure, it is necessary and sufficient for one to recount it," Jean-Paul Sartre said in his pre-blog times. I vowed to recount it—write about it—regardless of how it turned out.

A friend at work asked how I was feeling. I mulled the question momentarily. "Like a man about to go over a waterfall," I said. "Really excited."

I paused. "And really scared."

Part II
Breaking trail

WALDO'S WANDERLUST
The Judge's most ambitious trip was 160 miles from Diamond Peak to Mount Shasta in 1888.

PACIFIC CREST TRAIL

WIPED OUT
Toilet paper was an afterthought for me, which would prove to be a harsh lesson.

TRAIL TAGS
Acorn. Blood Bath. Blaze. We met an array of people who'd taken on PCT names, but nevertheless stuck with "Bob" and "Glenn."

*Have you swept the visioned valley with the green stream
    streaking through it,
Searched the Vastness for a something you have lost?
Have you strung your soul to silence? Then for God's
    sake go and do it;
Hear the challenge, learn the lesson, pay the cost.*

—Robert Service,
in *The Call of the Wild*

5. First steps

TRAIL LOG: Friday, July 22, 2011.   **Location:** Oregon-California border.
PCT mile-marker *: 1703.2.   **Elevation:** 6,100 feet.

* — *Miles from Mexican border.*

HIGH IN THE surprisingly-all-but-snow-free Siskiyou Mountains, we had barely stepped out of Glenn's Izusu Trooper when we saw them: two backpackers headed north, toward us. Both thirty-ish, both slim, both clearly trail-hardened. The biggest difference was his dark, Brillo-pad beard contrasted with her blonde ponytail. For a year we'd read about them, talked about, aspired to be like them. Now, I assumed, we were seeing them for the first time: PCT hikers.

In the same situation, Waldo may have nodded little more than a polite hello, not so much out of rudeness as shyness. "I do not advance to talk to strangers, as you know," he wrote to wife Clara from the mountains in 1883. Me? I was a reporter who got paid very average sums of money for engaging perfect strangers in conversations that could run on for hours.

"Are you guys actual PCT hikers?" I asked as we greeted the couple just a few hundred yards beyond where the trail crossed the Oregon-California border.

"That's us, mate," said the man.

"Welcome to Oregon," I said.

"Thanks, I'm Ben," he said, extending a hand, "and this is my partner, Kate."

OK, so much for trail names. Australians, they had started at the Mexican border in April and, among "thru-hikers" (technically, Glenn and I were "section hikers"), believed themselves to be behind only "Marcus," a hiker from Germany. The Pacific Crest Trail Association had issued 673 thru-hiker permits this season and, in a normal year, roughly half might make it. But this was not a normal year.

Glenn's wife, Ann, fetched the couple apples, pop, and red licorice—"thank you, thank you, thank you," they said as they shed their packs—and we talked for about fifteen minutes. About their journey thus far. About the trail ahead. And about the seemingly unending snow in the Sierra-Nevada Mountains; "at one point, I fashioned myself some crampons out of trail shoes and roofing nails," said Ben. He was, we'd come to learn, a do-it-yourself guy who eschewed trekking poles for tree-branch walking sticks that he'd found near the Mexican border more than three months earlier. He and Kate made it through the Sierras with no GPS, just a map and compass.

"It's not easy, the PCT," Ben said. "But it's a great place to be. Where you headed?"

"We're a couple of old farts just doing Oregon," I said. We were roughly twice the age of the couple.

"Maybe we'll see you at Callahans," Ben said. The hiker-friendly lodge was two days' walk from where we were, just off Interstate 5 south of Ashland. We'd planned on a hot meal, a shower and an overnight stay there.

We posed for a few photos—two veterans, two rookies—and bid the couple farewell. We headed south, down the trail a few hundred yards, to get to the official "Entering Oregon" tree. We were actually here, on the PCT. And there wasn't a cloud in the sky—nor, somewhat surprising given the Cascades' reputation for the annoying insects, a mosquito in the air. Glenn and I posed for cheesy photos at the border tree, put on our packs, and started hiking north. I took my first step at 12:34 P.M. True, it was only the beginning, but in my mind it was a moment as grandiose as Neil Armstrong's first step on the moon. A moment I figured I would never forget.

"Only about a million to go," I told Glenn. "Literally."

We headed up the hill, stopped at the car for Glenn to discard his full-body mosquito suit—after less than a quarter mile of Oregon, he was already convinced he wouldn't need it—and said our goodbyes. We wouldn't see Ann and Sally again for a week, at Crater Lake. Meanwhile, it was onward to the Bridge of the Gods.

In some ways, I would never be the same.

IT MIGHT HAVE been an omen. Within two miles, on the north flank of Observation Peak, we hit snow. Just like that, the trail vanished. We were faced with one of those straight-or-turn dilemmas. We saw faint footprints, but nothing decisive. I found myself on a thick-treed slope, already fumbling for the GPS on my iPhone. Glenn's face was already buried in his map. Eventually, we found the trail, but it had been a sobering lesson that struck with disquieting suddenness. Now I knew why Glenn had been so worried about what the snow could do to us staying on track. If such trail-loss became a common thing, we'd be lucky to make the Columbia by Halloween.

We met three guys known as "the Colorado Boys" heading north to Canada after having started in northern California. Beyond that, it was just us and a trail that stayed high enough on a ridge that we were afforded sweeping views of the Applegate Valley and Coast Range to the west and caught an occasional glimpse of California's Mount Shasta to the southeast.

At one point, the contrail of a jet pierced the Dodger-blue sky and I thought of the people up there, ripping through the air at hundreds of miles per hour with drinks in their hands. I was glad I wasn't among them.

By Wrangler Gap, seven miles into the trip, I felt what every long-distance hiker fears: a hot spot on my foot, specifically the left little toe. How could this be? I'd done dozens of hikes over the previous few months without blisters. Why now? I feared blisters like horses feared rattlesnakes: the villains were small but deadly. My spirits sagged. Suddenly, you're not only in pain, but your partner knows you're in pain. You're a liability. A problem. You're everything you don't want to be. I patched my foot with Second Skin and duct tape, and moved on, but not without a pit in my stomach. This, not snow, was my deepest fear: that something small—a blister, a twisted ankle, a "masto" flare-up—would turn into something big. But as darkness descended and we made camp at Long John Saddle, there was a certain satisfaction in having a day—OK, half a day—under our belts.

A "good tired" lulled my body toward sleep. I had a belly full of freeze-dried spaghetti with meatballs. The year-in-preparation adventure had begun. Life was good. Until, that is, I smelled something oddly suburban. Could it be? No, that's not a smell you encountered in the great outdoors. That's a raunchy stray-cat smell. That's a smell you don't want to smell anywhere, much less a foot from your nose on your first night on the PCT.

Cat spray.

The wall of my tent had clearly been sabotaged by a feline back home. Then I remembered: I'd left the tent hanging over the grandkids' basketball hoop the previous night to let the mosquito repellent dry. A neighborhood cat had obviously struck in the night.

"Great," I said to Glenn. "A cat sprayed on my tent last night."

From his nearby tent, he chortled in the darkness. Over. And over. And over. He couldn't stop laughing. I flipped over and faced the other way. In 1888, when Waldo had camped east of here as his small party of men headed to Mount Shasta, had he endured such humiliation? I don't think so. Alas, if this were my first humiliation—OK, second, counting the blister—it would not be my last.

THE LATE Oregon Governor Tom McCall would have loved it. Nearly every hiker we met on our first full day on the PCT was from out of state: People visiting, not staying. People just passing through. People not contributing to the demise of the state he loved. We met three hikers from Michigan, two from Minnesota, and one from North Carolina. And were passed by the Colorado Boys. Ironically, except for a few day-hikers, nobody we saw on this day was from Oregon.

As we gradually descended the eastern flank of the Siskiyou Mountains just south of Mount Ashland Ski Resort on this sunny Saturday morning, I saw the silver snake of Interstate 5. Saw the Oregon-California border where McCall had once posed at the "We Hope You Enjoy Your Visit" sign in 1982, his final stand in an attempt to protect the natural beauty of his beloved Oregon.

McCall's anti-growth-bomb-heard-round-the-world detonated in January 1971 when the Oregon governor was being interviewed by CBS News reporter Terry Drinkwater. In speaking engagements, McCall—the same age, fifty-seven, that I was now—had drummed home the point that Oregon wanted to avoid the runaway growth that, he felt, was ruining states such as California. He wanted Oregon to grow cautiously, smartly, on its own terms. But how, asked Drinkwater, do you stop people from moving to your state?

"Come visit us again and again," McCall said. "This is a state of excitement. But for heaven's sake, don't come here to live."

Pandora was out of the biodegradable box. McCall had spearheaded a Beach Bill in 1967 that gave public ownership to Oregon's coastline. He was championing the nation's first returnable bottle bill to cut down on litter. Meanwhile, he was looking for a way to articulate this new Oregon pro-environment doctrine. Now, with his statement to CBS, he had it. McCall's statement was the environmental salvo heard round the world. Within weeks, he'd been labeled both hero and villain. "The first person I've ever heard to place the environment over economics," wrote one letter-writer. Fired a dissenter: "The personal freedom to live where we choose is a cherished privilege."

Many Oregonians happily took up McCall's charge to defend Oregon, admittedly with a sort of smug defiance. Eugene artist James Cloutier designed a line of "Oregon Un-Greeting" cards and books to keep outsiders away, ballyhooing the fact that "Oregonians don't tan, they rust." The James G. Blaine Society formed to oppose development and unchecked growth. If much of the rhetoric was done with tongue firmly in cheek, foundational to the Oregon resistance was a serious belief that the state wasn't going to bow to the minions of mindless development. Out-of-staters who did move to Oregon, particularly Californians, learned to keep their geographic backgrounds quiet lest they endure subtle or not-so-subtle bias.

McCall, as gnarled and stubborn as an Oregon juniper, stood by his statement. No, he wasn't setting up border patrols, but neither was he backing off his concerns about unmitigated growth. A decade later, in 1982, McCall's successor, Vic Atiyeh, asked for a favor. Oregon was in the throes of a recession. Would McCall travel with him to the Oregon-California border at I-5 and, with the media on hand, say a few words after Atiyeh replaced the "We Hope You Enjoy Your Visit" sign with a "Welcome to Oregon" sign?

Then sixty-nine and wracked with cancer, McCall surprised more than a few when he said yes. But even then, the maverick governor got in the last lick in what he saw as a war to safeguard the beauty that made Oregon special.

"There's been a lot of bad mouthing about 'visit, but don't stay,'" he told reporters as I-5 traffic whisked by in the background not far from where I was now hiking. "It served its purpose. We were saying 'Visit, but don't stay' because Oregon, queen bee though she is, is not yet ready for the swarm. I am simply saying that Oregon is demure and lovely, and it ought to play a little hard to get."

McCall would be dead within a year. But he literally defended Oregon and its pristine beauty to his death, though he was not the first to do so. That honor belonged to a man who pleaded to safeguard such beauty nearly a century before McCall arrived on the scene: Judge John Breckenridge Waldo.

AS WE ZIGZAGGED east toward I-5 below, the freeway noise intruded like off-key notes in an Anglican hymn. Going from woodsy silence to freeway noise must have been the same sort of discordance Waldo experienced August 23, 1896, when he wrote in his journal: "There is a plain blazed trail from Diamond Lake to our old camp on the North Umpqua, and the grassy meadows along the river look like they had been struck by a cyclone—the sheep have laid all the grass flat to the ground they have not eaten. There are two thousand head of sheep at Diamond Lake."

We met the Colorado Boys again. They were high-tailing it to I-5 and hitchhiking into Ashland for rest and microbrews, clearly an anxious bounce in their steps after having not had a re-supply stop since the Seiad Valley some sixty miles earlier.

"Ten by ten, that's our goal," one told us.

"Ten miles by 10 A.M.—seriously?" I asked.

That seemed no more achievable to me than, say, running a sub-four-minute mile. As the Colorado Boys bid farewell and headed down the slope, Glenn and I joked about being the "Two-by-Four Boys." Joked, an hour later, about the Colorado Boys probably being in Ashland by now. Joked about how, at a water-and-pop cache for PCTers we'd found at Grouse Gap, we'd seen that Ben and Kate had jotted a note in the log book—and thanked the "Trail Angels" for the fluids— at 5:45 A.M. These guys were serious.

We continued heading east, one of few times the Oregon portion of the PCT headed decidedly that direction for north-bound hikers. As we neared the freeway, the trail nearly disappeared in brush. We crossed a road—this would prove to be the only "ugly" stretch of PTC I would encounter—and, just before falling off a steep pitch to I-5, saw the sign, spray-painted in green: "Callahans Mountain Lodge. First beer free for PCT hikers." Glenn didn't drink, I only sparingly. But the welcome felt good, even if we had been on the trail only two days.

We emerged from the woods into an opening framed by maintenance sheds of what appeared to be an old railroad yard. Something stirred in one of the sheds.

"Aaaaaaaaay!" Glenn, up front, jumped back. I recoiled. A deer sprang in front of us and bolted away. In the summer of 2011, fear would confront me in many ways, seldom with a sudden burst like this. At times, it was the subtle fear of strangers. In a few instances, it was the fear of being injured or getting sick. But the most prevalent fear would prove to be a variety that was seemingly stuffed tightly in my pack, poised to burden me every step of the way.

The simple fear of failure.

6. Left behind

TRAIL LOG: Saturday, July 23, 2011. **Location:** Long John Saddle.
PCT mile-marker: 1715.2. **Elevation:** 5,900 feet.
Days on trail, as of this morning: 1. **Portion of trip finished:** 2.7%

SOMETHING DIDN'T fit and by the looks on the faces of guests in tuxedos and black dresses, it was us: the two PCT hikers in sweat-matted shirts checking in at Callahans Mountain Lodge just before a wedding was to start. At the new-but-rustic-themed lodge, we obviously hadn't arrived with wedding invitations. But any sense of not belonging quickly dissipated in the "glad-to-see-you!" welcome from the Callahans folks, who told us about their "PCT Special": a shower, a dinner, a breakfast, and a place on the back lawn to throw our sleeping bags, all for $40. It was one of those deals that renewed your faith in humankind, as if you expected Opie Griffith's Aunt Bee might be in the kitchen scooping ice cream atop our pieces of fresh berry pie.

"With the wedding out back, if you wouldn't mind pitching your tents until a bit later that would be appreciated," an affable young man at the desk told me.

"Sure, no problem," I said.

Given that thru-hikers such as Ben and Kate had been on the trail for more than three months and we had been on it for less than two days, I couldn't help but feel a bit like Rosie Ruiz. She was the marathoner who appeared to have won the women's division of the 1980 Boston Marathon, only to be stripped of the title when it was learned she had joined the race only half a mile from the finish line. (No wonder she wasn't sweating.) To the untrained eye, perhaps we could pass for the real deal; Glenn's cobalt blue REI wind shirt was already so blotted with waves of white salt marks from sweat that it had taken on a tie-dyed appearance. And though we'd only done fifteen miles that Saturday, I was nearing that post-marathon fatigue stage. But we weren't about to fool any real-deal PCT hikers, who, I'm sure, could tell we were a couple of rookies who'd joined the race a half mile from the finish line.

Not that they treated us with scorn. *Au contraire.* When we bumped into Ben and Kate while waiting for a shower in the corner of a maintenance building, they welcomed us into the conversation like old friends. With a pair of tin snips, Ben was fashioning himself a metal wind break for his stove; the couple had already been into Ashland for supplies, checked in, and taken showers. Callahans' owner had given them free use of available tools.

"Good to see you, mates," said Ben.

"And you," I said.

We started sharing a bit about ourselves. Ben Dyer, thirty-one, was interested in hearing about the life of a newspaper columnist and, after learning I did a little sailing, boats.

"I'd like to sail," he said. "First, I'd like to kayak the Amazon River, then I've been thinking about sailing around the world. What kind of boat do you think I'd need to build? I'd like to build my own boat."

It was like asking for investment advice from a kid counting Chuck E. Cheese tokens.

"No, no, no, you don't want me telling you what kind of boat to build to sail around the world in," I said. "I sail a twenty-two-foot Catalina on a lake near Eugene that averages eleven feet in depth and feels like bath water. Much different from sailing around the world."

He laughed. Kate Manning grimaced. Manning, twenty-nine, was deep in conversation with Dr. Dull about what he seemed to believe could be a stress fracture in her foot, certainly not surprising after more than 1,700 miles of hiking often-rocky and -snowy terrain. Ben and Kate were roughly two-thirds of the way to Canada—and 7,500 miles from Australia—and didn't need this. But they were neither whiners nor obsessive jerks who were just in it to say they'd done it. Both were school teachers on sabbaticals. They were mellow, affable, and loved the trail.

"People help each other out," Ben told me. "Like in the Sierras. Marcus, the German guy, lost his sun glasses. We fixed him up with a makeshift pair."

But—make no mistake—the two were committed to getting to Canada. And had to be. The trail was so arduous that, over the decades, more people had stood atop Mount Everest than had reached Canada from Mexico via the PCT.

As the conversation continued, they reminded me—in so many words—that PCT hikers each had their unique styles, techniques, and equipment. On their trip to Ashland, Ben and Kate had stocked up mainly on fresh and dried vegetables, which were the staple of their on-trail meals but hardly common among hikers we'd read about. The exception: Ben also tucked a twenty-four-ounce can of Foster's Premium Ale into his backpack.

"I've got this little tradition," he said. "I get down the trail a ways, then leave one of these for a PCT hiker behind me. Just ask them to pay it forward down the line to someone else." I liked that kind of thinking.

We showered, doctored feet, off-loaded a little food into a hiker box for those following us, wolfed down two helpings of spaghetti in the restaurant, and watched the wedding reception kick into gear on the sprawling deck framed by firs.

When the July sky started fading blue to black, we rolled out our bags on the lawn—no tent tonight—as Ben and Kate set up a v-shaped homemade tarp with a speed and precision that suggested they'd done this a hundred times before, which, of course, they had. The sounds of the wedding reception cascaded off the deck and onto us like a loud waterfall emitting bad nineties music. Three shooting stars—a one-night record for me—flared above as I tried to ignore the spirited wedding reception.

I rolled onto my side and, with my headlamp, started reading my Pac-12 football magazine. Could Oregon repeat as conference champs? Would the Ducks' hated rivals, the Washington Huskies, finally return to respectability? I considered these questions for roughly eleven seconds before my eyes grew heavy and I stowed away the half-mag. The last thing I remember seeing before falling asleep was an automatic sprinkler head, ten feet away. It was aimed our way like artillery.

But, no, we would not wake to that rare PCT disaster of being soaked by an automated sprinkler system. We would, instead, experience a similar travail, the price you pay for a night of hot food, showers, and smooth lawns: a wedding guest, presumably a touch on the tipsy side, tripping on Ben and Kate's tarp lines and nearly landing atop us in the night. With villains like this, who needed bears?

GLENN AND I climbed east into the lower reaches of the southern Cascades, through a pine-oak woodland, the two of us fueled by stacks of Callahans pancakes and a desire to put the sound of the freeway behind us.

We hiked this Sunday morning with Ben and Kate. Good conversation. Nice views of Pilot Rock. And a short conversation with three PCT section hikers, one of whom introduced herself as "Dream Dancer."

"And your trail names?" she asked.

"Bob and Glenn," said Glenn. Mentally, I imagined a Dream-Dancer-esque trail name for Glenn: *Unicorn*.

"No, no, no," Ben interjected. "They're 'The Oregon Boys.'"

It was like being blessed by the Pope himself. Now that we'd been dubbed with an official identity, we were all the prouder to be hiking with Ben and Kate. But I knew that they were taking it easy for our sake and that we couldn't expect to hike much longer with them. We didn't. By noon, they politely bid us farewell, and I said the only words I could to a couple of Aussies who'd helped a couple of rookies find their trail legs.

"Goo' luck, mates," I said as we shook their hands. "Hope you make it to Canada."

"And hope you make the Columbia," said Ben before he and Kate headed up the trail.

By mid-afternoon, I couldn't see Glenn behind me so I stopped and lay down on my back beside the trail and looked up at the towering Siskiyou Mountain conifers. All was still. All was perfect. Timeless. My column deadlines had been left at the trailhead. All I needed to worry about now was the simple matter of survival.

Our next water source was listed in our guide book as "5. Water faucet," a spring twelve miles into the leg. We were hoping for about twenty miles total by nightfall and to camp at the trail's 1742.0-mile mark. (Miles from the Mexican border, based on Erik the Black's *Pacific Crest Trails Atlas: Volume 4 Oregon*.) Beyond maps on electronic devices, we were trusting two paper maps for our journey: The ones in Black's split-in-half book and a National Geographic 1:31,680 contour map in 8½-by 11-inch sheets that came complete with the PCT trail and other notes of interest by a California PCT hiker trail-named "Halfmile."

Both would prove invaluable; neither would prove infallible. We were high on a west-facing ridge when Glenn suddenly stopped. "Bob," he said. "I don't think we're on the PCT anymore."

"What do you mean?" I said. "Of course we are."

"Check it out," he said, looking at his GPS.

In Frostian terms, "two roads diverged into a yellow wood" a few miles back, and I was certain we'd taken the one that said "PCT." At the junction, so was Glenn. But his GPS showed us on some other trail. We were somewhere between lost and found.

"What's your iPhone say?" he asked.

I called up my TopoMaps app and followed the PCT north to where the split in the trail had been. Before we'd left, I'd downloaded twenty-seven quadrants to get us to Elk Lake, the end of Part I of our journey. Unfortunately, just before the recent trail-split junction, my on-screen map stopped. Apparently I should have downloaded twenty-eight. "I didn't think the trail was getting this far west here," I said, trying to justify my dim-wittiness.

My battery was low—eighteen percent—and cell phone coverage had been spotty since leaving Callahans, but I had a couple of bars. Whether it was enough to download a quadrant was another question. I called up the state map, organized in a grid of hundreds of quadrants. I pressed "full install high res" for "Emigrant Lake." Slowly, the blue bar of download progress began trucking. "We're in business," I said.

Outside of Salem, Judge John Waldo must have turned over in his grave. On his trip to Shasta in 1888—given his journal's reference to Johnson Prairie, Waldo traveled about ten miles east of us on his way down—he "entered the region without benefit of reliable maps, local familiarity, or guides," wrote Jeff LaLande in *Oregon Quarterly*. "In addition, the five men traveled north to south, hugging the mountains' crest, and this entailed miles of bushwhacking between marked trails."

The "Cary Map of 1806" was the first to depict Oregon's Cascades; in 1844, the year Waldo was born, a librarian at the U.S. Department of State, Robert Greenhow, published a map with more high-mountain specifics, but it carried forth mistakes earlier maps had made, including a southeastern, not north-south, trend of the Cascades. By the time Waldo hit the trail later in the century, he had access to far better maps. Even then, an 1881 map done by a U.S. Army engineer, Captain J.W. MacMurray, did not individually label such prominent peaks as the Three Sisters or depict the huge body of water that would be known as Waldo Lake. In other words, while the judge would have had access to good-for-their-times maps, Waldo had nothing close to the accuracy and detail of maps Glenn and I had, some done by individuals who had literally walked every step of the PCT.

"Yes!" In a few moments, the quadrant popped up. The blue pulsating ball located us on the map and showed that if we just continued north on this trail we could reconnect with the PCT. Apparently, there was a new portion of the PCT to the east—none of our maps had it—and, in another Frostian term, we'd "taken the road less traveled."

By the time we reconnected with the main trail, light was fading. Our destination was the exceedingly undistinguished "5. Water Faucet." We hoofed north, anxious to call it a day.

"Should be right here," said Glenn. No spring. No water faucet. No way to finish a twenty-mile day. It was getting darker. We saw a meadow ahead, which often meant water. Again, no faucet. We both had a little water left. But, if possible, the first edict of PCT hiking is to "camel up"—drink as much water as possible where it's available. And camping at water was a virtual given.

Glenn was already buried in his map. "Bob, we need to go on to Little Hyatt Reservoir," he said. I didn't want to hear that. Didn't want to hear anything that involved taking a single step more. But, of course, he was right. We trudged on and, half an hour—and a mile—later arrived in near-darkness at Keene Creek, dammed at Little Hyatt. (In 1880, when Waldo began his Cascade adventures, Oregon had only six dams; now it had hundreds.)

We'd been on the trail for twelve hours. I was spent, the living, breathing (sort of) embodiment of the cartoon in which a cow opens up the door to see her spouse standing there, carcass only. "Tough day at the office, dear?" Indeed, just filtering water was a chore, all the more so because the handle seemed to be getting harder to pump and the once-white cartridge was already the color of Oregon beach sand.

"I'm cowboy camping," said Glenn, meaning no tent. I agreed. We'd done twenty-two miles; who had the energy to put up a tent? It was a clear night. We spread our Tyvek drop cloths snug to the edge of a dirt parking lot. Beyond a few trailers in a mile-away meadow and a ranch house beyond, the place was vacant. We scarfed down our freeze-dried dinners, mine chili mac with beef.

I slid into my bag. No wedding parties tonight. No cat spray either. The smell tonight was distinctly different, though I was too tired to care what it was. Only in the morning, when we awoke drenched in dew, did

I realized that I had slept on it: the scattered remnants of horse dung.

The consolation prize for a rough finish Sunday night, for sleeping in horse manure, and for now carrying an extra pound or so of moisture in our sleeping bags was this: breakfast a couple of miles away at Hyatt Lake Resort. After a mile walk from the trail on a road, we spread our wet stuff on the new-but-rustic-looking restaurant's outside picnic tables so the sun could dry it while we ate. Inside, with permission, I recharged my iPhone—Glenn was packing a solar-charger but, as with water, you didn't want to waste a rare "resupply" opportunity; we wouldn't see another one until Crater Lake eighty miles away.

In some ways, that was just fine. A CNN reporter on the restaurant's television told of a madman having killed nearly a hundred people in Norway. For snippets of our first three days, we had still been tethered to the so-called "civilized" world; I was suddenly anxious for the deepening wilderness that we would be entering.

The real world had intruded on Waldo from time to time, too. He and his "tramping" buddies would pick up mail and send letters from remote post office spots here and there. On July 22, 1881, from Pamelia Lake near Mount Jefferson, he wrote: "Learned of (President) Garfield's assassination, or attempted assassination, but have not yet learned the result of the recount."

Beyond us, only two parties in the bare-bones restaurant were eating early breakfasts: a group that obviously knew the chef and waitress, and a couple roughly our ages. They were dressed in long-sleeved outdoor shirts and looked clean and organized. In other words, not the kind of folks who had slept in horse dung the previous night. They were, we learned after introducing ourselves, two Californians—married—headed north on the Pacific Crest Trail themselves, having started near Lake Tahoe seven weeks earlier.

"I'm Roadrunner," the woman said with a slight accent. We nodded.

"Cisco," said the man, holding out a hand to shake as a smile creased inside a salt-and-pepper beard.

The moment of truth had arrived. Did I dare introduce myself as QuackPacker or the two of us as "The Oregon Boys?"

"Uh, I'm Bob," I said. "And this is my brother-in-law Glenn."

"Where are you going?" asked Roadrunner. The accent was European. Swiss? German?

"Trying to do just Oregon," I said.

While the conversation was unfolding, my mind was distracted. Was my breakfast burrito coming? My stuff drying out? My iPhone battery getting charged?

The couple had, we learned, spent the previous night in one of the cabins next door. Given their fresh-looking appearances, I wouldn't have been surprised had they spent the previous night in a forty-five-foot motor home with high definition television and a stuffed sofa.

They said they were hoping to make Canada by mid-September. OK, so maybe they were out of our league in more than just the dress/cleanliness category. Glenn and I seemingly had little in common with these folks other than this winding trail called the PCT.

"*Goot* luck to you," said Roadrunner. "Maybe *vee* will *zee* you on the trail."

"And to you guys," I said. "Take care."

We next saw them on the mile-long walk back to the trail—on asphalt that was escalating my blisters from bad to worse. The two zinged past us, facing backward in a pickup truck. If they saw us, they didn't act like it. If they didn't see us, they should have.

7. In Waldo's footsteps

Trail log: Monday, July 25, 2011.
PCT mile-marker: 1752.2.
Miles hiked Saturday: 15.
Miles hiked Sunday: 22.
Total miles hiked: 49.

Location: Little Hyatt Reservoir.
Days on trail, as of this morning: 3.
Elevation: 4,600 feet.
Average miles per day: 16.3.
Portion of trip completed: 10.8%.

THE GLAMOUR of the Pacific Crest Trail had long belonged to California, where the trail began, where nearly two-thirds of it was located, and where it was at its most dangerous: water-starved deserts, snowy passes that reach to 13,153 feet, icy rivers that required water crossings, and the threat of bears and rattlesnakes.

Most first-person books about PCT experiences suggested the two Northwest states were the basketball equivalent of garbage time—the outcome essentially having been decided and participants now just going through the motions until time expires. Much as I enjoyed *The Cactus Eaters,* for example, Dan White spent only a fifth of the book on Oregon and Washington combined.

Not, of course that I was keeping score—*wink, wink*—but native Oregonians like myself grew up with an odd inferiority/superiority complex. We felt inferior, of course, because of the whole rain thing. ("What do you call three straight days of rain in Oregon? A weekend.") And we felt quietly superior because we secretly loved the rain and knew the deeper truth: even if the winter wetness nudged us toward the window ledges come April, our summer and fall were blissful makeup days. Having spent seven years in Washington, I believed the two states were similar in many ways, the two of us bound by regionalism, rain, and the relief that we weren't Californians.

Which is to say that if people's perceptions of the trail were California-centric, I was proud that the idea for the PCT had been hatched in the Northwest. It was January 13, 1926, when Catherine Montgomery, a teacher at Washington State Normal School in Bellingham (eventually Western Washington University) was meeting with a textbook salesman, Joseph Hazard. Knowing he was also an accomplished mountaineer, Montgomery concluded their textbook discussion with an out-of-the-blue comment that Hazard later recounted in his 1946 book, *Pacific Crest Trails*.

"Do you know what I've been thinking about, Mr. Hazard, for the last twenty minutes?"

"I had hoped you were considering the merits of my presentation of certain English texts for adoption!"

"Oh that! Before your call I had considered them the best—I still do! But why do not you Mountaineers do something big for Western America?"

"Just what have you in mind, Miss Montgomery?"

"A high winding trail down the heights of our western mountains with mile markers and shelter huts—like these pictures I'll show you of the 'Long Trail of the Appalachians'—from the Canadian Border to the Mexican Boundary Line!"

Six years earlier, in 1920, the United States Forest Service had routed a posted trail from Mount Hood to Crater Lake, called the Oregon Skyline Trail. It would become the PCT's first link, stitched together by old wagon roads, logging roads, and Indian paths. But Hazard would spread the idea to Washington. He sold Montgomery's idea to his fellow Mount Baker Club members in Bellingham, and soon other Northwestern outdoor clubs were blowing on the embers of it, too.

By 1937, the Skyline Trail was marked from the Canadian border to the California border. Meanwhile, Clinton Clarke, chairman of the executive committee of the Mountain League of Los Angeles County, proposed to the Forest Service and National Parks Service to "build a trail along the summit divides of the mountain ranges of these states, traversing the best scenic areas and maintaining an absolute wilderness character."

Finally, in 1968 the National Trails Act created the PCT, though it wouldn't be officially declared completed until 1993. From Montgomery's idea to complete fruition had taken sixty-seven years, a symbolic legacy suggesting that good things—like hiking the trail itself—take time and perseverance.

FROM THE BEGINNING the plan was to use the first half of the trip to prove we could actually do this, and, if we could, to invite *Register-Guard* readers along for the second half through online blog posts and photos. So, though I was posting messages and iPhone photos daily to my blog site, the updates weren't being read by the paper's 65,000 readers, most of whom had no clue I was embarking on this journey. Instead, my updates were being read by only family and friends and a smattering of folks who knew of this journey from my Facebook messages.

That said, I was beta-testing a daily report offering a numerical value on both our bodies and spirits. Regarding our physical well-being, "10" meant "brimming with life" and "1" meant "what life?" And for our mental condition, "10" meant "ecstatic" and "1" meant "ready to pin Dr. Dull to a tree with a trekking pole."

Physically, I was doing fine, other than that the shift to a trail diet had my stomach doing some gastronomical break-dancing that had me exiting the trail more than I preferred.

"Hey, Unicorn," I said while we skirted Hyatt Lake to the east, "I've got a new trail name for me."

"What's that?"

"Jiffy Poop."

I was doing worse on the mental scale. Day Four—Hyatt Lake-to-Griffin Pass—merited only a "5" on the spirits scale; as I wrote in my update, it was "my first down day." For starters, the snub—OK, the *perceived* snub—from Cisco and Roadrunner had gotten me off to a bad start. True, it meant only an extra mile on pavement, but it still meant extra walking on a surface that reminded me of how sore my feet really were. More than anything, it was the *idea* that they hadn't had their driver stop to give us a ride. Glenn, naturally, shook it off as no big deal. I tried, though with less success.

Because we'd picked up a resupply of food at Hyatt Lake, our packs were about eight pounds heavier than they had been when we'd arrived. By now, I'd learned that my "Necessary Water" chart had proven fairly accurate; in ten hours of hiking I was tube-sucking nearly two bladders of water—200 ounces. Meanwhile, our water filter was still balky. We could purify water, but each time we did so was proving to be far more of an ordeal than we'd imagined; the procedure felt like pumping up a basketball that was already full of air and required energy that, after hiking all day, was in short supply.

At a small creek that crossed the trail—barely big enough to dip our pump's weighted tube in—Glenn took time to take off his boots and check his feet. They looked like week-old pizza.

"Why didn't you say something?" I said. "Your feet are a mess." That was just Glenn: never one to complain. But, clearly, his feet were bad. Mine, after my first-day setback, were battered but not to the red-flag stage that Glenn's were.

As we rested at the creek, neither one of us had much gumption to press on. A butterfly featuring the three colors of a campfire s'more landed on the handle of one of my trekking poles. I barely had the energy to pull the iPhone from my pack's waist pocket and take a picture.

"How far we going today?" I asked Glenn, who, by now had patched his feet and had his boots back on.

He opened his map. "Not many options for camping by water," he said. "We've got a spring at Griffin Pass that'd give us a fourteen-mile day or we could go—let's see—eight miles more to Brown Mountain Shelter."

"I vote for Griffin Pass," I said without hesitation, slowly rising to put my pack on.

The previous day had been twenty-two miles. Beyond marathons, that was the farthest either of us had gone by foot in a single day, much less with thirty to thirty-five pounds on our backs.

"Griffin Pass it is," he said.

We stopped at Howard Prairie Reservoir for faucet water, lunch on a picnic table, and a quick nap. On a Monday afternoon, the campground was virtually deserted, the deadness of the place mirroring our moods. After struggling a tad to find the PCT trail again with a cross-country bushwhack, we pressed on.

A few miles up the trail, I saw something on a stump just off the trail.

"Hey, Glenny, Ben and Kate were here," I said. I pointed to the twenty-four-ounce can of Foster's Premium Ale sitting beside a small pile of "look-here!" rocks, beneath which a note said:

"Take it, fellow PCT hiker. Enjoy it. And somewhere up the trail, pass on a favor to another PCT hiker." It sparked my first full-blown smile of the day.

Glenn's face lit up, too. The sun-baked beer didn't appeal to either of us on this afternoon, though a cold one would have worked for me. What did appeal was the idea that we weren't the only ones going through this "you-asked-for-it" pain.

"Wonder how her ankle is doing," said Glenn.

Somehow, Ben keeping his promise with the gift beer lifted my spirits. The trail might not be easy, but I took some comfort in the reminder that we weren't the only ones on it.

AS WE CROSSED a Forest Service road—even these would become rare the farther north we got—I thought about Judge Waldo and how he, too, had walked these woods. At the end of the 19th century, plenty of trappers, sheep men, and miners knew pockets of the Cascade Range, but only a handful knew the north-south breadth of these mountains as did John Breckenridge Waldo.

His parents had journeyed on the Oregon Trail with the Applegate party in 1843, settling in Salem following a trip that was nearly five times the length of the Oregon PCT. John was born October 6 the next year, 1844, on the family's homestead east of the city, a year before his literary hero, Thoreau, would hunker down at Walden Pond to "live deliberately."

Waldo graduated from Salem's Willamette University in 1866, passed the Oregon state bar in 1870, and, seven years later, married Clara Humason of The Dalles, the daughter of other prominent pioneer settlers. She soon bore a baby girl, Edith. Waldo served on the Oregon Supreme Court from 1880 to 1886 and became, for all practical purposes, the state's first native-born chief justice. (Oregon didn't join statehood until 1859.)

If dogged by asthma-related illness into his adult life, Waldo wasn't feeble; the man summited 10,000-foot mountains, slept on bows of fir limbs, and rode horses. A bushy gray-white beard stretched south to his Adam's apple. In one of the few photos of him that remain, he resembles the suspicious snow-shoveling neighbor in *Home Alone*, his face exuding a certain sternness. But his journal writing was lively, optimistic, free-spirited, not the stuff that suggested even a glimmer of mean-spiritedness.

Wilderness brought out the boyhood in him. "What a feeling of youth I still have," he wrote from the trail on September 26, 1896. And the forest became not an escape but a second home. "As the drooping, boughy limbs brushed against me, I seemed as if treading the ground of some long gone ancestor, whose lineal descendant and heir I was. Indeed, in the woods I seem at home," he wrote on September 24, 1887, from Diamond Lake.

His life inspiration came from two places. The first was books. He was an avid reader of Thoreau, Emerson, Wordsworth, and Goethe. The other was the mountains. As a way to help alleviate his asthma, he retreated from the Willamette Valley to the Cascades come summer, apparently with wife Clara's blessings. For all but two summers between 1880 and 1907, Waldo left for up to three months to camp in the wilds.

"In good health," Waldo once quoted an Emerson poem, "the air is a cordial of incredible virtue." At the time, summer forays into the mountains weren't an uncommon practice for "wet siders"—Oregonians living on the rainy west side of the Cascades—who suffered similar plights, though most didn't pursue the arduous mountain tramping that Waldo did.

He and his men were believed to be the first European Americans to see certain mountains, lakes, and streams in the Cascades. "I am seated before a camp-fire, the shadows of night darkening the forest on the bear haunted shores of Waldo Lake," he wrote in August 1888. By then the lake had been named for him, and he was on a trip believed to have been the first recorded journey along the Cascade crest from Waldo Lake to Mount Shasta.

It was a segment that included the stretch Glenn and I now walked. "We hear the wild note of the Loon," Waldo wrote, "and the hum of the multitudinous mosquitoes near at hand. The fire blazes and crackles and shines upon us three—Ed, Harry and me.

"The lake looks beautiful lying embossomed in the evergreen forests—dark timbered peninsulas jutting into it, with the broad snow fields of Diamond Peak and blue mountains looking down upon it. Fire has not troubled its shores, and everywhere about it extends the green aromatic forest."

For inspiration to complement the beauty surrounding him, Waldo turned to words from John Greenleaf Whittier, a 19th-century Quaker poet, newspaper editor, and ardent advocate of the abolition of slavery.

> *Long be it ere the tide of trade*
> *With harsh resounding din,*
> *Shall break the quiet of these banks of shade,*
> *And Hills that wall them in.*

From poetry, he segued to Waldo-the-naturalist. "Here grows the graceful white pine, tall feathery hemlocks, and mast-like firs *(abies con-*

color) with white moss swaying from their branches and curving about their trunks. Here are evidences, too, of some of the wild inhabitants. The footprints of the timid deer denotes his recent presence and rapid flight. The blue grouse lifts himself out of the low huckleberry bushes at our approaches, settles himself among the hemlock branches and looks securely down upon us from his perch...." At this point, Waldo-the-naturalist transitioned to hungry back-country traveler who didn't have the luxury of mail-delivered food as did we. " ... But we have long arms he knows not of—they reach him, and down he comes for our breakfast to-morrow."

Waldo's 1888 trip to northern California, like ours now, was his most ambitious: a 160-mile exploration of the Cascade spine from Diamond Peak to Mount Shasta. To begin, he'd traveled southeast from Eugene—where we, too, had begun—on the Oregon Central Military Wagon Road. Like us, he had left in July.

Waldo and his men, however, traveled by horse. Their supplies were carried by pack horses tethered behind them, though at times he writes of wagons, too. At any rate, their supplies were as heavy as ours were light: iron skillets, weighty tents, pots and pans, lard, even a canvas boat. (Having twice gone on week-long elk-hunting trips to Oregon's Blue Mountains—as a columnist, not as a hunter—I had experienced that kind of camping. If allowing certain "luxuries," it still was a challenging experience that, in my case, included leading a mule to a stream, filling tin canisters on its flanks, and leading the sometimes-stubborn animal back to camp.) Waldo and his men might have stayed three or four days at a particular lake, hunting, fishing, climbing nearby peaks, resting the horses. It was common for them to travel only a few hours a day.

The Waldo party would have been a few miles east of us, camping at Lake of the Woods and soon skirting Klamath Lakes en route to a September 26 summiting of 14,180-foot Mount Shasta. "The climb was not difficult, but the altitude told on me somewhat before I got to the top," Waldo wrote. "The hot, sulfurous vapor was rising out of the crater, and cannot but be the first thing to attract attention on reaching the summit. Here was a living volcano beneath our feet."

At times, thinking of Waldo having once been in these same woods almost made me feel as if he were still here. At other times, however, his journal reminded me of how much water had run under the proverbial bridge since he lived. In 1888, from McKenzie Bridge, he made reference to "old Mr. Spores, a veteran of the War of 1812, who lives just below here." The man was ninety-three years old. In a state whose history was relatively young, Waldo had interacted with a guy who had been born in 1795.

"The old gentleman spoke highly of my father, and seemed glad that one of his sons should call to see him, tottering now as he is, all worldly cares over, on the brink of his grave … . He is one of the very few still among us of a former and interesting generation."

Just as I looked back on Waldo with the wonder of time—he was born 110 years before I was—so did the judge have a deep appreciation of the past. On September 19, 1890, Waldo discovered two names chiseled into a tree at Waldo Lake, a fairly common "we-were-here" tradition in those times. "(They) must have been put there nearly, if not quite, forty years ago—S. Bagley and Wm. Winkel—if the last two letters of the name were deciphered correctly. They gave little thought of the interest their names would excite long afterward or they would, at least, have added date. But that would still have left the inquiry who were S. Bagley and Wm. Winkel. Musty pioneer records must be stirred on their account."

Waldo had the same curiosity about these etched-in-a-tree names as I had about his name being similarly carved into a tree up ahead near the PCT. Indeed, it was strange thinking how deep in history Waldo and his men lived, so distant from Glenn and me, and yet sharing much in common. Waldo had come for the adventure, for the challenge of getting to certain places, for the chance to escape into, as he wrote, "the unaltered wilderness." Like us, he had left a family in the valley. Like us, he spent long stretches of time without seeing another human being. And, like us, he sought to camp each night where clean water was available, which brought us to a meadow at Griffin Pass early in the evening.

We found a flat spot near a cluster of fir trees for our tents. I headed for what I could hear was the spring that our map had indicated was nearby. I threaded my way through another clump of trees, spotted the blessed site of a pump handle, and, suddenly, noticed something bright to my left: a bright apricot-colored tent—the kind a thru-hiker used.

Outside, four trekking poles were neatly planted in a row, each handle covered by a hiking sock obviously placed there to dry. From inside came the quiet exchange of conversation, which stopped as I snapped a twig. The fly zipped open; whoever was in the tent had heard me. A woman stuck her head out the flap and offered a welcoming smile.

It was them: the Californians.

8. From whimsy to worry

Trail log: Tuesday, July 26, 2011.
PCT mile-marker: 1766.2.
Miles hiked Monday: 15.
Total miles hiked: 63.
Days on trail, as of this morning: 4.

Location: Griffin Pass, about 20 miles south of Highway 140.
Elevation: 5,650 feet.
Average miles per day: 15.7.
Portion of trip completed: 13.9%.

THE DAY BEGAN with a frightening realization.

"How you fixed for toilet paper?" I asked Glenn after my traditional post-wakeup outing to Commune With Nature had left me doing the math: a two-inch-thick toilet paper roll divided by four—the days we had until picking up resupplies at Crater Lake. I didn't like the answer. But improvisation is a hiker's best friend; I'd figure something out. And, I assumed, this was not a big problem. Alas, the day would end with another frightening realization that was a big problem.

"You getting low?" Glenn asked as we stuffed our tents, bags, and other stuff in our packs with the illumination of head-lamp light.

"Yeah," I said. "I should have grabbed some back at Hyatt Lake. I'll be OK."

I crammed down my traditional three Svenhard's danishes and headed back to the spring to top off my water supply. The Californians weren't stirring yet. Figured. The differences between Californians and Oregonians were imprinted in our DNA, some believed. Or at least deeply rooted in the two states' histories. On the Oregon Trail back in the mid-1800s, a fork to California split in western Wyoming. After gold was discovered in 1849 the trail to California became a nineteenth-century Santa Ana Freeway. Those who weren't gold-crazed stayed on the northern-most route, headed for Oregon's less materialistic Promised Land, even if it did prove to be a soggy Promised Land. Because the Oregonians valued people, place, and a hard day's work—not the hollow promises of get-rich-quick thinking—they became a simple, independent lot, their souls marinated in the sauce of low expectations and endless winter/spring drizzle. On the other hand, those who took the trail to California became, in generations to come, movie stars, beach bums, and participants of a second rush, not for gold but for Botox.

So, no, it didn't surprise me that it was already 5:45 A.M. and the Californians weren't stirring. I got my water, and Glenn and I hit the trail.

LONG-DISTANCE hiking, I started to realize, not only brought you in touch with nature and your soul, but also brought you in touch with your body—in the most literal of senses. After four hot days on the trail, certain parts of my body started coming in contact with other nearby parts of my body. At first the friction was just a casual "hello-how-are-you?" But as the miles passed and the temperature increased and the legs slid back and forth, the relationship deepened to a dangerous level of social interaction, leaving me only one choice: Anti Monkey Butt.

Monkey Butt, as I called it, was like baby powder only for adults with, uh, chaffing issues, front or back. Sally had stumbled across it and, at the last minute, I'd poured sixteen ounces of it into a zip-lock sandwich bag, momentarily flustered about whether to categorize it as "Toiletries" or "Emergency." On this day, as I let a smirking Glenn go by so I could make a Monkey Butt application, I definitely would place it in the latter category. And was thankful that I'd brought it.

That little challenge aside, the morning proved to be the smoothest, fastest, coolest stretch of hiking we'd had thus far. Once we got over 6,339-foot Old Baldy, which afforded our last glances of Mount Shasta behind us, we were trucking slightly downhill through a cathedral of towering trees—Oregon's proverbial "green tunnel"—in the Fremont-Winema National Forest. Trees covered almost half of Oregon's total land area but dominated the Cascades. The mountain range stretched from Northern California into British Columbia, Oregon's tree-thick portion representing about one third of that.

Amid the quiet, a dead tree crashed to earth somewhere in the forest, jolting my heart. "Heard a tree fall a short time ago," wrote Waldo on August 16, 1905, from near Mount Jefferson. "Silently it has grown and is heard only when it falls. 'Silently,' says Carlyle, 'the oak has grown in the forest for a thousand years.'"

It was here, in these woods, where Glenn announced we would be "going through a little lava later today," a prediction that, in hindsight, was akin to the captain of the Titanic predicting a "little water in the bilge this evening; nothing to worry about." It was here that we first noticed the PCT had teeth.

In deference to the dry, rocky lava spread before us on Brown's western flank, a view of Mount McLoughlin emerged to the north-northwest like an unexpected guest, all rock and cinder with a splash of snow near the top. It was nearly symmetrical, taking on a sort of Mount Fuji look as we hiked farther north. In Waldo's day, the 9,495-foot peak was known as Mount Pitt and, earlier, as Mount Shasty. Call it what you will, it was beautiful. And, if all went well, by nightfall we would be camped on its eastern flank, close to where Waldo had begun his ascent of it in 1888.

But first came the lava fields beneath 7,311-foot Brown Mountain. For the first time, I started appreciating my wide-brimmed Columbia hat with its rear neck flap; the sun was intense. And, looking at a trail that wound through rocky chaos, started appreciating the volunteers who kept up the PCT; in 2010 alone, they contributed time that had an in-kind value of nearly $3 million—so people like me could walk ourselves into blistered-foot weariness.

The trail through the lava was a series of horseshoe-shaped loops wrapping around the mountain's lower flanks: in and out, in and out. To keep my mind off the monotony I began counting them: *Ten, fifteen, twenty.* The trail had become a seemingly endless snake of burnt-red cinder. *Twenty-five. Thirty. Thirty-five.*

Up and down, around and around. The sun seared the tree-less spread of lava rocks, sapping my internal battery as if I were a cell phone on "roam." The rocky trail twisted my ankles in ways they'd never been twisted; in places, the challenge was like walking across a swimming pool filled with cinder-studded golf balls.

After we'd rounded thirty-nine such loops—as if to convince myself that, if not method to this madness, there was at least an *end* to it—I boldly made a prediction about when the red monster would return to the lushness of forest.

"Forty," I said. "We'll be out of this stuff after one more loop."

We trudged on. "OK, forty-five," I said when forty came and went with no reprieve. At forty-five, I predicted fifty. As the afternoon wore on, the waiting game became like that scene in the movie *Airplane!* "Flight 209 now arriving, gate eight ... gate nine ... gate ten ... ." Finally, the plane actually landed. Sixty-four loops.

Blessedly, we stopped to rest beside Cascade Canal, a well-shaded creek that intersected the trail at Highway 140, which wound its way from Medford to Klamath Falls. I soaked my feet in its chill, then lay on my back with my aching nubs propped on a log. In an e-mail before we'd left, Glenn had said it well: "Face it. At any given moment, some part of our body will be aching." Prophetic man, Glenn.

I tilted my head sideways. That's when I saw them: Cisco and Roadrunner, bounding across the highway, through the picnic area, and on up the trail, with all the zeal of Julie Andrews twirling on an Austrian hillside in *Sound of Music*. Or, in my state, so it seemed. Probably empowered by organic fruit that they'd grown and dried themselves. Too far away for a hello, too tired for a happy face, I raised an unenthusiastic wave and reached for another handful of Good & Plenty candy.

If the sight of the two Californians brought regret regarding the past—leaving us in pickup dust as they headed for the trail at Hyatt Lake—the Messenger of Doom brought fear regarding the future. I saw her just after crossing Cascade Canal, coming south toward us, with warnings of deep snow on the steep pitches of Devils Peak.

"We nearly died."

The words slammed me like an icy snowball to the side of the head. She and her husband had been so shaken by what they'd encountered that they'd aborted their cross-Oregon PCT trip.

The news changed everything. The trip we'd planned for a year was suddenly at risk of falling apart. Earlier in the day I had used humor as a reserve tank to get me through the pain. Now, my humor tank was south of "E."

Things only got worse when, two hours later, we realized we had overshot Freye Lake, where we planned to camp, by at least half a mile. We had already put in twenty-two miles; we had been on the trail for more than thirteen hours. And darkness was suggesting it was closing time.

Our marathon suddenly became a marathon with steeplechase barriers. Over blow-down. Under blow-down. Fighting through fir limbs. Pushing through bitter brush. My shirt was soaked, my legs scratched, my heart pounding. But, somehow, I was going to find this lake. Like a madman, I stretched ahead of Glenn, iPhone-with-GPS-app in one hand, my two trekking poles in the other. I increased my pace, fueled by weariness and desperation.

A huge old-growth tree lay on its side, chest-high, crossing my northbound path. I planted a boot on a branch and, with whatever energy I had left, leveraged myself to the top of the log. I started walking—almost stumbling—atop the fallen tree like an Old West bandit atop a hijacked train, looking for the right place to jump off with the bags of gold. My eyes darted from the blue dot on the iPhone map to the hope of seeing water through the trees.

That's when I tripped. With my eyes looking for the lake I hadn't seen the snag. I fell off the log, toward the forest floor, into the gathering gloom of uncertainty. Just before hitting, I instinctively raised my fists slightly and landed on elbows and torso, saving my iPhone and wrists. I scratched up my arms and legs and pretty much punctured any last vestiges of pride I'd had after having to make the Monkey Butt stop. Other than that, the only thing wrong with me was bag-of-bones weariness and aching hunger.

Soon I'd add a third: The realization that the reason we hadn't seen any mosquitoes to this point was that they'd all gathered here for a delayed "Welcome to Oregon" party. We were the guests of honor for hosts who, with snow-clogged trails, hadn't seen much in the way of fresh meat this summer.

Though we found Freye Lake, I slunk into frustration, whatever energy I had left used to don my mosquito-net hat and gather some purified lake water through our balky pump. When a mosquito slipped between neck and net and flew into my mouth—apparently on a dare from his pals outside—I made the mistake of spitting. Bad idea with a mosquito net covering your face. Glenn, beat to the bone, wasn't Mr. Happy either.

"How's this spot for the tents?" he asked, pointing to a piece of ground less sloped than others.

"Yeah, whatever," I said, hardly looking up.

The lake sat in something of a bowl. Unless we wanted to traipse over blow-down to the far side, our only choices of tent spots were, in catalog terms, "steep," "steeper," or "steepest." I pulled off my boots and put on my camp flip-flops, which had proven to be a horrible choice from the trip's opening day; the stem in the middle irritated my aching toes and my feet were continually sliding off the rubber soles.

Glenn had his tent up and was boiling water for dinner about the time I found my sleeping bag deep in the caverns of my pack. "I keep sliding toward the lake," he said.

Everything slid toward the lake that night. My sleeping bag was atop a slippery Therm-a-Rest Z-Lite pad that was sliding down the nylon tent's seemingly siliconed floor, which lay on a piece of Tyvek so slick that kids could have use it as a sled—all on a downward slope. I semi-slept scrunched against the tent's lake-side wall all night long.

The only saving grace of the night's misery was this: It kept my mind off worse thoughts, namely Devils Peak.

9. Calm before the storm

Trail log: Wednesday, July 27, 2011.
PCT mile-marker: 1788.3.
Days on trail, as of this morning: 5.
Miles hiked Tuesday: 22.
Total miles hiked: 85.
Location: Freye Lake, just above Highway 140.
Elevation: 6,200 feet
Average miles per day: 17.
Portion of trip completed: 18.8%.

I HAD LOBBIED for sleeping in but Glenn wouldn't have it. Even though we had agreed on a light day—thirteen miles—he thought it best we get up at 5 A.M., as we had the last few mornings, and get our miles in before the afternoon heat. I had no energy to debate, so acquiesced.

By now, the morning routine was worn into me like a well-traveled trail: Wake to the 4:50 A.M. soft beep-beep-beep of my watch, purposely set ten minutes before I announced to Glenn it was time to get up, thus giving me a necessary head start over Mr. Eagle Scout. Pray for strength, endurance, and wisdom. Pray for my family. Find headlamp. Find four-ounce container with water ready to go. Take four ounces of liquid Gastrochrome for my mastocytosis. Take five pills that were in a one-inch-by-one-inch plastic bag labeled by day and "morn" or "eve." Slip off warm long-sleeve sleep shirt, tug on damp, smelly, long-sleeve hiking shirt. Put on down jacket and stocking hat. Take off long-john bottoms. Slide on cold, damp hiking pants. Find foot tape and powder. Doctor feet. Slide on cold, damp socks. Pull on boots. *Ouch!* (The anti-blister fairy apparently hadn't come in the night.) Stuff sleeping bag into nylon pouch not much larger than a sleeve of tennis balls. Gather any remaining items and make sure they were either in my pockets or in the pack. Slide pack out of tent. Wake Glenn, who had no idea that I had been getting up ten minutes before he has.

"I can't figure out how you get ready so fast," he would often say, much to my failed-Scout delight.

Commune With Nature. Wash hands with mini-antiseptic towelettes. Cram down two or three Svenhard's danishes. Organize all items in pack. Affix accordion foam pad to back of pack. Stretch left arm over head. Stretch right arm over head. Bend at waist, left, center, right. Stretch hamstrings. Watch Glenn finish folding up his tent and placing it in his pack. And, with the prelude over, do it: Take the first of what would be about 25,000 to 50,000 steps on this day.

"Wonder what happened to the Californians," I said after we'd bushwhacked our way up a hill and caught our breath after reaching the PCT.

"Yeah," said Glenn. "Not like there's a lot of water up here. Freye Lake is about it. Thought they'd be camping there, too."

After a couple of hours, we were paralleling Fourmile Lake, on which Waldo had camped on September 15, 1888, while headed for Mount Shasta. Glenn was up ahead. Suddenly, I heard footsteps. I turned. There was a young man in shorts, T-shirt, and a pack that couldn't have weighed much more than twenty pounds.

"Scared me," I said.

"Sorry," he said, extending a hand. "Blood Bath's the name."

Scared me more, I thought. He was a thru-hiker from Maine, the first Full Meal Deal hiker—Mexico to Canada—that we'd seen since first encountering Ben and Kate at the border some eighty-eight miles and six days before. He had already hiked thirteen miles. It was 9:30 A.M.

"And how did you get the name?" I asked.

"At the PCT Kickoff Party in Warner Springs last May," he said. "They had this relay involving carrying bear canisters. I cut my hand on one. It was a mess."

Fortunately, bear-resistant food storage containers weren't required in Oregon as they were some places along the PCT in California. We chatted but his eyes kept darting up the trail. "I need to roll," he said. "I told myself I'd try to get in at least one fifty-mile day. This is it."

Glenn and I watched as he headed north with near race-walker strides. We just looked at each other. *Fifty miles?* "Hey," I said, "how many other nearly sixty-year-old guys are out here like us?"

"Not many, Bob," said Glenn. We pressed on. "Because," he said, "they've got brains." Then burst into his customary "aren't-I-funny?"

laugh. It felt good to laugh again. For all we joked about being a couple of dinosaurs in Merrells, we were quietly proud to be on the trail. Waldo, in 1903, near Fish Lake, had written about encountering an eighty-five year-old man—my mother's age as I write—who "believes coming to the mountains does one good." If he could do it, we could do it—if, of course, we could get beyond Devils Peak, the thought of which I was subconsciously hiding beneath a veneer of whistling-in-the-dark humor.

After the Blood Bath encounter, we'd barely regained whatever stride we had when we noticed a couple of hikers sitting trail-side up ahead. A man in a neat blue shirt, a woman in a neat mauve shirt. *Them.*

"*Goot* morning," said Roadrunner, who, with Cisco's help, appeared to be preparing some sort of exotic brunch. "*Vee meets* again."

They had a mini table cloth spread on a log. Who does that on the PCT? Goodness, the previous night, amid my slipping and sliding, I'd awakened to feel lumps beneath my back and realized I'd slept on a couple of my Svenhard's danishes. No wonder my breakfast tasted flat.

Cisco was stirring dried mushrooms into a dish they were concocting. In our entire time on the trail, we never concocted anything more exotic than freeze-dried dinners made by pouring hot water in a foil pouch, shaking it, and letting it set for eight minutes.

"How did we miss seeing you last night?" I said. "Freye Lake is just about the only place up here with water. Where'd you guys camp?"

"About two hundred feet north of Highway 140, just off the trail, near where we saw you guys," said Cisco.

We learned a little more about them. Learned that they were from the San Francisco area. That Roadrunner, fifty-two, had gotten her trail name because of her speed and Cisco, sixty, from a nickname he'd been given at birth. His father, a surgeon, had been called that, based on the movie *The Cisco Kid*; Rich, his real name, had inherited the moniker.

The two learned a little more about us. Learned that I was a newspaper columnist and that Glenn was a family-practice physician, albeit one who, with the bill of his hat flipped skyward, now looked a bit like Elmer Fudd of 1960s cartoon fame. And that we were concerned about getting around Devils Peak. OK, *really* concerned.

"The problem, as with most mountains, is the north face," said Cisco. "With the sun in the southern sky, it's shaded much of the day. Steep and melts slowly."

"Normally you would have switchbacks on that face," said Roadrunner. "But those switchbacks will be buried in snow. Instead, you'll have a sheer wall that falls into a glaciated bowl."

She laced the phrase "glaciated bowl" with a sense of trepidation, not as if she feared it herself but that other, less experienced types, might. *Glaciated bowl.* It sounded like something you'd read in *Into Thin Air,* the best-selling book by a 1972 Corvallis High classmate of mine, Jon Krakauer, about the eight climbers who died on Mount Everest in 1996. It sounded like a repository for bodies, a final stopping place for those who either didn't have ice axes or those who couldn't use one to stop a slide. Interestingly, if you check the *Atlas of Oregon's* "Ice Age Glaciers" two-page spread, those glaciers are shown as beginning in the southern Cascades within a few miles of where we now stood. The journey was about to change, the stakes to rise.

I needed to move on. Devils Peak had my full attention; I didn't need any more convincing. I needed to somehow get beyond it so we wouldn't have to slink back to Highway 140 in defeat.

"Bon appetit," I said, masking any fear. And we headed on.

"SHE'S A BOOK editor," I said. "He works for some sort of environmental agency. No kids. Second marriages for them both. And total outdoors nuts."

"What?" asked Glenn.

"I'm just guessing about Cisco and Roadrunner," I said. "And what do you think?"

"I don't think, Bob," he said. "I just walk."

Yes. That's what we did, wasn't it? We walked. More than 200,000 steps thus far, I figured—one more way to keep my mind off the blisters and fatigue. The good news: I hadn't needed Monkey Butt lately. The bad: Conserve as I might, I had my doubts as to whether my toilet paper was going to last me to Crater Lake.

We reached our off-trail camping spot, Deer Lake, in the heat of mid-afternoon. I slipped on my running shorts and plunged into the lake for a swim. I hadn't showered in four days. At 6,200 feet it was ice cold but cleansing, the smell and taste of lake water bringing back an array of good childhood memories of our family's annual camping trip to Cultus Lake in Central Oregon and college-day backpack trips to other lakes sprinkled along the PCT.

At dusk, Glenn got a fire going, our first of the trip. For once, the experience felt like actual camping. I read a few more team previews from my Pac-12 football magazine—Oregon State, Stanford, and Washington State. For some reason, I put off reading the section on Washington, which was a nasty word in Eugene.

After our freeze-dried dinners—beef teriyaki with rice for me—we leaned against logs and talked. There was a long pause while the fire occasionally spit a spark. I looked into the night sky splashed with stars, which triggered a thought.

"You ever see that *Twilight Zone* episode about the hitchhiker?" I asked Glenn, realizing in mid-question that he, of course, hadn't. He had the pop-culture IQ of a monk. Entire fads—bell-bottoms, pet rocks, Sony Walkmans—had come and gone without him noticing their presence. He couldn't name all four Beatles or recognize the theme song from *The Brady Bunch*. Not surprisingly, he didn't answer my question. I was too tired to look his way.

"So, this woman is driving across the country, right, and she sees this old guy hitchhiking," I began. "No big deal; she doesn't stop. But on up ahead, there he is again. Strange, but possible; she'd made a stop for gas so maybe he'd gotten a ride with someone else and they'd dropped him there. But then it happens again. He's there, out in front of her as she drives by, holding out his thumb with this innocent yet slightly sinister look on his face. Again. And again. He's always there, appearing out of nowhere. And she's going crazy."

"Glenny, don't you get it?" I said, pausing for dramatic effect. "Cisco and Roadrunner are the *Twilight Zone* hitchhikers of the PCT. They just pop up out of nowhere. It took us two hours to slog up that mountain last night, and yet there they are, *ahead* of us by mid-morning today but telling us they stayed down near the highway. What did they do, start hiking at 3 A.M.? I mean, did they really leave from Sierra City like they said or did they just morph out of nothingness behind those two breakfast menus at the Hyatt Lake Restaurant?"

He didn't answer.

"Glenny?"

I looked his way. He was fast asleep.

10. Going to meet the devil

Trail log: Thursday, July 28, 2011.
PCT mile-marker: 1802.0.
Days on trail, as of this morning: 6.
Miles hiked Wednesday: 13.8.
Total miles hiked: 98.8.

Location: Deer Lake.
Elevation: 6,150 feet.
Average miles per day: 16.5.
Portion of trip completed: 21.9%.

THIS WAS IT. Shortly after the 4:50 A.M. wakeup beep from my Casio, I lay in the darkness and thought: *By day's end we will either be triumphantly past Devils Peak or heading back to the highway, our trip in shambles.* In 8.6 miles, we would know our fate. I prayed, then slid on my headlight and reached for my still-damp clothes that hadn't been washed in nearly a week. Show time.

Each year, particularly in California, snow spoiled hikers' PCT dreams. Sometimes it only delayed those dreams. People with flexible time schedules might hop ahead to a lower-elevation section, then return at trip's end, after significant snowmelt, to finish what they'd missed earlier. We had no such flexibility. This was it. By this afternoon, it would be either on to Crater Lake for a triumphant reunion Saturday with our families—and fresh supplies—or a marathon-distance trudge back to Highway 140, knowing we'd failed.

The uncertainty gnawed at me. The more I tried to ignore it the more it returned to pester me. I desperately wanted to complete this cross-state hike as we'd planned, border to border. On the other hand, Glenn and I weren't seasoned adventurers willing to risk all for a notch in the belt. Nor were we willing to put our lives on the line just so we could say we "did it."

The morning's hike was a quiet one, the only revelry muted recognition that we had hit the hundred-mile mark of our journey. I took my mind off Devils Peak—and its prelude, a peak known as Lucifer—by thinking of Judge Waldo. In September 1888, he had come south near the present PCT, camping at Island Lake, a cutoff to which we had passed the previous day.

Waldo spent most of his summers in the 110-mile stretch between Mount Jefferson and Diamond Lake. But in 1888, at age forty-three, he and four others ventured this way on a trail far cruder than the well-maintained PCT we now followed.

Waldo was Oregon's John Muir, the naturalist from California who founded the Sierra Club—and whose mountain journeys, too, once took him north through this area, to Crater Lake. For Waldo, the high-mountain experience was religion without church. "Here I am at Pamelia Lake, breathing the pine scented air and already feeling much stronger, both in body and spirit," he wrote in 1907. "Blessed be the mountains and the free and untenanted wilderness."

When something threatened that experience, however, Waldo got angry; "at Crane Prairie once more," he wrote on August 9, 1886. "Quite well but my fine Summer Resort has been discovered and turned to base uses—nearly four thousand sheep have dispossessed us and the deer and bear from a great part of our possessions—driven us into the nooks and corners of its wide expanse, still undisturbed, but with such occupation of a part, the charm of the whole is gone."

Given his love for the Oregon Cascades—and the efforts he would take to keep that wilderness wild—it struck a sour, if not intriguing, note with me to learn what Waldo and his pals had done at Island Lake: chiseled a foot-high marquee into a tree on the southeast corner of the lake and carved their names and the date they'd been there. "*Sept. 13, 1888.*" In our modern-day eco minds, in a time when some purists would have frowned on me for not packing out my human solid waste, the idea seemed reprehensible. But the tradition of arborglyphs—tree writing—dated back centuries. Wrote Robert H. Cox in *The Pacific Crest Trailside Reader:*

> Trees have been used to express love, as message boards and boundary marks, as location maps, and as artist's palette. Cherokee Indians tagged beech trees along portions of the Trail of Tears in the 1830s; Civil War soldiers would carve names and dates in trees as they passed; pioneers left their mark as they migrated west; and

> Basque sheepherders etched images on the high-country aspen of Nevada, Oregon, and California beginning in the late nineteenth century.

The idea that I could have touched Waldo's name etched into a Shasta red fir the previous day had been inviting. And given another pass on that portion of trail, I would take the Red Lake Trail, a western spur of the PCT. I would bushwhack my way to "The Waldo Tree," clearly marked, and surrounded by a split-log rail. But the side trip looked to be at least a two-hour proposition. On paper, before the trip, the idea had seemed practical. But with a depleted body and a concerned mind, I hadn't even brought up the idea to Glenn. For now, Devils Peak had to be our priority. Waldo would have to wait.

ABOUT THREE miles from Devils Peak, patches of snow started dotting the trail, the first we had seen since the day we left the Oregon-California border. We had ascended about 500 feet since leaving Deer Lake about three hours before.

The snow patches gradually rose and fell like whale backs: perhaps two to five feet high, deeper in the well-shaded areas that precluded a faster melt. Each foray over snow widened my imagination to the challenges of what lay ahead—challenges iced with a certain foreboding. At one point, we stopped to look at our maps. The tightly spun brown-on-white contours etched a four-point challenge: Luther Mountain, Shale Butte, Lucifer and, finally, Devils Peak. Glenn was the one who'd studied the maps in detail; I had never imagined the trail chiseled this high into the ragged flanks of mountains.

When we reached the dicier spots, what I wanted was a clear sense that we were safe to proceed or foolhardy to do so. Cut and dried. Black or white. Head on or turn back.

As we rose higher, to the timberline, Mount McLoughlin rose majestically behind us, its north face far whiter than the south face we'd seen while crossing the diabolical lava fields below Brown Mountain. Devils Peak's north face, I was reminded, would be similarly chalked in white.

We moved on. I took the lead. Wildflowers fronted jagged shale, a reminder of the Cascades' beauty-and-the-beast nature. Glenn stopped to take some pictures on this cloud-free morning, particularly of feathery flowers that seemed to defy the rugged land and lofty elevation. (Waldo, by the way, mentioned taking pictures, too. In 1888, George Eastman had introduced the Kodak, a square box camera using roll film, and, overnight, photography had become a practical hobby for Americans.)

At 7,000 feet, on the west flank of Luther Mountain, we reached our highest point since the trip started. What impressed me, besides a sprinkling of red, purple and yellow wildflowers, was the sheer *bigness* of the land beyond: Massive mountains splashed with sheer walls of shale, craggy peaks here and there, rolling buttes of timber speckled with white-bleached snags that may have watched silently as the Waldo party jostled down the spine in 1888. Geographic features that we'd never heard of and were small potatoes compared to, say, Mount Jefferson or Mount Hood or the Three Sisters, and yet scattered 360 degrees around us in a display so large as to humble me, a mere ant amid God's sprawling grandeur. About four percent of Oregon was designated "wilderness," another eight percent publicly owned forests wild and unprotected. But from this perch it seemed the whole state were untamed wilds.

"MORNIN.'"

I mentally lurched. The guy seemed to have materialized as if beamed here from a *Star Trek* teleportation machine. He was up a slight hill to my right, amid a clump of trees, in front of two tents. Like me, he looked late fifty-ish. He had what appeared to be a cup of coffee in his right hand and seemed no less casual than if he'd been my neighbor standing on his porch and seen me going to fetch the morning paper.

"Hello," I said.

"Acorn," he said, extending a hand.

Huh? Oh, of course, his trail name. He was, I realized, a PCT hiker. We hadn't seen many.

"Uh, I'm Bob," I said. "That's my brother-in-law, Glenn, back there. You thru-hiking?"

"Doing a section with my daughter, from Ashland to Crater Lake. Got turned back by Devils Peak. Too tough. Too much snow. So far, four have made it past. Four have turned around."

Exactly what I didn't want to hear. I wanted something definitive one way or the other, not the kind of information that necessitated a coin-flip call. When Glenn arrived, the three of us chatted some more. It was now nearing noon. A glance north suggested that this was where the trail wound out of the woods for good and lay buried, in many spots beneath deep snow shrouding ridges that arced into an "S" ending with Devils Peak.

"We didn't have ice axes or crampons so decided to hang out here for a while," he said. "See if it gets better. We didn't even make it to the back side."

Certainly he wasn't waiting for snowmelt; some of this stuff wouldn't be gone for a month. What he was actually waiting for, I assumed, was a fresh set of footprints from a couple of guinea pigs like us. We obliged. The Welch-Petersen unspoken plan was simply to go slowly, be cautious, and talk things through.

"You see a couple named Cisco and Roadrunner?" I asked.

"Yeah, they were by here a little earlier," he said.

I turned to Glenn. "How did they get past us again?" I asked.

"Must have gone up ahead of us yesterday after we'd peeled off for Deer Lake," he said.

"Yeah," Acorn said, "I think they said they camped at the Snow Lakes Trail junction."

That was six miles above where we'd stayed. If so, they'd done twenty-four miles to our fourteen the previous day.

"One step at a time, Bob," said Glenn after we'd bid goodbye to Acorn and his back-at-camp daughter—a college student—and headed on.

I was happy to let him lead, even after Acorn said, "Uh, the trail goes *that* way," pointing west instead of north.

"Hey, thanks," said Glenn, laughing at himself. "We're off to a great start, Bob, now that we're actually going the right direction."

Partially melted tracks creased the snow ever so faintly; probably Cisco and Roadrunner's. But who else's? Ben and Kate's? Blood Bath's? Trekking poles firmly anchored, Glenn planted each foot with caution, then moved forward. I followed suit, willing myself to look forward, to focus on each step, not on what would happen if I slipped. After a quick glance down, I'd already calculated the result wouldn't be death—this wasn't Mount Everest's Khumbu Icefall—but some broken bones and scrapes on a shale outcropping a few hundred feet down the slope.

On August 19, 1905, while on the east side of Mount Jefferson, Waldo got into a danger zone. "Some very steep snow banks," he wrote. "We crossed one laterally by making steps with the butt of Heideck's rifle, where a slip would have been dangerous to life. Heideck persevered amazingly in finding his way among the crevasses of the glaciers, making five attempts before finally succeeding in finding a way across. He assisted me twice in dangerous places." Almost two years later, to the day, Waldo wrote of his party trying to ascend Mount Jefferson but "being driven back by the snow and ice—too dangerous to proceed without mountain climbing appliances."

Focus. Not on the danger, but on the process necessary to avoid that danger. It was the only thing that had carried me through a scarier experience when, for a two-part *Register-Guard* column in 2002, I'd climbed a 180-foot high crane that was doing work on the University of Oregon's Autzen Stadium addition. I was neither afraid of heights nor totally comfortable with them; I was a tweener. The only way I'd survive the rung-to-rung climb to the cab—then, through a hatch in the roof, for the final twenty feet—was concentrating on where I was at, not where I'd been or where I was headed.

As we traversed the lip of Shale Butte, Glenn broke the cadence of boots punching into snow. "Great sled run," he said, then nodded to exposed shale at the bottom. "Tough ending."

I liked that. Humor was good. In a few minutes, we again hit a rocky trail. Pausing to rest, we could see Devils Peak a mile north-northeast: a craggy rock, lacking the aesthetics of so many other Cascade peaks. It was not the pile of sugar that, say, a wintry Mount Hood appears as; instead, it was more like something a child on the beach would make with a bucket of wet sand. Only a few splotches of snow remained on the sun-facing south side, which was comforting and, we would soon find, deceptive.

We swung around to 7,474-foot Lucifer, which presented a totally different challenge than Shale Butte. Because the PCT ran through a fat swath of the ridge, there was little danger of slipping down a snowy slope. On the other hand, at one point the dirt-and-rock trail disappeared into a mass of snow that appeared to have been dumped by a semi truck's covered trailer. Huge.

Neither of us said anything. We just stared at a mass of snow a few feet taller than us. Glenn took his trekking poles in one hand and started chiseling steps straight up the block of snow. He looked like Spiderman on the side of the Empire State Building. While he began his slow ascent, I mentally shook my head and headed downslope and around the mass of white. Better to stay out of the stuff, I figured, even if it meant some cross-country trekking.

I was wrong. Within five minutes, I wasn't even within shouting distance of Glenn. I scrambled up the hill, duly chastened by my stupidity for leaving the trail, and fell in behind Glenn. Still, if this were the new normal, it was going to be a difficult normal. But after trudging through a handful of such snow masses, we popped into the open. In fact, we traversed the south face of Devils Peak as if on a freeway.

"Not bad at all," I said.

"No, we can deal with this," said Glenn.

Of course, just as music is really about the pauses between the notes, so is communication about what isn't said, not what *is*. Neither one of us was mentioning the north face, though the more I tried not to think about Roadrunner's words, the more I thought about them: *"Those switchbacks will be buried in snow. Instead, you'll have a sheer wall that falls into a glaciated bowl."*

DEVILS PEAK TOWERED above us, a remnant of some eons-old volcano. The trail snaked from the south side of the ridge to the north on the Devils Peak/Lee Peak Saddle. After two days of stewing about what lay beyond, it was time for us to peer over the edge and learn our fate.

The ridge fell dramatically off into a quarter-mile slope of white that ended with a peninsula of trees and a snow-fed lake: Roadrunner's "glaciated bowl"—or half bowl. With an icy veneer to the dropoff, I realized how dangerous traversing down could be. But my spirits soared when I saw we didn't have ice. The mid-afternoon snow was sun-washed and soft. The marks left by others suggested a few had post-holed their way down with deep steps into the snow; others had thrown caution to the wind and glissaded on their butts or backs. Some, it appeared, had skied on their boots.

"Wow," said Glenn, a view suddenly opening up distant peaks to the north.

"This isn't bad, is it?" I said, looking for some assurance. "I mean people clearly got down this thing."

"Sure did," he said. "Looks like good sledding."

"The question is," I said, "can we stop once we get going?"

I already was thinking about technique. Whether we should be dragging our trekking poles to slow us down and to prevent us from getting out of control. And how we had one shot to get down and, if we underestimated our speed, we'd wind up in the trees or the lake. If reasonably certain we could get safely down, I was still nervous.

"We need to be careful about this," I said. "Should we take our hands out of our pole straps? Should we dig in our boo—"

Glenn apparently hadn't heard the questions. He'd already plunged down the slope, using his boots as skis in a sort of semi-controlled slide.

Within a few moments, I saw he was already home free, having reached a less steep part of the slope and stopped. "Hey, come on down," he yelled, "and I'll get some video of you!"

Until now, I realized, I'd worried so much about the dangers of Devils Peak that I hadn't been able to let them go even when the empirical evidence screamed, "All safe!" I was *The Wizard of Oz's* Cowardly Lion, still trembling even when realizing Oz, the Great and Terrible, was nothing but a little old man with a bald head and a wrinkled face.

I launched forward, leaned back and slalomed left and right, partly out of control but knowing the worst I could do was make a face plant in soft snow. When the two of us reached the bottom, I surged with unbridled joy. It was as if two days of fear had melted into a lake of relief as large as the greenish pool spread beneath us.

Long after the trip was over, this moment would stay fixed in my memory as one of my favorites. Not only because it was a common triumph for us but because of how our reactions to it so perfectly defined our dramatic, and humorous, differences.

I looked back up at Devils Peak, and pointed an accusing finger at it. "Is that all you got?" I screamed. "You couldn't stop us! Nothing can stop us!"

I turned back toward Glenn. His face was buried in a map. "So, Bob, I think we can pick up the trail if we head almost due east from here," he said, then pointed to where the glacial bowl met with trees.

Trail? Who cared about a piddly thing like that? We'd gotten past Devils Peak. Never mind that we still had more than three quarters of the state to go, including peaks far higher than this one. I could practically see the Bridge of the Gods spanning the Columbia River.

Part III
The disappearing trail

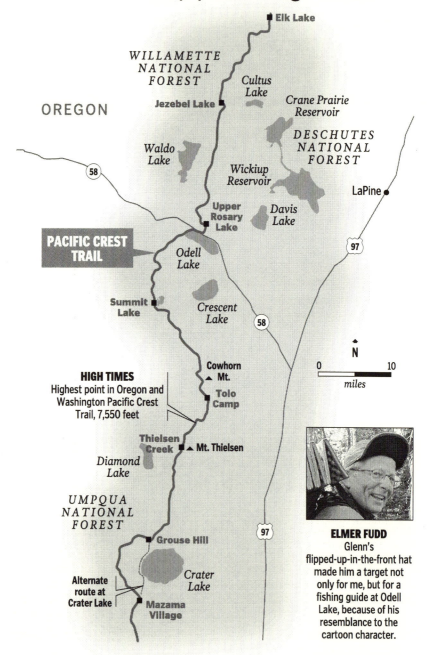

PACIFIC CREST TRAIL

HIGH TIMES
Highest point in Oregon and Washington Pacific Crest Trail, 7,550 feet

ELMER FUDD
Glenn's flipped-up-in-the-front hat made him a target not only for me, but for a fishing guide at Odell Lake, because of his resemblance to the cartoon character.

The snow doesn't give a soft white damn whom it touches.

—e.e. cummings

11. Enlightenment

Trail log: Friday, July 29, 2011.
PCT mile-marker: 1820.4.
Days on trail, as of this morning: 7.
Miles hiked Thursday: 19.
Total miles hiked: 117.2.

Location: Jack Spring.
Elevation: 6,200 feet.
Average miles per day: 16.7.
Portion of trip completed: 25.9%.

NEVER MIND that after Thursday's up-and-down nineteen miles, we had no choice but to camp in a ghostly forest with trees charred by fire; that to find water we'd had to hike off the Pacific Crest Trail for a steep drop of more than half a mile, each downhill step reminding us of an uphill step we'd need to take in the dark the next morning just to return to the main drag; that the outsides of my two little toes, despite my having bought extra-wide boots a half-size larger than normal, had by now been rubbed raw; and that I'd had just enough toilet paper to get through my morning session, but not a square more.

Never mind all that, because today we would be reaching Mazama Village below Crater Lake's rim, where we'd get a shower and a restaurant meal. And Saturday, overlooking the lake itself, we'd meet our families and get clean shirts and pants, fresh underwear and socks, a new supply of food, Monkey Butt, and, of course, toilet paper. Nothing like family, real food, and adult baby powder to raise the spirits, which, despite the Devils Peak triumph, had ebbed a bit in the afterglow.

After the Devils Peak passage the previous day, we had been joined by Acorn and his daughter, Hillary, a congenial pair with whom we'd hiked for about five miles. At day's end, they'd gone with us in search of Jack Spring, whose location proved difficult to find until my blue-dot iPhone GPS pulled through. But, unlike us, the father-daughter team chose to trudge back up the hill Thursday evening and to camp on the trailside. That proved wise because, we later learned, the mosquitoes weren't nearly as bad away from the spring. Weariness, I learned, could lead to bad decisions.

In an uncharacteristic mini-meltdown, Glenn had poured a giant bag of gorp out and left it for the wildlife. "Take it all, squirrels!" he'd yelled, "because I can't take it anymore!"

Wow. That was refreshing: Glenn showing frustration. He was the proverbial canary in the coal mine; when he went nuts, you knew things were getting bad. But, secretly, it was kind of nice to see the mild-mannered guy go bonkers, if only for a moment. It reminded me that I wasn't the only one teetering on the edge at times.

Waldo had his moments, too. From Davis Lake, in south Central Oregon, he wrote on July 25, 1882, that "mosquitoes annoyed us so much that we struck into a trot which we kept up until we got back to the ford at 11 o'clock."

Glenn and I had decided to cowboy camp, but we hadn't been in our bags more than five minutes when I realized mosquitoes were attacking with the vigor of Kamikaze pilots. Without any sort of announcement, Glenn got up, popped up his tent, and was soon seemingly fast asleep inside it. I hated that. His doing so meant it was a wise thing to do. But I didn't want to do it. I deemed it necessary, however, when swarms of mosquitoes made me feel like Gulliver being attacked by millions of Lilliputians wielding high-pitched drills confiscated from millions of really small dental offices. Forget Waldo and his euphemistic "hum of the multitudinous mosquitoes," these miniature monsters had clearly been released by the Dark Forces of Devils Peak as payback for our successful conquering of it.

I slapped on my headlamp and for the next fifteen minutes, morphed into a crazed man in long johns, the ordeal of setting up a simple tent seeming no less ambitious than erecting an entire Barnum & Bailey circus while blindfolded. The crowning moment was me stepping on a tent stake. Needless to say, I did not sleep well.

On Friday morning, Acorn and Hillary were ready to go when we swung by for our agreed-upon 5:45 A.M. departure. It was cool to see a father and twenty-something daughter taking a journey like this together, even if she was attending the University of Washington, along with Oregon State, one of the University of Oregon's rival schools. Glenn had a similar close relationship with his three slightly older daughters: Katie, a missionary in Africa who, with her husband David, had returned to southern California this summer and was due to deliver a baby, and the two others, Molly and Carrie, who would join us at Crater Lake to hike four days with us.

As darkness faded, we headed north through the burn, invigorated by the thought of Crater Lake, even if my inspiration came more from the idea of an all-you-can-eat lunch buffet than from the more nature-oriented muses of Waldo as he tramped nearby in August 30, 1901.

> The morning was splendid, and the walk in the light air, up the rather steep ascent to the summit, through an open burnt woods, was a delightful lung exercise, and the effect that of a grand moral sermon. Here were the berries, and young and everywhere lofty peaks, shadowy forests, untrodden solitudes, and inspiring pine-scented air. To gather the luscious berries far from "the madding crowd's ignoble strife" was like converse with the Gods.

While I had talked with God earlier, for now my conversation was with Acorn and Hillary. As a reporter, I had an almost innate craving to know a person's story. I soon had learned that Acorn was from Washington state and had bumped into Noah Strycker, the son of my *Register-Guard* colleague, Bob Keefer, somewhere deep in southern California. Acorn had re-jiggered his PCT plans when hitting the heavy snows of the Sierra Nevada. Delving into our respective pasts, I also learned he had not only enrolled at the University of Oregon in the fall of 1972 as I had, but spent his freshman year in the same Bean Hall dorm complex where I had.

"I was the 'Beverage Boy' at Hamilton Hall, where we ate," I said. "I probably poured your fruit juice for you every morning."

"Seriously?"

"Yeah, and remember the smell of bread from the Williams Bakery next door?" I asked.

"We'd go over there at night and the guys would give us free samples."

"It's gone now," I said. "The new basketball arena is there. But enough of you asking all the questions. I've got one."

"Shoot," he said.

"How could you, a proud Duck, allow your daughter to become a Washington Husky?"

He laughed, a nice sound amid the rhythm of boots and trekking poles on the trail—and, until now, rare the last few days.

THE MORNING wore on. The miles were easy until patches of snow started becoming wide swaths of snow, then like the white overturned hulls of fishing trawlers. In my mind, once we'd passed Devils Peak, the trail was going to all but make a pine-needled bee line for Cascade Locks. Instead, as we climbed the west flank of the 7,124-foot Goose Egg, the trail started to get hard to follow through a forest of thick lodgepole pine. Acorn and Hillary passed us; who knew when—or if—we'd see them again. That got me thinking of how we hadn't seen Cisco and Roadrunner now for two full days—above Freye Lake—and probably wouldn't see them again. But with them, you never knew. "They're like spirit people," said Glenn. "They just materialize out of nowhere."

In the same way, I noticed, the PCT could just "un-materialize" out of nowhere. We would be on a well-defined path of dirt when the trail disappeared beneath snow. The challenge was figuring out where that trail went after vanishing. In my naivety, I assumed you could just keep trudging due north and the trail would pop out at the end of a snow patch. Sometimes. However, the PCT wasn't a yardstick, but a snake. After disappearing into the snow, the trail might abruptly turn east or west in a single bend. But, without blazes or tree markings, how could we tell?

The Oregon Pacific Crest Trail twisted and turned 452 miles; as the crow flies, 257 miles. That's how crooked the squiggly line was. True, in the snow you could often follow footsteps of others who'd gone before you. But they were few and as the day warmed, obscured by snowmelt. And, besides, what guarantee was there that the hikers who left them had a clue where the trail was themselves? They could have been made by a couple of rookies like Glenn and me, heaven forbid. I'd expected tree blazes to mark the PCT and, true, I found them—and palm-sized diamond PCT markers—on occasion. But there could be literally miles between such occasions.

"Remember when I laughed at you when, before we left, you said your three biggest concerns were snow, snow, and snow?" I said.

"Yeah."

"I thought you were crazy," I said. "I still do; don't get me wrong. But you were right about the snow."

I occasionally saw a bumper sticker back in Eugene that reminded folks that, "Not All Who Wander Are Lost." I agreed. But, for at least part of this day, we were.

Judge Waldo and his buddies found themselves in similar predicaments, though with few trails to follow, "lost" may not have quite described their status. They were, in essence, trailblazers without much more to go by than a compass, the sun, and some maps that included large geographic features but nothing very specific. At times, he and his boys rolled up their sleeves and with shovels and pick axes from the wagon, made their own trails.

On September 8, 1888, Waldo was heading south. From the same southwest Crater Lake rim that we would scramble up to in the morning, he wrote:

> This morning we filed down the rugged, furrowed sides of the high bowl which holds Crater Lake toward the Southwest. Half way down, as we entered a glade in one of the small hollows, a doe and two fawns started up and stood watching our approach out of the evergreen woods. They were an easy mark, but we let them go unharmed, protected by a game law of our own enactment. On the summit we turned off from the Fort Klamath and Ashland road, and went Southward through an open forest of hemlock and black pine. The summit of the Cascade Mountains became our highway. Travel soon became delightful over open mossy ridges and flats handsomely dotted with scattering hemlock and pine. Fragrant winds blew over us fresh from evergreen mountains.

Despite such bliss, Waldo certainly experienced snow, too. On July 28, 1887, from Breitenbush Lake north of Mount Jefferson he wrote: "Unexpectedly, we find our camp surrounded by snow; and where thought to find grass knee-high we find the grass but little up out of the ground with snow lying around several feet deep on the Northern slopes." Later, they trudged through a foot of it on a ridge near Summit Lake. Indeed, his 1887 sounded as if, in terms of snow, the modern era's 2011.

BACK ON THE trail, I was heading up a blessedly snow-free incline when I heard them: footsteps. I turned. Coming up the trail like a Maserati in overdrive was a twenty-something kid, clearly a young man on a mission. But he stopped. Briefly.

"Blaze," he said, introducing himself.

"Bob," I responded.

I didn't have to ask how he got his nickname—the kid was fast—though I later learned his name was actually Blaze Greene. Age twenty-two. From Toronto, Canada. Lean. Handsome. Full of more energy than a senior-discount guy like me could relate to at the moment. We chatted. I learned that on a day off, he'd climbed 14,161-foot Mount Shasta. Twice. (If I had a day off—or a "zero day" as they called it on the trail—I would attempt something less ambitious, like taking off my boots.)

"Yeah, I'm hoping to bag Hood, Adams, and Rainier en route to Canada," he said as if he were just mentioning that he were going to the bank, the post office, and Home Depot. "Who's ahead of me?"

"Near as I can tell, four people," I said. "Some German guy named Marcus; The Aussies, Ben and Kate; and Blood Bath."

He knew of them all. We talked a bit more, but, like Blood Bath, he too, was in a hurry. "Maybe we'll see you at Mazama," I said.

"Sure." And, poof, he was gone.

Suddenly, I got a sinking feeling. A literal sinking feeling. Like in my lower intestines. It was an impromptu time to Commune with Nature. I dropped my pack and reached for the toilet paper, whose location was well memorized by now: outside netting, halfway down, starboard side.

Argh! The tube was like a barkless tree. Now I remembered: That morning I'd used the very. Last. Square. My stomach lurched, triggering a panicked memory of the Turbo-Lax scene in the movie *Dumb and Dumber*. I needed a backup plan. Fast. I fished around in the outer netting. *Got it*. The Pac-12 football magazine.

It would need to be my port in this embarrassing storm. I found a good tree, communed deeply, and buried it just as deeply. I washed my hands with a handi-wipe and stuffed the magazine back in my pack, quickly rationalizing the loss.

Was anyone really going to miss the Washington Huskies' section?

GLENN CAUGHT UP. The dirt trail disappeared into snow again, the most consistent of the trip. Drifts rose to eye level. I fired up my TopoMaps program to make sure we were on track. By now, five days since getting an iPhone charge at the Hyatt Lake Restaurant—and thick forests precluding much sunlight getting through to Glenn's solar charger—my battery was as thirsty for Mazama's electricity as I was for its food. I had only fifteen percent charge left.

Like a couple of pin balls, Glenn and I bounced left and right in the white-carpeted woods as we tried to keep on track. Near as we could tell, we were closing in on the junction of the Stuart Falls Trail, about six miles south of Mazama Village.

"Well, if it isn't *zee* doctor and *zee* newspaper man."

Roadrunner? The German accent was unmistakable. She and Cisco were sitting on a log, in a snow-less patch just off the junction, much like we'd seen them three days before. Glenn and I exchanged quick glances whose meanings we instinctively knew. *Spirit people.* They looked no less weary or dirty than when we'd seen them above Freye Lake or at Highway 140 or at Griffin Pass or at Hyatt Lake. It was uncanny. In computer terms, it was as if they were able to copy and save clean, vibrant versions of themselves from day's past and paste those versions to anywhere on the trail they wished.

"We took the cutoff and stayed the night near Stuart Falls," said Roadrunner. "It was beautiful."

I dared not describe our night in the fire-charred, mosquito-thick reaches of Jack Spring, including Glenn's crazed parting of ways with his trail mix and my middle-of-the-night meltdown while setting up my tent.

"Wanna join up?" asked Cisco.

My pride said no, we could make it just fine. We may have looked pathetic—I hadn't shaved in a week and Glenn was still going with the Elmer Fudd flip to his hat's bill—but we'd made it this far by ourselves. We'd spent a year prepping for this trip. We'd just brought Devils Peak to its knees. And, heck, we were *Oregonians,* not lightweight Californians.

"Uh, sure," I said, giving Glenn a "might-as-well" look whose nonchalance he saw straight through. Face it, beneath my muted bravado was a growing sense of desperation. The snow wasn't going away—and finding our way through it was costing us serious time. These two probably knew what they were doing; they'd been finding lost trail since Sierra City. Glenn and I? We were two blind mice in hiking boots. Through what was now a forest thick with snow, we happily followed the Californians into the boundaries of Crater Lake National Park.

Cisco had a GPS superior to those that Glenn and I were using. And he and Roadrunner had something even more valuable: instincts. "The trail," Cisco would say, "has a mind of its own. It goes where it wants to go." They had been on it now for about five hundred miles and could, as Cisco would say, "Think like the trail would think. Where would I go now?"

They taught us to look for cut logs; in wilderness areas, a log sliced thusly always indicated trail. They taught us to look for water drainage from snow masses, which often followed the confines of a trail in the same way a river stays within its banks. They taught us to spread out laterally; if we lost the trail, four sets of eyes increased our chances of re-finding it—as opposed to us walking single file.

"Where are you staying tonight?" asked Roadrunner..

"We have reservations at the Mazama campground," said Glenn. "And you?"

"The same place," she said, "but we have no reservations."

BY MID-AFTERNOON we hit Highway 62 and, across the road, dipped into Mazama Village, tucked hard to the base of Crater Lake's rim. It was a return to civilization that proved terrific and terrible. Terrific because there was a store, a restaurant, a shower, and a camp site reserved for Glenn and me, complete with a picnic table at which you could actually sit. Terrible because it represented civilization, which I hadn't been missing much. I felt like a scuba diver surfacing too fast and suffering from the emotional bends. I had gone five days—since Hyatt Lake Monday morning—while seeing only trees, lakes, and a trail—and no cell coverage. Suddenly, I was in a place with recreational vehicles, gift shops, and sightseers in Hard Rock Cafe shirts. All I wanted to do was scarf down an all-you-can eat lunch buffet, grab a shower, and hunker down like a hermit crab to nap.

As I walked toward the store, I remembered something Craig Mayne, the guy who had done the Oregon PCT the previous year, had written me about his arrival at Crater Lake.

> You hike into a place filled with tourists, you've been on the trail for days, you're dirty, ragged, and tired. Your face and legs are covered with dust. Your diet has consisted of freeze-dried food, Clif Bars and filtered lake water. People look at you as they go by in their cars, as they walk around in their expensive clothes—clean, spotless, and pressed—and holding their cameras and eating their ice cream. You stand out like a sore thumb. But as they pass you, you can see it in their eyes, that touch of envy, that little feeling of inadequacy, that desire to feel what you are experiencing. You feel the exhaustion that comes from hiking for days on the trail, you look down at your wrinkled clothes, your dirty pack and boots, and you feel a sense of pride.

I had once been on a cruise ship in Alaska and, seeing sailors below, envied their being at water level. Cruise ships were nice and this particular trip was a gift from parents-in-law celebrating their fiftieth wedding anniversary; I was grateful for the experience. But hiking or sailing offered an intimacy with nature, a doing of something, instead of observing from a distance. I liked that.

However if I felt that quiet pride Craig described, it was muted by other feelings: hunger, fatigue, and thirst. I downed a thirty-two-ounce Mountain Dew in roughly thirty-two seconds while Glenn got in line at the double-sided kiosk to check in for the campground. In front of the store, Blaze finished off a power drink. "I'm moving on up north of Crater Lake for tonight," he said to a small group of other hikers. A female thru-hiker in a jean dress arrived in a huff.

"I'm through," she said to Blaze as she peeled off a ULA Catalyst pack just like Glenn's. "Can't stand it anymore. Oregon is nothing but trees. No views. I've got claustrophobia. Gotta get back to California."

It wasn't an uncommon criticism from thru-hikers who'd been used to California's wide, high vistas. Some called Oregon "The Green Tunnel." The sad irony for the young woman was that she was only a few-miles hike away from one of the greatest views on planet earth, Crater Lake, and the start of a 125-mile PCT stretch that afforded views of, and from, a half dozen majestic peaks. But, again, weariness could bring out the worst in people. I was reminded of that, regarding myself, as I joined Glenn at the kiosk.

Just as it was Glenn's turn in line at the south window, Roadrunner arrived at the north, where she was told, sorry, there was no room in the inn.

"But we're PCT hikers," she said. "Isn't there someplace we could—"

"I'm sorry," said the park ranger.

"How about if they stay with us at our site?" Glenn asked the ranger from the opposite window.

"That's fine," said the ranger. "So, four people total?"

Now hold on a minute, I wanted to say. My feet were blistered, my body parched, my mind a mess. What about my blessed nap? No offense, but socializing, which this new setup would no doubt require, was not what I needed. My weariness had worn me down to my selfish core, even if I hadn't noticed it at the time.

We headed for the restaurant, a new-to-look-old motif replete with massive rock walls and natural wood paneling. A waitress, after quickly assessing our appearance and stench, led us to a far corner, a safe distance from the more refined tourists who weren't stowing thirty-pound packs beside their tables and didn't smell like the riffraff at a 1980s Grateful Dead concert.

It was an all-you-can-eat luncheon buffet. Though choosing decidedly different items, the four of us went through the line with gusto, if not piranha-like, not exactly Miss Manners either. We sat down and began eating. When Roadrunner—her real name, we learned, was Baerbel—told of her decision to move permanently to the United States to marry Rich, aka Cisco, my bone-weary sarcasm got the better of me.

"Well, hey, it must have been easy leaving Germany for a guy who can follow a trail like Rich," I said.

Her face froze. Clearly, I'd hit a nerve. "It is not easy leaving your home, your family, your friends, in essence, for *goot*," she said while tight-roping the wire of tears. "Not easy at all."

There was an awkward pause. I don't think Glenn or Cisco even noticed it, deep, as they were, into their mounds of food. I did. And I wasn't particularly proud of what that pause signified. It was, in retrospect, a moment of clarity akin to seeing my reflection in the waters of a high-mountain lake—and noticing I didn't particularly like what I saw. Ever since I'd met Rich and Baerbel, I'd shoved them neatly into a category that, even if seasoned in humor, precluded me from seeing more deeply into who they really were. Not Californians. Not L.L. Bean models. Not *Twilight Zone* hitchhikers. But human beings, one of whom I'd just hurt with my lack of sensitivity. I'd heard Roadrunner's accent more than I'd listened to what she was actually saying.

The more I thought about it, the more I realized an interesting—and humbling—reality. My trail weariness was translating into a certain insensitivity toward people we were meeting, as if I were too tired to care about anyone other than my poor-me self. Meanwhile, the trail had brought the usually reserved Glenn out of his shell. He was no less tired than I, but seemed to be relishing these new relationships in a way I wasn't.

We found our camp site a few hundred yards away from the camp's "business district." I set up my tent, then headed to the coin-operated shower—ice cold, but wonderful—and then to the pocket-sized laundry mat next door.

My load had just started churning when Roadrunner walked in. For the next hour, she washed and dried her and Rich's clothes; I did mine. We talked. Laughed. Learned, more deeply, each other's stories. Then headed back to the camp site.

"You know," I said. "I owe you an apology."

"For what?" she said.

"For being an insensitive jerk at lunch about how hard it was for you to leave Germany and move to the states," I said. "Sometimes, I get carried away with my sarcasm. I'm sorry."

"Not to worry," she said. "But as I said, it is not easy leaving all that you know for what you do not know."

For the first time, I was hearing her, not her accent. "I can imagine."

But hardly on a scale that she had experienced. The PCT was "Unknown Lite." Yes, it was unlike anything I'd ever done. It was leaving much of what I knew for a lot that I didn't know. But it was short-term. What the two experiences shared in common, I supposed, was adventure. Seeing things you'd never seen. Meeting people you'd never expected to meet. Facing obstacles you never thought you'd face. But the PCT took nowhere near the courage leaving one's country did.

Back at camp, I pulled out my iPhone and took advantage of a recharged battery to create a short iMovie birthday greeting for granddaughter Avin, who was turning four the next day. I would send it once we got up to Crater Lake's rim Saturday and had cell coverage. I also tried to compose a blog post that I'd send, but got frustrated and quit. Too tired. I slipped into my tent and rested.

"I could write you a great many pages about our camp life and make it almost as interesting to you in the reading as it is to me in the acting," Waldo wrote the day after a stop at Crater Lake, September 25, 1887. "But while the sun shines I am too much in motion to write much, and in the evenings the pleasure of lying in my little bed overcomes my desire to write by the flickering light of our camp fire."

Outside, I heard soft talking among the other three about what lay ahead, about how Ann and Sally were leaving water for us—and Cisco and Roadrunner—north of Crater Lake, at a point where the trail nudged Highway 138. Then, Glenn spoke up in a voice intended for me. "Bob, you ready for Round II?"

"Say what?"

"It's time for dinner," he said.

"Hey, didn't we just eat?"

"That," he said, "was the lunch buffet. Now, it's time for the dinner buffet."

I popped my head out and looked at Roadrunner. Her eyes brightened. Rich's head bobbed "yes" like one of those spring-loaded play horses ridden by an enthusiastic toddler. It was our last chance for a real meal before the end of our trip's first part.

"Well, OK, then," I said. "Let's go."

The evening meal was fun, festive, and, of course, fulfilling, even if I caused some furrowed brows when I asked the waiter for a handful of those small plastic tubs of jam. I wasn't eating toast or muffins.

"I'll explain later," I said. "All I can say is there's method to my madness."

"If this were Glenn, I would see the method," Roadrunner said. "With you, Bob, only the madness."

Everyone laughed. Glenn and I would leave early the next morning to meet our families. Later, after picking up resupplies at the post office, Cisco and Roadrunner would go their separate way. But for now, we raised our glasses in a toast. "To the PCT," said Roadrunner.

"To Canada for Roadrunner and Cisco," I said.

Cisco nodded his appreciation and raised his glass of beer. "And to the Columbia River for Bob and Glenn," he said.

In this unexpected moment of unity, forgotten were all thoughts of blisters and fatigue and snow and myriad other obstacles that might dampen our dreams of completion. For the moment, all things seemed possible, all snow-choked slopes passable, all the days ahead destined to bring us to our respective destinations: for Glenn and me, the Bridge of the Gods, and for Roadrunner and Cisco, Canada's Manning Park.

Alas, by summer's end, only two of the four of us would reach those places.

12. Adoption

Trail log: Saturday, July 30, 2011.
PCT mile-marker: 1833.6.
Days on trail: 8.
Miles hiked Friday: 13.2.
Total miles hiked: 130.4.

Location: Mazama Village, just below Crater Lake.
Elevation: 6,200 feet.
Average miles per day: 16.3.
Portion of trip completed: 28.8%.

IN THE SUMMER of 1882, his third year of exploring the Oregon Cascades, Judge John Waldo stood across the water from where I now stood and gazed over one of the most beautiful lakes in the world. From the rim 900 feet above, the sheen of the lake appeared so blue it seemed postcard-enhanced.

It was hard to believe such jaw-dropping serenity was created from chaos: the eruption of Mount Mazama around 5,000 B.C. So widespread was the blast that it coated Washington's Mount Rainer, 280 miles to the north, with three inches of ash and dusted points deep into Canada and northern California with lesser amounts. The eruption was forty times larger than Mount St. Helen's in 1980. It left what's now, at 1,994 feet—nearly half a mile—the deepest lake in the United States, and one of the clearest in the world.

Waldo saw the water's clarity up close on his trip to Shasta in 1888 when he and two friends made the perilous zigzag trip down to the lake's edge and boated to Wizard Island. "The blueness of the water as one rows over it, even when sitting so close as to be able to touch it with the hand, is remarkable," he wrote. "It seems to be actually colored. When dipped up, however, it is perfectly clear, and tastes well."

The Crater Lake area fascinated him on other trips, too. "This is the most interesting spot I have yet met with in my mountain travels," wrote Waldo on August 7, 1882, less than thirty years after the first person of European descent is believed to have seen the lake. "The lake itself is rather exceeded by the scenery in view from the summit of the mountain wall which surrounds it and from the top of Mount Scott, which lies just to the east, and to the summit of which we all climbed this morning."

Glenn and I had no aspirations of trying to summit Mount Scott. It had been challenge enough getting up extra early so I could top off my iPhone battery from an outlet in the men's bathroom. I was surprised how many guys had to go to the bathroom between 4 A.M. and 4:30 A.M.—and who looked at me with a little suspicion as I explained my pre-dawn presence. (Waldo, too, relied on the occasional brush with civilization to have travel needs met, but instead of iPhone battery recharges his stops often involved literal ax-grinding sessions provided by farmers.)

With my iPhone ready, Glenn and I had scrambled up, mainly through trail-less snow, the lake's west rim, to get to where we now stood at 9 A.M.

"Unbelievable," said Glenn, his eyes scanning the lake.

Indeed, seeing Crater Lake—only my second time here—gave me the sense of being on top of the world. It was like seeing the grandest body of non-ocean water I'd ever seen from the loftiest lake view I'd ever had while breathing the freshest air I'd ever breathed.

Slowly, tourists began to thicken along the lake's rim. For now, we appeared to be the only two PCT hikers here, though, as we waited for our families to arrive, I noticed a young couple with packs headed our way: a guy and girl, mid-twenties. Multiple piercings and tattoos, looking more like they were hitchhiking a ride to Eugene's hippie festival, the Oregon Country Fair, than hanging out with camera-clicking tourists at Crater Lake. But not grubby or weary, and clearly not people who had been on the trail.

"Are you guys doing the PCT?" the young woman asked.

"Yeah, just the Oregon portion," I said. "South to north."

The two seemed anxious—and not in a good way.

"We just got dropped off to hike south from here to Highway 140 by Fish Lake," the woman said, meaning the trailhead where we'd gotten the Devils Peak warning. "How's the snow?"

"Lots of it," I said.

"Really?"

"Yeah," I said. "Slow going. You have to work to stay on the trail."

They had, we learned, lots of enthusiasm, little experience and, most importantly, no GPS.

"What do you think?" the young man said. "Are we crazy to be doing this?"

I envisioned a newspaper headline after the bodies had been found weeks later. Glenn beat me to a reply.

"It's a slog," he said. "And you'll have to go up the north face of Devils Peak in the snow. Going north, you can just slide down."

I could tell how badly they wanted to do this, but was experienced enough to know that youthful enthusiasm—or any enthusiasm for that matter—was a poor substitute for lack of preparation in the outdoors.

"Put it this way," I said. "If you were my kids and they had no GPS, I'd say no. Don't go. Not worth the risk."

They stared down at their boots.

"Sorry," I said. "But you asked."

"No, that's cool," he said. "Thanks."

They walked off—to where I never knew.

Decisions. The PCT was a winding, twisting series of choices that presented themselves each week, each day, each minute, beginning with: To go or to stay? How can we get to the Columbia River by this date? What do we take? What do we leave? Where do we stop for water? Where do we camp? In the snow, where do we presume the trail is? For the next step, where do I chisel my boot into this snow bank so I won't slip?

As we waited, I pulled off my boots, took out my single-blade pocket knife—light—and proceeded to cut holes in the sides of each roughly the size and shape of orange slices. My little toes needed their freedom. Glenn shook his head sideways.

"What about stuff getting in your boots, Bob?" he asked.

"I've already thought about that," I said. "Duct tape. When they dry out, I'm going to wrap them in duct tape."

"But won't your toes just rub against the duct tape?"

"I'm one step ahead of you, Glenny," I said. I reached into the netting of my pack and pulled out the plastic jam tubs from the restaurant the previous night. "Once my boots dry out, I eat the jam, clean out the tubs, then duct tape a couple of these over each hole. The toes have room to wiggle. The duct tape keeps out debris. Meanwhile, I'm getting a two-for-one bang for my buck in terms of weight: nutritional sustenance and foot protection from a few light items."

Glenn shook his head sideways and smiled.

"You scoff now," I said. "Next year, everyone on the PCT will be wearing Merrell Moabs—With Jam-Tub-Enhanced, Duct-Tape-Fortified Extra Breathing Room."

AFTER EIGHT DAYS of being apart, hugging Sally felt good. She had arrived with her sister and our two ready-to-hike nieces, Carrie and Molly, and, of course, lunch. Carrie was the administrative assistant to the Linn County sheriff, though soon headed to law school in San Diego. Molly, back from teaching English in France, worked in a retail store in Seattle.

Over sandwiches, chips, and pop at a secluded picnic table, we updated the four on the trip thus far: mosquitoes, blisters, snow, Cisco and Roadrunner, and the Aussies, which made me wonder how Kate's ankle was holding up since we hadn't seen them in six days. Ann and Sally updated us on home: Ann and Glenn's other daughter, in Los Angeles, was getting along well with her pregnancy; our granddaughter Avin was turning four today, though I was disappointed I couldn't get enough cell connection to send her my video birthday poem.

The Crater Lake-to-Summit Lake stretch for which the girls were joining us afforded little water. On their way to the lake, the women had left some gallon jugs for us and for Roadrunner and Cisco at Grouse Hill, just off Highway 209 to the north, where, after thirteen miles, we planned to camp that night. (We weren't sure about Cisco and Roadrunner's camp plans, but, regardless, Glenn had arranged with Ann by phone to make sure water was left for them.)

The Saturday morning meeting was part family reunion, part picnic, and part NASCAR pit stop, the latter more frenetic than I expected. Back-dropped by tourists much cleaner than us, we unloaded stuff from our multi-colored stuff sacks—spent DEET containers, for example—and replaced it with new stuff, such as toilet paper. What to keep? What to throw? When I had made my choices, I'd be leaving with a pack about eight pounds heavier, mainly because of food to get me to Summit Lake on Tuesday, where Ann would return with fresh supplies.

Amid the crazed transition, expectations swirled in an array of varieties: Glenn and I, trying to reconnect with our respective spouses while making sure we weren't leaving anything we needed to bring or bringing anything we needed to leave; Sally and Ann, trying to be supportive amid the chaos but knowing, in a few minutes, they'd be PCT Trail widows again for the second of four weeks; Carrie and Molly, upbeat as they readied to join us on the trail.

Photos. Hugs. Final checklists. Then goodbyes.

If the park was beautiful, the transition out of it was ugly. It was hard leaving Sally. Meanwhile, the rim was packed with snow—and precarious given that one slip to the east took you lakeside 900 feet below—so we were forced to walk miles along Rim Drive. The shoulder was narrow, the vehicles annoying, the temperature heating up. After a week of incessant silence in the woods, I couldn't get off this road fast enough. It was extra hard on the feet; Carrie was already reporting blisters.

After seven miles, about half of it on the road, we crossed the highway and headed north on a pumice desert that transitioned into scattered trees, wilderness, and something I thought would disappear on this side of Crater Lake: snow.

I found it annoying how my mind translated maps into an image in my head that was often far different from what I actually found. The map-to-reality image was never as accurate as the cartoon I once saw in which a man driving down a road comes to a giant crease across the highway. "Wow," he says. "Just like the map shows!"

The map showed the area north of Crater Lake as open plain—lots of sunlight to melt snow, I figured—and, with a full day before we'd get to the higher reaches of Mount Thielsen, I assumed this would be snow-free. Not the case. Glenn and I were soon relying on our respective GPS devices. And Carrie and Molly were getting a rude welcome to the PCT, though their spirits stayed high. Better than mine, which sagged with the unexpected snow.

At one point, Glenn and I were consulting the map when I heard the faint sound of a voice in the distance. On a gradual ridge, perhaps three-quarters of a mile away, I could barely make out the criss-cross wave of someone in a light blue shirt.

"Is that who I think it is?" I asked Glenn.

"Yeah," he said. "Cisco."

The guy was marking trail for us, something he didn't have to do, but did anyway. Saying, in essence: *Follow us.* We did. But if he and Roadrunner's occasional arm-waving helped keep us on track, Glenn had already seen the handwriting on the wall. He seemed deep in thought, which wasn't unusual, because he wasn't exactly the trail chatterbox. But this was something more. With Molly and Carrie far behind, he stopped.

"Bob," he said. "I think we need to adjust our plans."

Sounded to me like the second coming of the "we-nearly-died" warning regarding Devils Peak, an ominous intro to something that was going to threaten our making the Bridge of the Gods by summer's end.

"Meaning?"

"This is going to be tougher for all us," he said, "and I'm concerned for Carrie and Molly. They have only four days to hike and, chances are, this snow is only going to get worse up around Thielsen."

Where was he headed with this?

"There's a cutoff northwest to Diamond Lake paralleling Mount Thielsen," Glenn continued. "I'm thinking tomorrow I take them down there, a thousand feet lower than this, where there's not likely to be snow. The three of us hike around Diamond Lake for three days. Ann picks us up Tuesday, when, in our original plan, she was going to bring us food to Summit Lake. Instead, she picks me and the girls up, takes the back roads and drops me off at Summit, then takes the girls home."

"And I'm where during all this?"

"Going over Thielsen with Cisco and Roadrunner on the PCT," he said, then paused. "Assuming they'll have you, which is a big assumption." He then broke into one of his trademark bursts of laughter. "Seriously, Bob, this way you maintain the integrity of your PCT hike and the girls get a better experience. You can take my solar charger."

What he didn't say, of course, was who, in this scenario, was the odd man out: himself. Just like him, to think only of others.

"Glenn, the idea was the two of us doing this together," I said. "Where's the integrity of *your* PCT hike in all this?"

"That's OK," he said. "I can come back and do this stretch some other time. I'll still do the entire Oregon portion of the trail."

I still didn't like the idea. Not that I liked the idea of Molly and Carrie being dragged through more snow; it was one thing for Glenn and me to face some tough stretches on our month-long journey, another for my nieces' entire four-day trip to consist of essentially cross-country skiing without skis.

"Cisco and Roadrunner are an hour ahead of us," I said. "What if they don't stop for the night at Grouse Hill so we can discuss your plan? We might have already seen the last of them."

"We'll cross that bridge when we come to it," he said. "But they didn't get a great jump out of the park today and the next water stop is eighteen miles beyond Grouse, so I bet they'll be staying there."

OK, I thought, what if Cisco and Roadrunner weren't keen on a three-day guest, particularly one whom they knew wasn't a snow-hiking veteran, one who'd wounded Roadrunner the previous day with his insensitivity, one who had holes in his boots? What if I infringed on the integrity of *their* trip? Slowed them down? Got hurt? Or was simply so annoying they wanted to duct tape me to a tree and flee? Like revving an engine in neutral, the questions churned in mind even if they never left my mouth.

"All I know," said Glenn, "is I'm not leaving you unless they're willing to have you join them. You're not going it alone, not in the snow."

I'd already briefly considered that and dismissed the idea. Without snow, sure. But losing trail was too easy to do with it covered. And with five days on a thickly forested trail before an electrical outlet at Odell Lake, meaning little direct sunlight, Glenn's solar battery wasn't going to be transferring much juice to my iPhone for GPS purposes. Cisco and Roadrunner's trail instincts were integral to my continuing.

In the end, I understood what was happening. Glenn was making a decision as our team leader, yes, but, more importantly, as a father. And, as I weighed it, I realized it was a good one. Good for Molly and Carrie. Good for me, though, unfortunately, not good for Glenn.

I nodded an OK. "I'm game," I said.

AS TRIBAL COUNCILS go, it was decidedly low key. Cisco and Roadrunner had, indeed, stopped for the night at Grouse Hill. We gulped down our freeze-dried dinners, watery scrambled eggs after I accidentally used twice the amount of water the exotic recipe called for. We learned, from Molly, that the reason our filter was so hard to pump was that we'd failed to insert a small, came-in-the-package filter at the end of the intake tube. (Whoops.) And learned, from Cisco and Roadrunner, that they'd met Sally and Ann back at Crater Lake. They had been hiking past a tourist-thick viewpoint when two women in a Honda Pilot offered them some snacks.

"By any chance are you two Cisco and Roadrunner?" Sally had asked.

It was one of those what-are-the-chances moments. "Trail Magic," they call it. Serendipitous deeds of goodwill offered to PCT hikers along the way. The way, for example, we were able to get some fresh fruit to Ben and Kate, an opportunity they would have missed had we arrived even three minutes later at the border.

Now, at Grouse Hill, we replayed their leaving Crater Lake. "We couldn't understand how two such wonderful women had gotten stuck with, er, wound up with Bob and Glenn," said Cisco.

People were in good moods. Glenn, in private, had told Carrie and Molly about his plan. If they were disappointed to leave the PCT for Diamond Lake they didn't say so. No grumbling. No complaining. A lot like their father. Cisco and Roadrunner seemed to enjoy the addition of Glenn's daughters. So did I. I'd just finished washing my dishes, a task that took about five seconds given that those dishes consisted of a plastic spoon and a plastic fork, the former which I seldom used.

In flip-flops and wool socks, I shuffled over to my pack. Evenings got cool. I was wearing black long johns, with socks and running shorts over the bottoms; a pea green down vest; and a stocking cap. I looked like the camp jester, even if my propensity for humor seemed to wane with each passing mile, meaning by evening I had, in cell-phone lingo, ebbed to one bar.

Carrie and Molly laughed at my outfit, my appearance topped off, of course, with nine day's of scrub on my face. In the eyes of Cisco and Roadrunner, I must have appeared as some sort of trail freak, though even they were enjoying the fashion show. Then came the moment of truth. When things quieted down, Glenn shared his proverbial New Deal with Cisco and Roadrunner.

"But as I told Bob," he said to the couple, "it's contingent upon your willingness to let him join you for three days."

In the slight pause all you could hear was a mosquito or two—million.

"So, you're asking us to adopt Bob for three days?" Roadrunner asked.

I felt a little like one of the last kids picked for a team being offered to a coach who might not want me. But a smile creased her face.

"Well, of course," she said. "We'll take Bob."

Rich nodded. "Sounds good to me," he said. "Maybe I can pick up some writing tips."

"Or fashion tips," said Glenn, then laughed louder than the one-liner deserved.

Everyone laughed. Even I laughed.

But, later as I slipped into my sleeping bag, I realized that, in the morning, everything was going to change. In our year of planning this trip, who expected anything like this?

The Oregon Boys were going their separate ways.

13. 'Mount Sielsen'

Trail log: Sunday, July 31, 2011.
PCT mile-marker: 1846.8.
Days on trail: 9.
Miles hiked Saturday: 13.2.
Total miles hiked: 143.6.

Location: Grouse Hill, just north of Crater Lake.
Elevation: 6,500 feet.
Average miles per day: 16.2.
Portion of trip completed: 31.8%.

ROADRUNNER WASN'T called that for nothing. She didn't have the speed of a Blaze or Blood Bath, but on a snow-less open trail, which we were delighted—and surprised—to have on this Sunday morning, she gobbled up miles. With her leading and Cisco on her heels, I hung on like some rickety, out-of-place caboose hitched to a bullet train. But I hung on. We had eighteen miles to go—Thielsen Creek, just beyond Mount Thielsen itself—and couldn't afford to come up short. It would be our only chance for water.

Glenn, Carrie, and Molly were, I assumed, far behind. We hadn't left camp with any particular "goodbye plan"—say, a meet-at-the-fork-to-Diamond-Lake agreement. So, when, after eight miles, we came to the cutoff, I took a pea-sized morsel of duct tape—more precisely, Duck tape, because it was literally duct tape with a green-and-yellow University of Oregon design—and placed it on the PCT sign. I wanted Glenn to be assured we'd gotten this far.

When I last saw him at Grouse Hill, Glenn had looked more comical than usual: beyond his flipped-up-in-the-front hat, he'd tied a handful of the now-empty one-gallon water jugs to the back of his pack in order to drop them in a Diamond Lake recycling container. He looked like part pack mule and part recycling truck.

The lack of snow was wonderful, if not rare. We had gone nine miles in a little less than three hours, a pace about fifty percent faster than the two-miles-per-hour pace that Glenn and I averaged. I felt better than I had since early in the trip and was pleased that I didn't seem to be slowing down Cisco and Roadrunner.

What's more, during lunch, I found a flaw in Roadrunner: She couldn't say "Mount Thielsen." With her German accent, it kept coming out "Sielsen." It wasn't that I needed something to lord over her, but she and Cisco were obviously so proficient at this thru-hiking stuff—and I so inept—that it made her ever so much more human. And she was able to laugh about it.

At lunch on the trail, she and Cisco were anxious to learn more about Glenn, his family, even me. Meanwhile, I learned that she was a material scientist who'd worked for large international companies in Switzerland and Germany.

"Darn," I said. "I told Glenn I thought you were a book editor."

Cisco, meanwhile, had spent three decades with the Lawrence Livermore National Lab, primarily working on their laser program before retiring recently. As a hobby, he was an amateur astronomer who built his own telescopes and led star-watching parties. Who builds their own telescopes as a *hobby*? That made my hobby of browsing used bookstores pale by comparison.

"And here I had you pegged as working for some environmental agency," I said. "Who knew?"

I finished off a summer-sausage-and-string cheese pita wrap—dry, and not nearly as good as it sounded—and was fastening down my pack to leave when Roadrunner spoke.

"No, Bob," she said. "Now we nap. A short one. But we nap."

I could get used to these guys. Presumably, Waldo could too. "Have stopped about three hours at noon every day," he wrote on July 25, 1894, presumably with zzzzz's involved.

"OK," I said. "Now we nap."

I leaned my head against the sleeping bag at the bottom of my pack. "Then," I said, "we take on Mount Sielsen."

JUDGE JOHN WALDO climbed most of Mount Thielsen on August 25, 1886. "Today," he wrote in his journal, "ascended to within a hundred feet or so of the summit of the peak known as the Emigrants or the Cowhorn, now frequently called Mount Thielsen." (It was named to honor railroad developer Hans Thielsen.)

Waldo had spent the previous night "under Mount Scott" on the southeast side of bowl-shaped Crater Lake. Because Thielsen is essentially due north of Crater Lake and the pumice desert serves as a fairly smooth approach to the mountain's base, it's likely he and the boys had guided their horses up the very stretch we were on now before dismounting for the ascent.

If they traveled with pack horses, Waldo and his pals were hardly high-mountain lightweights. The day after their near-ascent of Thielsen, says Waldo's journal, he climbed 8,368-foot Mount Bailey, which rises just west of nearby Diamond Lake. The next day, he summited Thielsen: three mountains in three days.

We, of course, were not interested in getting to the top of the 9,182-foot mountain, so narrow at its peak that it was known as "the lightning rod of the Cascades." Only a handful of climbers could stand on it at a time. We were only interested in getting around its snow-shrouded western shoulder on a trail that would reach to 7,350 feet, roughly the same elevation we'd encountered at Devils Peak.

Soon after lunch we hit the snow I'd expected far earlier, particularly in the tree-shaded portions of the trail. Few people had been through here; in fact, in the sixty-mile, four-day stretch from Crater Lake to Summit Lake, we would not see a single hiker. The few footprints visible—probably those of Ben, Kate, Blood Bath, and Blaze—were, like melting candles, their distinctiveness rounded at the edges. And were easily camouflaged by swaths of natural dips in the melting snow, called sun cups, which made for an undulated pattern not unlike the decorative swirls you might find in the whipped cream atop a lemon meringue pie. Add to that branches, twigs, moss, and needles, and making out such footsteps was seldom easy.

About two miles from where Thielsen jutted into the sky, Cisco, up front, stopped.

"Your turn, Bob," he said. "You take the lead."

Me? I remembered an old first-person story in *Sports Illustrated* about a basketball player who sat on the bench the entire year. Never played. Suddenly, in a crucial game, the coach yelled to him that he needed his help. The guy, naturally, was incredulous. *Me? You want me in the game?* No, not in the game. To the locker room. Turns out the star player's jock strap had broken. "Give him yours," said the coach.

In other words, I was wary about being called upon for the wrong reasons. And yet this seemed to be a legitimate offer. *Lead us.* At first, the new hiking order was so unfamiliar to me that I immediately burdened myself with thoughts of failure. To hike with Glenn, often in the lead, was to flow with the familiar; we knew each other well. Certainly, neither one of us wanted to let the other down, but there was little sense of "succeed-or-else." Beyond that, we were slow, meaning the standards weren't particularly demanding.

With Cisco and Roadrunner, it was different. This was more than my father letting me drive the boat alone for the first time at Cultus Lake; "point her at Irish Mountain's nub and you'll hit our camp," he'd say. No, in *Hoosiers,* this was Coach Norman Dale (Gene Hackman) turning over his Hickory High basketball team to Shooter, the town drunk (Dennis Hopper). Just like Shooter, I momentarily froze. *Me? Now? Here?*

"Lead on, Bob," said Roadrunner.

I've never been a "never-let-them-see-you-sweat" guy; instead, I'm more of a "what-you-see-is-what-you're-stuck-with" guy.

"OK," I said. "If you're really that desperate."

But an interesting thing happened as we crunched our way through the tree-clumped snow: I started to believe I actually belonged here. On this trail. With these people. In the lead. And as I began believing that, my fear of failure melted and my enjoyment of the experience rose.

That, of course, was followed immediately by pangs of guilt. Below to our left, we were afforded view after view of Diamond Lake, where Glenn and my nieces were. And I felt badly that he wasn't having this mountain-top experience I was having. But, then, he made his choice. And, knowing the three of them, they were having a great time, right? OK, end of guilt.

The trail was carved into the western flank of Thielsen, though now lost below up to six feet of snow. The challenge was staying atop what amounted to a giant version of that pliable, exhaust ducting that wraps from your dryer to the outside vent. The whitened trail snaked amid trees. It dipped, rose, twisted, and turned. As such, you were safest to stay centered atop the "tube," lest you slip down one of its sides. It was all like being on a slow-motion roller coaster, say Disneyland's Matterhorn, though my metaphorical abominable snowman was not a wild-eyed monster but the fear of letting down Cisco and Roadrunner. Spraining an ankle. Getting sick. Something like that.

As we continued, I was reminded that for all its beauty, nature ruled. The trail and snow felt absolutely no obligation to arrange themselves for us hikers in any sense of order that might be to our liking. Every now and then, the actual dirt trail would emerge from a waning snow bank. Then, after a short stint of walking on rare earth, I'd find myself having to edge my way sideways, up a new mountain of snow. By now, trekking poles, beyond Cisco and Roadrunner, had become my two best new friends. Sometimes, the snow might sweep into a pitch roughly the slant of an A-frame's roof. Without trekking poles, I'd have been constantly slipping.

Even with the poles, my legs and arms were being stretched and strained in ways I'd never imagined back in my pre-trip vision. I'd visualized a nice, neat, left-right, left-right, hiking cadence. As it was, I might take three wide sideway steps to dig up a snow bank, tip-toe carefully across its upper ridge, slide down a six-foot snow ramp, then take some more of the traditional right-left steps before encountering an entirely different challenge.

At one point, amid a stretch that was like frozen sea chop, I splayed out like a new-born colt on ice, limbs here and there. I hit the snow hard. My sunglasses popped off and I rolled onto them, snapping off the left band. It was late afternoon. We'd been on the trail for nine hours and sixteen miles. Roadrunner took a hard fall, too, though bounced back with a grittiness that impressed me. Cisco trudged on, a quiet soul now even more quiet.

We stopped to rest, grab a snack, and plan a final route down. The late afternoon sun was still on our shoulders. I sucked in some water and threw back a handful of Good & Plenties as Cisco munched on dried fruit. Now to fix the sunglasses: I unwound "Duck" tape from one of my trekking poles and fashioned myself a splint from a six-inch twig, then modeled the final results.

"Hey, you'll never find these in your L.L. Bean catalog," I said.

They smiled and shook their heads, either enjoying my lightheartedness or too tired to express anything else regarding a guy who now had holes in his boots, twig-splinted sunglasses, and, of course, yesterday's dirty socks safety-pinned to the outside of his backpack to dry.

Grooved step by grooved step, we wrapped around Thielsen. Then came a timely payoff: An awesome view of its spindly peak unveiled itself, rising some two thousand feet above us. Somewhere near here, Waldo and his men had tethered their horses to trees, organized their knapsacks, and headed for the summit.

Now, I looked at a mountain whose peak was too steep to hold snow in July. But on this shoulder, we had plenty. I'd never imagined such a scene: being in deep snow on the edge of a mountain, the lower reaches of the Cascades stretched out far and wide beyond. The feeling was one part exhilaration, one part pride, and one part unmitigated fear. Because as we wrapped around the mountain's northwest slopes, we found ourselves on some snowy precipices that brought to mind a reverse-mirror-image of Devils Peak, when we first encountered its "glaciated bowl."

By now, I had happily returned the lead to Roadrunner and Cisco; this was a dicey stretch where the penalty for a misstep was growing with each foot plant. We were just at timberline. If not the do-or-die territory of higher reaches, the pitch to our left was steep enough so a slip could send us flailing down a slope whose backstop was a swath of juvenile firs. Despite growing weariness, I planted my boots with extra caution.

At the mountain's farthest northwest reach, we came to a shelf. Looking down, I was fifteen again, staring at a mogul-pocked run at Hoodoo Ski Bowl's top called "The Dive." A run I never thought I could make but did. And, really, wasn't that adventure's grandeur, the idea that overcoming something once made it easier to overcome other fears in the future?

I'd recently seen a greeting card that showed a backpacker high on a mountain, looking down. "What would you attempt to do if you knew you could not fail?" it said. The inference was that we'd take risks. But isn't the opposite true? Isn't the essence of adventure, be it big or small, the very idea that we *might* fail? Isn't it the tension that gives meaning to a story, the obstacles that steel us for the journey of life? I could plan a trip around my block, knowing that, in all likelihood, I wouldn't fail. But what was the value in that?

We started down the edge of the glaciated bowl. I traversed a bit. Boot-skied a bit. Slid on my butt a bit. Lower, lower, lower. After about twenty minutes we were into the more gradual slope of trees. Between Cisco's GPS and mine, we picked up the snow-shrouded trail again. Somehow, I wound up out front. I looked at the tiny blue dot on my screen, all but on the creek. Then I heard it: the sound of rushing water.

"Thielsen Creek!" I yelled.

It said something about PCT hikers and small victories that coming across a tiny creek after nearly twelve hours on the trail not only triggered whoops and hollers, but a twenty-second video (by me) and a pronouncement of the precise time of discovery: 6:12 P.M. (by Roadrunner). At last: water, food, and blessed rest.

The creek trundled cold and clear beneath the snow—the epitome of fresh—and only showed its face in short portions. We watered-up and made camp on a shelf a couple of hundred feet up from the creek, an island of dirt in an ocean of snow, backdropped dramatically by Thielsen's pointed peak to our south. The day's final light brushed the spiral summit in pink. An evening chill set in. It seemed more winter than summer, more Yukon than Oregon. I had never camped in a place that felt more untamed, more isolated, more chillingly close to the soul of wilderness than this.

When returning by myself for more water, the soft riffles of the creek were broken by what sounded like a rock slide on Thielsen's northeast slopes. The sound was jaggedly loud against the quiet. My adrenalin pumped. Quiet returned, save for the cadence of the creek. Then, again, more rocks clattered. A mountain goat loosening shale? Another hiker? An unprovoked slide, nature on the move?

It was only later that night, alone in my tent and on that uneasy cusp of sleep—when the real and imagined are as indistinguishable as is the place where a fresh-water river ends and the salt-water ocean begins—that I remembered: Hadn't there been the clip-clop of hooves before the rumble, as if made by horses? Sure, it was the sound I'd heard often when I'd joined a group of elk hunters in the Blue Mountains for a series of stories: hooves on shale.

Of course, it was the judge. Waldo and his three pals were making their descent from Thielsen to join us for the rest of the journey.

14. Reunion

Trail log: Tuesday, August 2, 2011
Days on trail: 11.
PCT mile-marker: 1899.6.
Miles hiked Sunday: 17.6.
Miles hiked Monday: 16.4.

Location: Tolo Camp.
Total miles hiked: 177.6.
Average miles per day: 16.1.
Elevation: 6,200 feet.
Portion of trip completed: 39.3%.

HAVING WRITTEN a few books on the subject, I had learned that war, though often portrayed as non-stop action, was largely about boredom: short bursts of excitement followed by long droughts of maneuvering into position. Of setting up camps and taking down camps. Of waiting.

At times, so it was with life on the Pacific Crest Trail. I'm sure PCT purists would argue that every step was replete with meaning, every view filling some hungry void in the soul, every hiker's thought pulsating with the sustenance of inspiration. But for every person who holds such views I would let them hear the monotonous sound of step after step, breath after breath, click after click of trekking poles on rock and dirt—the in-your-ear high-pitched buzz of a mosquito flapping its wings at 250 times per second, seemingly having been with us since we hit Freye Lake a week ago.

I would show them the weary young trail-maintenance worker who, as we chatted with her supervisor near Windigo Butte, leaned against a tree in the late-morning heat, eyes fixed in combat's "thousand-yard stare."

I would let them taste their twentieth Clif Bar or 200th handful of trail mix or 2,000th sip of purified creek or lake water.

And I would let them feel the quiet discontent of realizing that what they thought was some milepost along the way—a lake, a trail junction, a spring—was not.

On the PCT, everything you wanted to get to was farther up the trail. Rarely did you get anywhere before you thought you should be there. Instead, such destinations were always "just a little farther," even if the mind could play tricks and make you think otherwise. Once, I was looking for a spring and saw a concoction of branches that I was sure some Trail Angel had configured as a giant arrow to point to the water. When I arrived, however, I realized it was just a random collection of branches that only meant dashed hopes.

All of which is to say that our two days of hiking to reunite with Glenn at Summit Lake leaned decidedly to the monotonous side, at least for me. Oh, the company was great. Mount Thielsen had galvanized my relationship with Cisco and Roadrunner in a way that only overcoming a challenge can; it was the same reason why, after a week in a Haitian medical clinic with total strangers, you leave feeling as if you're friends for life.

But the exhilaration that had powered us past Thielsen was gone, replaced, as it were, by a Monday morning emotional hangover. Our reunion with Glenn was still thirty-five miles and two days away, so it wasn't as if that could become instant inspiration. Our destination Monday—16.4 miles away—was only some nebulous spot on the trail marked "Tolo Camp," whose only known virtue was a spring of sorts, an oasis at the end of what was an otherwise ho-hum trail with no water. The splendid views we'd had the previous two days—Crater Lake, Diamond Lake backdropped by Mount Bailey—were long gone, replaced by a winding tunnel through trees. Finally, in what was becoming the PCT Summer of 2011's "we're-not-out-of-the-woods-yet" mantra, snow hung on like *Christmas Vacation's* Cousin Eddie overstaying his visit with the Griswolds.

We no longer were chiseling our way along a steep mountainside. Instead, we were slogging through snow in dense woods where the danger diminished and the chances of losing the trail increased. On a timberline slope, it was easier to see where the trail at least might go next; it tended to stay fairly even, rising or falling steadily. Deep in the woods, who knew? Blazes or markers were rare, and, without the intuition of Cisco and Roadrunner, I would have been lost. Quite literally.

The foundational layer of this snow had probably fallen eight to nine months earlier, in the late fall of 2010. Now, it was still four to five feet deep in places and dipped sharply at the bases of trees, which, in number, were thicker than I'd remembered since somewhere in southern Oregon. As such, negotiating this section was like being an ant trying to get from one end of an empty egg carton to the other. An egg carton, by the way, that would be eight miles long on this day.

We zigzagged up the side of the Sawtooth Ridge. By late morning, 8,324-foot Howlock Mountain came into view and, farther north, near Tipsoo Peak, we broke into a white-swathed meadow.

"This is it," said Cisco. "Highest point on the Oregon-Washington PCT." We were at 7,550 feet.

After another few hours working our way down the east side of a ridge, we discovered something I'd almost forgotten existed: dirt. A regular trail. It was a two-foot-wide manifestation of Joni Mitchell singing "you don't know what you've got till it's gone." Having gone twenty-four hours with no semblance of an actual trail, the return to dirt was like Columbus spotting land.

"Whoo-hoo!" I said.

Around the next bend, the snow was back.

"Argh!" I said. "Enough already."

Finally, it ended for good. For now.

The pace picked up. Our spirits picked up. My water supply dwindled as my craving for food—I mean serious food, not Clif Bars—rose amid my late-afternoon weariness. That's one thing I'd learned: The only food that really satisfied me was the Costco-bought Svenhard's danishes and the evening freeze-dried meals. My snacks had grown as bland as prison food. (I'd spent a night in one for a story.) And no matter how much I ate, I always seemed hungry. After we finished Part I of our journey, I had to remedy that.

By late afternoon, we arrived at Tolo Camp, nothing more than a literal wide spot on the trail with room for two or three tents. The air was thick with mosquitoes; I put on my mesh mosquito hat. While Cisco made camp, Roadrunner and I followed steep switchbacks a quarter-mile down a slope to get spring water. Other than the first hour of the day—putting on damp, sweaty hiking clothes in the darkness of your tent—it was the PCT procedure I liked least: arriving at your destination, totally gassed, then not only having to get water, but sometimes having to get it on steep descents that threatened to rip off whatever skin you had left on your feet.

Waldo knew the feeling. "Climbing with painful steps and slow up steep and rocky slopes," he wrote about a July 22, 1880, slog up Elk Mountain near the North Santiam Pass. At times, his back gave him trouble. "I can still walk well enough," he wrote about that same trip, "but can do little at packing."

Ever the poet, Waldo loved to sit and read and philosophize, but work came first. "The mind takes satisfaction in carrying out its plans and exceeding them, as I understand Thoreau," he wrote on August 22, 1894, from about twenty miles north of where I now was, "yet the most important of my plans to-day must be deferred. In the morning after getting breakfast, making bread, and getting some wood, I must use that ax handle made to-day to cut boughs for the tent and make bough pillows."

The spring proved to be pathetic. Still water. Muddy bottom. Mosquitoes gyrating on the surface like ice skaters high on crack. But eleven days into our journey, I was gradually learning that on the trail you either conformed to lower standards or went nuts in your refusal to do so. I dipped the pump's hose in the least ugly portion of the swamp and began pumping.

WE AWOKE TO renewed purpose: a scheduled reunion with Glenn at Summit Lake 18.8 miles away.

"What time are we meeting him?" asked Roadrunner.

"Four o'clock," I said.

"We will be there, waiting for him," she said. "So, Bob, how did you sleep?"

"Fine," I said. "Once I got beyond the cat spray and horse dung and wedding drunks and, of course, Devils Peak, I've had no problem the entire way."

Roadrunner laughed.

It always surprised me how weary you could be at night, going to sleep with the thought that you couldn't walk another step, then the next day walk, say, 40,000 steps. As Waldo wrote in 1881: "Have tramped over the mountains pretty wide and lain down weary at night and rose in the morning seemingly wholly refreshed."

At mid-morning, fortune shined on us in the form of a trail crew whose boss invited us to stop at their camp near Windigo Butte for water. We rested at a picnic table. As with rediscovering the beauty of dirt, hiking the PCT reminded you of what an utter privilege it was to sit down at a table and eat. I had a Clif Bar and trail mix; Cisco fired up his jet-boil stove to make the two of them pancakes. I mentally shook my head. These two could be dangling from a rope atop Half Dome and they'd be slicing dried mushrooms for quiche. That said, I had to smile when Cisco nudged up to me later after a quick glance at Roadrunner.

"Hey, got anymore of those Good & Plenties?" (We all had our skeletons in the closet.)

From Windigo, the trail climbed again, another pattern that was starting to become ingrained in my memory: every day you basically went up and down the flanks of mountains, buttes, or ridges. By now, the rarest thing on the Oregon PCT was a long, flat stretch. The PCT was a tree-lined roller coaster, occasionally coated with snow.

By the time we got to 7,100 feet—1,200 feet up from the break we took at Windigo—we were back in patches of it. For lunch, I downed my fourth—and last—sausage-and-cheese tortilla wrap of the trip as we gazed across a saddle to 7,864-foot Cowhorn Mountain, which Waldo had climbed August 27, 1886, and which, two years later, gave a scare to his pals, Harry and Felix. "(They) had some severe and exciting experiences in attempting to ascend the Cowhorn," Waldo wrote. "They missed the only path to the top, and wandered among the cliffs and sheer blood-curdling heights all afternoon, and were lucky to have gotten safely back to camp."

As we began our descent to the northwest, I envisioned snow vanishing soon. Ah, but again, the trail gods gently reminded me that they, not I, would decide when the snow would end. It stayed with us all day, at times Cisco piece-mealing together alternative routes so we could avoid snowy lips that hung over drop-offs like white-frosted muffin crusts.

THOUGH WALDO ventured to California's Mount Shasta—and spent some time in the Diamond Lake/Mount Thielsen area—we were now entering what generally were the southernmost reaches of his summer sojourns: the Crescent, Odell, and Summit Lake area. As we made our way down to Summit, all three lakes came into view. This was the beginning of a sixty-mile stretch of the Oregon Cascades with the most lakes.

Waldo first camped at the most eastern lake of the three on August 5, 1883. "Here we are under the black pines on the shore of Crescent Lake," he wrote in his journal. "We did not get here until it was getting dark, and now, 9:15, have just finished supper by the light of the camp-fire, and I am now trying to write by the same uncertain light, but I must give it up until morning."

I could relate. My evening blog posts on the Internet had proven more difficult than I expected. Splotchy cell service and low batteries curtailed some would-be sends from my iPhone. A total lack of energy on my part didn't help. At day's end, it was all I could do to get water, set up the tent, and eat my freeze-dried dinner. With fingers worn by the grips of trekking poles, tapping out even a few sentences on a gumstick-sized keyboard proved challenging, all the more so because it was done most easily when able to prop my elbows on something—even my lap, while sitting—but such opportunities were rare.

At times, Waldo sounded more upbeat about his writing setup than I did about mine. "I am writing on my knee, sitting on a boat stool, with a fine, old barkless log to rest against," he wrote from Fish Lake on August 30, 1903. "All in good spirits," he finished up that "out-of-light" message from Crescent Lake a decade earlier. "Supper was eaten of biscuits, baked in the reflector, and spiced with some jolly conversation."

Not that he and his boys didn't have their challenges. The next day he wrote about one of their wagon's wheels busting through a log bridge, forcing a delay. And mentions a threat that, nearly 130 years later, I hadn't even thought of: fire.

"There is too much smoke, under present circumstances, to make the Crater Lake trip, or even to Mount Thielsen, which is barely visible," he wrote.

Snow, mountains, mosquitoes, blisters, and a fifty-seven-year-old body had proven plenty challenging for me. The recent realization that dirt and pebbles were getting inside the self-inflicted holes in my boots wasn't helping.

Who needed fire?

"YOU'RE SURE that the meet time was 4 p.m.?"

"Positive," I told Roadrunner as we waited in the late afternoon heat at a campground on Summit Lake's northwest reaches. The lake was large, the water turquoise in spots, and the view south, toward the mountains from which we'd come, gorgeous. Islands of trees popped out of the water here and there.

Such beauty aside, we were bushed after nineteen miles; even aesthetic appreciation required some energy, of which I had little. Once again, what I had imagined and what I found were two different things. I'd envisioned a large, well-maintained campground with picnic tables, blessed picnic tables. And, oh yeah, Ann waiting with taco salads, cold drinks, and fresh underwear and socks. What I found instead was a half-dozen scattered camp sites, an outhouse, no running water, underage kids squirreling on ATVs, and no tables. No Ann. No Glenn. No Molly. No Carrie.

"Glenny!" I yelled as I made my way on a dirt road beyond the lake. "Glenny!"

No response.

We poked around more. I yelled out some more, undoubtedly irking a few of the campers. But, with no cell coverage, what else could I do? Finally, the three of us plopped down on a log near the lake. This was not the reception I had in mind. This was like 1869 at Promontory Summit, Utah: Union Pacific Railroad officials anticipating the completion of the first transcontinental railroad only to realize the Central Pacific was a no-show. Plus, I was starved and thirsty.

"Wanna beer?"

A guy camped by the water made the offer. As consolation prizes go, it wasn't much but we each accepted a cold can. It was nearly five o'clock. The bigger challenge, I'd figured, was those of us on the trail making the agreed-upon meeting time, not the ones arriving by Izusu Trooper. What could have happened to them? Car trouble? An accident? Could they have gotten lost? I quickly ruled out the latter; Glenn and Ann were logistical Mensas, folks who could safely lead two dozen volunteers to a rural clinic in Haiti. Summit Lake was a slam dunk for them.

My mind wandered. The dirt road to Summit Lake from Highway 58 was a seven-mile snake for which high-clearance vehicles were recommended; I remembered my folks talking about taking it in the 1970s, and I'd heard it hadn't been improved much. Could they have gotten high-centered?.

In 1853—Waldo was nine years old—650 covered wagons got lost just miles from here when leaders tried to find a shortcut to the Willamette Valley. Finally, rescuers found "The Lost Wagon Train" and guided the group to the Willamette Valley, including Eugene where 1,500 settlers immediately doubled the town's population.

Behind us, a low rumble broke the quiet. Through the trees, I saw it: the Trooper. The reunion party burst forth with such spontaneity that there was no time for explanations. Seven people. Three days apart. There was too much catching up to do. Too many group photos to be taken. Too much garbage to give to Ann and too many fresh supplies for her to give to us. Clean clothes. Fresh DEET. Fresh Svenhard's danishes.

Top and left: Aussies Kate and Ben happened by just as Bob and Glenn arrived at the Oregon-California border. The two states' meeting point was marked by a sign whose mileage to Washington, 498, suggested a much longer trip than the guide book said: 452. (Ann Petersen.) Below: The red lava trail at the base of Brown Mountain offered loop after seemingly endless loop of rugged hiking. (Bob Welch.)

Top: After nineteen miles, Bob props up his feet to help ease the swelling after a soak in nearby Cascade Canal on Highway 140. (Glenn Petersen.) Middle: Bob boot-skis down dreaded Devils Peak. (Glenn Petersen.) Above:: Markers such as this, right, came along about as frequently as wildflowers, left. (Bob Welch.)

Top: Glenn exhalts in the grandeur of deep-blue Crater Lake. (Ann Petersen.) Middle: Cisco, left, and Roadrunner with their "adopted son" at Summit Lake. (Ann Petersen.) Above: Bob's twig splint on broken sunglasses at Mount Thielsen. (Bob Welch.) Left: In the same area, Bob hikes a trail choked with an awkward swath of snow slanted like an A-frame's roof. (Rich Combs.)

Top: Relieved to be past Mount Thielsen, Bob celebrates finding one of the few patches of dirt on which to place his tent just north of Thielsen Creek. (Rich Combs.) Right: Cisco and Road-runner on a Mount Thielsen ridge that falls off decidedly. (Bob Welch.)

Top: On the first full day of Part II of the trip, Glenn heads up pumice-thick Wickiup Plain, beyond a trail junction. (Bob Welch.) Middle: Later that day, a fire breaks out near Mount Washington. (Bob Welch.) Left: Final light of the day paints the sky above Sisters Mirror Lake. (Bob Welch.)

Above: A foggy sunrise featuring Black Butte. (Bob Welch.) Right: Glenn and Bob share a laugh after reuniting at Summit Lake. (Ann Petersen.)
Below: Lava thickens as Bob heads toward Collier Cone, near the North Sister. (Glenn Petersen.) Lower left: Wildflowers by Glacier Creek in the Three Sisters Wilderness Area. (Bob Welch.) Lower right: Bob's "Duck tape" job to keep debris out of "holy" boots. (Bob Welch.)

Top: Near Three Fingered Jack, Bob points a trekking pole toward a sea of clouds. Middle: At chilly Shale Lake, Bob dines on freeze-dried food. (Glenn Petersen.) Lower left: Three Fingered Jack. (Bob Welch.) Lower right: A congratulatory fir-cone message left by Bob for Glenn at the 400-mile mark just short of Timberline Lodge. (Bob Welch.)

Top: Glenn crosses a makeshift bridge on Mount Hood's Newton Creek. (Bob Welch.) Middle: Punch Bowl Falls on Eagle Creek, a spot where Bob's father, Warren, had taken photos when he was a young man. (Bob Welch.) Above: Bob with Natsuki "Mij" Tsuboi, of Japan (Glenn Petersen), at, lower left, Timberline Lodge. (Bob Welch.)

And blessed taco salads.

Never mind that my pack and its contents were spread out in a disorder that had become uniquely me; my nieces were having a field day with my messiness. Never mind that Roadrunner, the material scientist, had pooh-poohed my idea of patching my boots with silver duct tape to keep out the dirt. "It will come off before the end of the day tomorrow," she predicted. Never mind that the mosquitoes were having a feast of their own—with us on the menu. After Ann, Carrie, and Molly had left, I savored every bite of that taco salad.

If it tasted great, I felt great. Tomorrow night we would be camping so close to my home county, Lane, that you could hear a rock slide from it. Life was suddenly wonderful.

"But, Glenny," I said, "what took you guys so long?"

"We were here on time," he said. "We said five, right?"

"No, we said four."

"I think we said five, Bob."

As college kids, we'd once wrestled in Eagle Creek while backpacking with Ann and Sally, a lighthearted tussle that began when someone intentionally splashed water in the other guy's face. Our manhood was on the line. Now, nearly four decades later, not so much. I was too tired to argue. Besides, I figured I'd lose; he was probably right. The important thing was that his plan had worked. The Oregon Boys were back together again—thanks to two Californians.

Darkness descended. We were, with the compulsion of chain smokers, scarfing down the red licorice Ann had left. And at least one of us— I— was already looking forward to cinnamon rolls and orange juice for breakfast, another treat from Ann.

"Glenny," I said, loud enough for everyone to hear, "let me tell you how I dragged Cisco and Roadrunner across Mount Sielsen."

Amid some chortles, I reached for the duct tape to prepare my boots for the morning. The jam-container idea, as it turned out, did not work as I'd expected. But I was committed to the duct tape, even if, as I wrapped, Roadrunner shook her scientific head.

"As I said, by the end of the day tomorrow, it will be gone," she said. "It will not work, Bob. Trust me."

15. Waldo's vision

Trail log: Wednesday, August 3.
PCT mile-marker: 1899.6.
Elevation: 5,600 feet.
Days on trail: 12.
Miles hiked Tuesday: 18.8.

Location: Summit Lake,
   on the Willamette Pass.
Total miles hiked: 196.4.
Average miles per day: 16.4.
Portion of trip completed: 43.4%.

FOR ALL HER highfalutin scientific background, Roadrunner proved to be horribly wrong in her prediction that my duct tape would peel off by day's end. It actually fell off after only two hours, much sooner than she—or I—had expected.

Mike Jones, a fishing guide at Odell Lake for four decades, took one look at my air-conditioned boots and headed for his pickup truck.

"That ain't gonna do, my friend," said Jones, who, pushing seventy, reminded me of Wilford Brimley (*Cocoon*, Quaker Oats ads).

We had arrived at Shelter Cove Resort—with a few exceptions, "resort" in Oregon means any lakeside store with bug spray, beer, and boat rentals—after a beautiful eighteen-mile hike through lodgepole pine; early on, I passed my 200-mile mark, though didn't notice it at the time. I looked at Odell Lake, where Waldo, in 1891, talked about taking "two soundings of the depths, below Otter Point, each reached a depth of 335 feet. ... No wonder it is the home of such great trout."

En route to the lake, my mood had been as glorious as 8,744-foot Diamond Peak, which rose to our west. I found cell coverage and ordered a dozen red roses to be delivered to Sally. Took a quick dip in Diamond View Lake on our lunch break. And, boots off, waded my first creek out of necessity. Now, after a rest at Odell Lake, we planned to climb another five miles to the Rosary Lakes, perched above Willamette Pass's Highway 58. For now, at Shelter Cove, Glenn was on his third ice cream, Cisco and I were powering up our smart phones in the store, and Mike Jones was walking out of his truck with a roll of—

"Turquoise duct tape?" I asked.

If regular duct tape made a certain PCT fashion statement that I was willing to endure—"I'm a hiking dweeb"—then turquoise took that statement to the tenth power. Nobody wore turquoise on the trail, particularly wrapped around their boots. This was an earth-tone crowd. A tread-lightly crowd. A one-with-the-woods crowd. Goodness, wrap that around my boots and I'd be no less conspicuous than the *Dumb and Dumber* boys walking into that Aspen ski lodge with their knee-high, shag moccasins.

"It ain't the color that matters," said Mike. "It's the strength."

I got the idea you didn't mess with Mike Jones, figuring he probably knew his stuff. Fishing guides lived or died on their promises, and anybody still in the business after forty years must be making good on his.

"Whatever you say," I said, then took another deep swig of my Mountain Dew.

A horseshoe-shaped beard hung on Mike's face like tree moss. Suspenders held up his jeans, into which was tucked a T-shirt featuring hunters' camouflage. On the store's wooden front deck, he sat on a rough-hewn wooden stool and pulled up a second.

"Your problem," he said, "was you didn't go completely around the boot with your tape. Watch this. Prop your foot up here."

How could you say no to Mike Jones? I sat. He taped with the diligence of an athletic trainer. Clearly, he enjoyed having a good time with people. I couldn't resist.

"So, Mike," I said. "Let's test your judgment of people. One of the four of us is a doctor. Who would you say is most likely, and who is least likely, to be that doctor?"

He was game. His head quickly spun left to right like a Rainbird sprinkler. "Well," he said, nodding at Roadrunner, "she's your doctor. And the least likely? That's simple. Elmer Fudd over there."

I nearly spit out my Mountain Dew. Mike's one-liner sent my laugh-o-meter needle to its highest point since we'd taken our first step twelve days ago, nobody enjoying it more than Glenn himself. On a warm, early-August afternoon, the laughter bound the four of us together as tightly as Mike's wrap job on my boots.

I thanked him. Behind the trees, a late-afternoon wind picked up the chop on a mile-wide lake that stretched for five. "No miniature pond is Odell Lake, but one of the fairest of the Cascade's liquid eyes," wrote Waldo on August 1, 1890, almost the same time of summer at which we'd arrived here.

Now, it was sprinkled with summer cabins, its waters plied by fancy inboards, its guests a long hour—not two-day trip—from Eugene. In 1883, Waldo wrote: "It is the least visited and the most out of the way of any of the lakes in this neighborhood. I saw a solitary trapper's cabin among the pines near the outlet of the lake. The little black pines had grown to be nearly three feet high on the dirt roof, showing that it had been long deserted. We will leave here about Friday and take the direction of the Three Sisters."

We were going the same way, though he would have no more stores at which to stock up on junk food. This would be our last re-supply opportunity before reaching Elk Lake, just south of the South Sister, where Glenn and I would be finishing Part I of our trip.

"Sign our PCT book?" asked the woman behind the resort's woodsy counter.

Cisco signed us in. More than a dozen hikers had been through before us. But, surprisingly, beyond the Colorado Boys—three days ahead of us—we didn't recognize a single name. No Ben or Kate. No Blood Bath. No Blaze. Either they hadn't stopped—the resort is two miles off the trail—or had stopped but hadn't signed in or had quit, not that I expected that at all. For thru-hikers who'd survived one of the deepest snowpacks in Sierra Nevada history, Oregon—particularly from here on—was a hiker's autobahn, albeit an autobahn with lava and a handful of peaks larger than anything we'd seen in Oregon thus far.

Still, what could possibly stop the Mexico-to-Canada folks? Or, for that matter, Elmer Fudd and me?

AS I LAY in my tent that night between the Middle and the Upper Rosary Lake, I was, in essence, back in the old neighborhood. Sally and I, with my folks, had camped on a rocky shelf above the Middle Rosary some thirty-seven years ago. In winter, we'd cross-country skied into here, gliding across snow that had coated the frozen lakes.

Now, I was two days from Sally's arms. Sixty-five miles from Eugene. Half a mile from the Lane County boundary—and, yes, enough of a regionalist to know this and appreciate the fact. Finally, I was a mere six miles from the lake for which my historic inspiration was named: Waldo. At 6,300 acres, Waldo Lake was second-largest in the state to the Upper Klamath in terms of non-alkali bodies of water and, at 420 feet, second in depth to Crater Lake.

A lot of thoughts bounced around a mind that, usually by this time of day, had melted into sleep. I thought about Waldo. About how my sense of this place wasn't all that different from what his had been more than a century ago. "Our party is enthusiastic over Waldo Lake," he wrote August 27, 1889, "and I myself never saw its beauties so strongly before. It is a noble Lake—water almost as blue as Crater Lake—deep, and the wooded mountains about it wild and untrodden. What more appropriate than that the Waldos of Waldo Hills should have a Summer Resort Seat at Waldo Lake in the Cascade Mountains."

The year before, he and his buddies had gone to Mount Shasta, a journey that included the glorious Crater Lake. "The most memorable part of our trip," he nevertheless wrote, "has been our stay at Waldo Lake."

Judge John B. Waldo was something of a rough-hewn renaissance man. A poet who quoted John Greenleaf Whittier. An outdoorsman. A naturalist who, in 1880, went to hear John Muir lecture in Portland. And a preservationist who'd seen pockets of destruction in the Cascades when the mountains were left unprotected: illegal homesteading, timber theft, and herds of sheep trashing mountain meadows, polluting streams, and destroying tree seedlings, after which the sheep men often set areas on fire to enlarge them for future grazing. Waldo was a lawyer. A judge. And, following his long trip to climb Mount Shasta in 1888, a politician with a new-found agenda: save the Cascade Range that he so dearly loved.

He had particular scorn for sheep men whose animals, he wrote, had turned many a previously unspoiled lakeshore into dusty, foul-smelling bedding grounds. He'd been north to Eagle Creek in the Columbia Gorge—down which we planned to finish our trip—and to Mount Hood. His trip to Shasta gave him an overview of the entire range.

Now was the time to protect what he loved. He had forged a friendship with a certain William Gladstone Steel, an Ohio-born Oregonian who had taken one look at Crater Lake in 1885 and never been the same. The former post-office employee wasted no time launching a campaign to establish it as a national park and, while in pursuit of such, met Waldo. He learned he and the judge had a common desire to protect such places through political action. But when Steel suggested national park designation for Crater Lake, Waldo asked: Why stop there? Why not protect the entire Cascade Range as a reserve, a designation being used in other states by now?

"Taking it as irony, I made a factitious reply," Steel later wrote. "He assured me he was dead earnest and asked me to call at his office, which I did. We talked the matter over at considerable length and I was deeply impressed with his knowledge of the situation and the value of such a move."

If Waldo had the love, knowledge, and passion to preserve the Cascades, what he needed was a partner steeped in the skills the shy judge lacked: the ability to back slap, hobnob, and cajole those in power. Waldo was a poet who thought with his heart. He needed a lobbyist who could grovel with a gesture or pound a congressman's table with a fist. And Steel was just that. He went to Washington, D.C., and—convincing Waldo to protect Crater first and the Cascades later—met President Grover Cleveland. He lobbied the Oregon congressional delegation. Though unable to get full national park designation for Crater Lake, Steel convinced Cleveland to give the area a "hands-off" designation for local townships. If the designation was soft—a future president could rescind it—the move was at least a step in the right direction.

Now, following his 1888 trip to Shasta, Waldo upped the ante. At forty-four, he ran for a seat in the Oregon State Legislature and won. Immediately, he sprang into action. On January 14, 1889, he introduced House Joint Memorial No. 8, which petitioned the U.S. Congress to create a forest reserve along the crest of Oregon's Cascade Range. The protected land would run virtually the length of the state for a distance of twelve miles on either side of the Cascade crest.

Given the times, it was no less dramatic than a bolt of lightning striking the tip of Mount Thielsen. For the previous four decades, Americans had swept west like starving men in a chuck wagon line; ethics gave way to grabbing whatever they could. Drunk on the 1845-born spirit of "manifest destiny," they saw their role as a noble taming of the wilds. They chopped trees, mined minerals, and ran sheep roughshod wherever they pleased. Waldo's plan flew in the face of such thinking, particularly against sheep men who held considerable power in the state; indeed, from 1870 to 1890, an estimated three to four million Oregon sheep were driven to range land in Idaho, Montana, and Wyoming, and sold for top dollar.

Waldo didn't care.

> Your memorialists would most respectfully represent that that portion of the Cascade Range of mountains in the State of Oregon hereinafter described consists of the summit of said range and a portion of the slopes extending down on either side thereof.
>
> That the same is high, rocky, much of it precipitous, unfit for cultivation, largely covered with forests, and during the winter and spring with snow varying in depth from three to thirty feet.
>
> That within this mountainous region lie the chief sources of supply of the streams watering the rich agricultural valleys of the Rogue river, the Umpqua and the Willamette on the west, and the great Klamath lake and the Deschutes and its tributary valleys on the east.
>
> That the said region contains many lofty peaks covered perpetually with snow; the famous Crater Lake and many mountain lakes and streams stocked with the finest fish, and is the rendezvous and hiding-place of the once numerous but fast-perishing herds of elk, deer, antelope and other game ... .
>
> That the altitude of said strip of land, its wildness, game, fish, water and other fowl, its scenery, the beauty of its flora, the purity of its atmosphere and healthfulness and other attractions, render it most desirable that it be set apart and kept free and open forever as a public reserve park and resort for the people of the State of Oregon and the United States.
>
> Your memorialists therefore suggest and earnestly request that your honorable body pass an Act withdrawing the whole of said strip of land from sale or entry and granting the same to the State of Oregon, to be held in trust for the people of the State of Oregon and of the United States, to be used as a public reserve or park, and for no other purpose.

His petition was unabashedly passionate and personal, as much a plea from the heart as it was a political ploy from the head. "The whole idea," wrote Bobbie Snead in *Judge John Waldo: Oregon's John Muir*, "was nothing short of revolutionary."

LOGGING, STRUCTURES, grazing, and commercial hunting and fishing would be prohibited. Mining would be allowed, but not if a claim went unworked for two years, in which case it would be considered void. Railroads could cross the preserve, but the only timber that could be cut was that used in building tracks.

After some modifications to appease "wool-growers," the bill unanimously passed the legislature's House. But the sheep men, particularly those from Jackson and Klamath Falls in southern Oregon, dug in their boots. Who was this newcomer from Salem to be cordoning off a mountain range from everyone else?

If Waldo's bill to preserve the Cascades had been flowing smoothly down the political channels, the Senate spun it into a shore-side eddy from which it never returned. The bill was soon tabled and died.

As I lay in my tent, it was with the realization that Waldo knew defeat like the rest of us. In my life as a writer, defeat manifested itself in turn-downs from agents—twenty-six before someone bit on *American Nightingale*; aborted book projects—two years in a row I'd been stiffed by professional athletes whose agents contracted with me to write their clients' stories but the jocks proved too preoccupied, or lazy, to help; and book signings that drew more people accidentally than on purpose. For Waldo, defeat was his quest to preserve the sanctity of the Cascade Range essentially dying of neglect because of a group of politicians who, even if they shared a smidgen of his passion for such preservation, were apparently more interested in appeasing a small group of ranchers.

I wondered if he felt like a failure. Like a crazed voice in the wilderness that nobody else heard but him. Like it would be wiser to bag the idea and enjoy the mountains he'd come to love in whatever time he had left; never mind if the "purity of the atmosphere" might be ruined for generations to come.

The more I got to know Waldo, the more I appreciated the man who had once traveled these same forests, and had camped year after year at the nearby lake which bore his name. As I turned off my headlamp it was August 3, 2011. On August 1, 1888—probably a mild summer night like this one—Waldo had concluded his journal with these words: "The fire burns low, I must draw my sleeping bags over me, and hope to sleep well in the free, unaltered wilderness."

I did likewise.

16. Farewell to friends

Trail log: Friday, August 6, 2011.
PCT mile-marker: 1943.6.
Days on trail: 14.
Miles hiked Wednesday: 21.2.
Miles hiked Thursday: 22.8.
Location: Jezebel Lake.
Elevation: 5,650 feet.
Total miles hiked: 240.4.
Average miles per day: 17.2.
Portion of trip completed: 53.2%.

IF I NEEDED any further reminders that I was, indeed, "home," I got it mid-morning Thursday. The four of us were working our way north, just beyond the Willamette Pass Ski Area and paralleling the shores of Waldo Lake that was about two miles west. The footsteps from behind came upon me quickly, as did the dog, whose playful yip nearly popped me out of my Merrells. I turned.

"Welch?" the runner said. "Bob Welch!"

"KC Taylor!"

I'd coached his son, Blake, in KidSports baseball fifteen years ago.

I had always had the sense that Oregon, though larger in size than all but nine other states, was just one, big family. I'd once been atop the state's third-highest mountain, the South Sister, and started chatting with a guy who had on a "Summit High" T-shirt. Turned out he was the principal of the Bend high school. And, not incidentally, was a former college roommate of Jay Locey, the best man at my wedding. Then, of course, there had been my meeting with Acorn, who had lived in the same UO dorm complex as I had in 1972-73.

"What are you doing up here?" asked KC.

I explained the Oregon PCT trip.

"That's a long way," he said.

Not that he didn't understand long distances on foot. He was an ultra marathoner. On this day, he was running nineteen miles, followed by a planned dip in ice-cold, but exhilarating, Waldo Lake. In Eugene, we lived about two miles apart, but I'd seen him only a time or two in the fifteen years since those baseball days—until meeting up here in the wilderness. Only in Oregon.

"Good for you," he said. "Hope you make it."

"Yeah, great seeing you, KC," I said. "Happy trails."

We moved on. We saw two more PCT thru-hikers that morning. One was the only unfriendly PCT hiker I would meet on the trail the entire trip, a serious young man who didn't even laugh when I made fun of my ineptness at staying on the snow-blotched trail. The other was a young man trail-named Malto. Rail thin. A white towel under his golf visor and draped over his neck as if he were an Arabian sheik. Fingerless gloves wrapped around his trekking poles. And a diet that made me cringe—essentially, nothing but sips of some power drink he'd concocted, the basis of which was pure maltodextrin—thus, his trail name—with added electrolytes. He kept it in individual packets that could be mixed in 1-liter water bottles.

As if a symbolic nod to my speed-hiking inferiority, my back pack's waist belt snapped as I went to put it on following the visit with Malto. We jury-rigged a fix and moved on. As with the case of Malto and his liquid diet, the trail motto was simple:

Whatever it took.

IT WAS A THURSDAY. Originally, we had planned on arriving at Elk Lake on Saturday, which would have meant three days of about fourteen miles each. But the previous night, over our freeze-dried dinners (lasagna for me), the four of us had decided to put together back-to-back twenty-one mile days and do it in two. The four of us would meet Sally and Ann on Friday evening for a celebratory dinner at the rustic Elk Lake Lodge. Then, Glenn and I would head home for a three-week break while Cisco and Roadrunner continued on toward Canada.

I was pumped. Seeing KC was like a land-hungry sailor seeing a shore-based bird with a twig in its beak; the first half of our trip was almost over. But as the day wore on, my feet started going south, taking my spirits along for the plunge. I changed socks. Soaked my feet in Charlton Lake. Added tape. No change. By the time we hit a burned forest northeast of Waldo Lake, the bleached or blackened trees mirrored my mood.

I was dead. By now, I was far behind the other three; the separation between me and them grated on me like a boot on a blister. I slipped into self-pity, part of me mad at myself for not being able to keep pace, part of me mad that they weren't waiting.

Did Waldo ever get pouty? Somehow, I couldn't imagine it. He seemed invulnerable, much like Glenn, whose feet could be blistered badly and yet never complained. Me? I liked to think that my cross-country years in high school helped build a thick pain threshold; there were summers when I'd run in the early morning, rake beans onto a cannery conveyor belt for eight hours, then run again in the evening. That translated into mental endurance for my later-in-life book projects, one of which took four years before I saw a copy on a Barnes & Noble shelf.

But now, my reservoir of perseverance had dried up. The late-afternoon heat added a desert-like sense to the desolation of the burnt woods. Step by dusty step, I trudged on, losing any semblance of Waldo's ability to think of the positive. On October 14, 1891, he wrote to Clara: "Think of me in this lonely cabin to-night with the wind howling around me. But think of me without this cabin. Indeed I am very comfortable." Four years later, at a place less than ten miles from where I now was, he lamented that it had been thirteen years since his last visit to Crane Prairie and "the wilderness is in a great part gone that made it so attractive at the time. It was then the haunt of wild animals; now, it is devoted to sheep pasturage." And yet a few sentences later he chastised himself for apparently taking out his anger on a horse. "No more ill temper from this day toward a horse," he wrote. "And I have not said toward anything else: not toward things, for they care naught about it, as Mr. Aurelius has said. It is God-like never to feel or at least exhibit it toward persons."

At the moment, I could not muster such God-like thinking. Somewhere amid that black forest, a thought arrived that I hadn't entertained since my meltdown at Freye Lake after the fall from the log: *I just want to be home.*

BETWEEN THEIR waiting and my picking up the pace, I caught up with Glenn, Cisco, and Roadrunner soon after we got out of the burn. The plan was to stay at Brahma Lake, about three miles away. I couldn't get there soon enough. But, en route, Roadrunner started lobbying for a lake a mile beyond, Jezebel, to shorten our distance for the homestretch Friday.

Really? A twenty-one mile day was about to become twenty-two. By now, I had a motto: A mile in the morning was a mile; a mile at day's end was five. The only solace in this homestretch was the smell of the pines and sandy soil, which nudged memories from long-ago places I'd been near here, though my pain and weariness kept shooing them away.

We arrived at Jezebel Lake. A couple had already popped up a tent near water's edge; there was a campsite near them but, I realized, a more private one a few hundred feet north. I headed that way, thinking it obvious that we wouldn't want to intrude on the couple's privacy.

"Here's a decent spot up here," I yelled back.

Nobody followed me. Or seemed to be listening to me. The three of them discussed things in voices I couldn't hear. Clearly I hadn't been selected for the site committee. Roadrunner liked to camp where there was a log to place kitchen stuff, I was about to discover. The spot next to the other couple had a log. Decision made.

I returned, found a tent spot beyond the others, and, with all the enthusiasm of a robot with drained batteries, set up my nylon abode. I then laid out my foam pad, pulled off my boots—a chore in itself—and crawled inside my sleeping bag. I closed my eyes, too tired to zip up the tent fly. Mosquitoes buzzed. I might as well have hung up an "all-you-can-suck" blood buffet sign.

"You're going to get eaten alive," said Glenn.

I pretended I was asleep. I didn't close the fly. By now, it was a pride thing. Hey, if I wanted to be stupid, nobody was going to stop me. Later, I got water from the lake, hating every step with my stupid flip-flops; I should have listened to my heart and gone with the Crocs. Meanwhile, at the log-accented dining room, Cisco, Roadrunner, and Glenn prepared their dinner with way too much enthusiasm; never mind the folks next door.

Glenn returned to his tent next to mine to get a forgotten spoon or something. Seven straight days of mosquitoes and other things had pushed me over the edge of my own private Devils Peak.

"Just so you know," I said, "I've hit the wall."

In some situations like this, Glenn might have retorted with a joke. Like: "So, how about if your new trail name be 'Cuckoo's Nest.'" And followed with his predictable burst of laughter.

He didn't this time. "Pretty beat, huh Bob?"

"Yeah."

"And your feet?"

"Toast," I said. "I'm getting up really early and heading out on my own so you guys don't have to wait on me."

"I don't think that's such a good idea," he said.

I couldn't tell him the whole reason why I wanted to go it alone.

"Glenn, I can hardly walk. I don't want to slow everybody up. And we need to be there when Sally and Ann arrive."

"I'll hang back with you."

"Thanks, but I just need to do this," I said. "The trail is good. We only go up five hundred feet. There won't be much, if any, snow."

I hadn't convinced Glenn about the wisdom of my walking alone, but he grudgingly nodded his head.

"OK," he said.

It wouldn't be the last time I'd take off by myself.

I HIT THE headlamp-lit trail at 6:30 A.M. for the twenty-mile hike to Elk Lake. Nobody else was stirring. This was just what I needed. Nobody was at fault; I just needed to be alone for a day. And the more I walked, the more comfortable I was with the decision.

Maybe it was because the day was cooler and the swelling had abated. Maybe because I'd managed to drain and wrap my blisters properly for a change. Whatever the reason, my feet felt far better. I was soon lost in the trail, in the memories, in my father. That's what I hadn't been able to tell Glenn the night before: that another reason I wanted to hike alone was to get lost in the past. And, like a group visit to a cemetery, it's hard to do that with others around.

We had pitched our tents the previous night three miles due west from Cultus Lake, where our family had camped for two weeks every summer in my boyhood. Smell, I've read, is the most evocative of senses. When I breathed in the pine trees and trail dust of Central Oregon, it was as if I were twelve years old again. As if I were at the wheel of the fourteen-foot Dillabah boat my dad had built from a kit and aimed at the nub of Irish Mountain to return to our campsite. As if we were hiking up the trail to the Teddy Lakes or Muskrat Lake for an evening of fly fishing. Or traipsing cross country in search of the elusive Comma Lake.

I'd grown up, headed off for college, and started a family of my own. My father died. But in 2006, on the ten-year anniversary of his death, I found myself alone in the woods near Cultus Lake: Backpack on—essentially, for the first time since college days. Compass around my neck. Map in hand. I was trying to find Comma Lake. In his honor.

I thought of borrowing a friend's GPS, but my father-the-purist might have considered that cheating. And I didn't want to disappoint the guy who was as much a part of the Comma Lake Expedition as I was.

Off the beaten trail, I headed into a tangle of downed trees, scattered thick on a semi-steep, upward slope. Decades' worth of blow-down was strewn across the forest floor. I walked over it. Crawled under it. Went around it. And on top of it. I checked the map. Checked the compass. Took a drink. Then repeated the sequence.

My breathing got heavier, my shirt wetter, my hopes dimmer. The temperature was nearing 80. I crested a hill and headed down. Then I saw it: a glimpse of blue. Water. This had to be it. I had arrived at the lower tail of Comma Lake.

I wanted to whoop and holler, but it didn't seem right amid a quiet punctuated only by a few birds and bleached-white trees rubbing against each other in death. The summer heat had evaporated about half of what's up to sixteen acres of water, probably not more than a few feet at its deepest. On the dried mudflats, I made my way up the comma—a writer literally *in* his element—toward the lake's center. I saw no human footprints.

I had thought of bringing something to leave in honor of my father, but he was big on leaving a camp better than you found it, so I nixed that idea. I looked around. A half dozen stones lay scattered near me. So, I built him a poor-man's pyramid. I knew that by October the lake would fill from autumn rains. By November, the monument would be encased in ice and covered in snow. Regardless, it would be my little reminder: We were once here. We had finally found Comma Lake.

My father and I.

NOW, FIVE YEARS LATER, the miles came and went in a blur, partly because my mind was elsewhere, partly because my eyes were moist with memory. I did notice the ominously named Cougar Flat. And I hit a bit of snow at higher stretches, but on this day the PCT was easy to follow. So was the past.

At Mac Lake—seven miles from the campsite I'd left—I remembered swimming with friends John Woodman and Jay Locey. In 1975, just two weeks before Sally and I were to be married, the three of us had climbed the South Sister, then, with a night's rest, hiked some twenty miles south to my old haunts at Cultus Lake over the next few days. (My sentimentalism came at an early age; I was only twenty-two.) Along the way, we had taken an afternoon dip in Mac Lake. And hiked the very trail I was on now, though then it was known as the Skyline Trail.

I was lost in the past. So lost, in fact, that before I felt the need to take off my pack and rest for the first time I'd already traveled fourteen miles; I'd been hiking for seven hours, the day as smooth as the previous afternoon had been rough. At Island Meadow I ate lunch, took a few photos, caught some light sleep, and finally had time to put things in perspective.

Waldo did it often. On July 30, 1885, from alongside the North Santiam, he wrote:

> I sit among the boulders strewn along the stream, the new silent witnesses of its tireless toil, listening to the story of the wild regions through which it has come, while it hurries onward as if bent on some mission of heroism which will admit of no delay. Its story is indeed a tale of travel and urgency. Silent specters on either hand, the rank and file from which the undefiled and untrodden forests—untrodden except by the wild creatures of the wood—look down as if infected with some mysterious awe, on a procession of waters which never end; whose front ranks have gone on ages before while those still in the rear will continue to file by for countless ages to come.

And less than a week later, from what he sometimes referred to as Jefferson Lake and sometimes Pamelia Lake:

> It is now four years since we were camped at this lake, having left August 6, 1881.
>
> Those years have not been such years of usefulness as they might have been—too many hours misapplied or feebly grasped; too little of improvement in wise living; too little of knowledge acquired.
>
> There is certainly a great or at least a considerable change—a change apparently for the better—more strength of character; more aptitude for reflection. But there is something like the approach of age, as if the time might come when I would prefer to sit by the camp fire, rather than roam the forest or climb the mountain—but certainly that time has not yet arrived.

I EXPECTED the three other hikers to catch me anytime. Instead, a couple hours later, I neared the one-mile "exit" to Elk Lake, from which an incredible vista opened up: the South Sister and Broken Top.

The end of our journey's first half was reason enough to shoot video. "Right now I'm about a mile short of Elk Lake after 258 miles," my narration goes, the jiggly iPhone camera showing what I was seeing. "Oh, my goodness. Mount Bachelor. A sweet reminder that we're almost home on this halfway segment of our walk across the state. Right on schedule."

I was anxious to see Sally. Waldo left his wife, Clara, and daughter, Edith, for one to three months a year. His letters don't shed too much light on their relationship, but indications are that they remained close despite their time apart. In one letter, he referred to the beauties in his life beyond nature: "a beautiful, sweet wife, a wise little daughter, and a home of light." Once, he returned from one of his summer outings with a roan pony to give to his young daughter. Of the little girl, he wrote to Clara: "Remember what a rare, sweet, intelligent child we have in Edith and don't let her get too long out of your sight."

Soon, Glenn, Cisco, and Roadrunner arrived. It was good to be reunited, even if I'd thoroughly enjoyed the day alone. I didn't tell them about my traipse down memory lane, only that I'd had a good day and I appreciated their understanding my need to leave early. Everyone seemed fine with that choice. They, too, had had a good hike.

By now, we'd made cell-phone contact with Sally and Ann, who had arrived at the rustic resort on the lake's western edge. As we approached them on one of Central Oregon's lava-red dirt roads, I turned on the video camera again to memorialize the moment. "Here we are at the end of the trail, and here's our welcoming party. Glenny, get over here."

"This is the swat team," said a mosquito-riddled Cisco. "We've been swattin' all week."

Sally came to me with a hug and two words. Not "missed you." Not "love you." Not "great job." Instead, a reference to my two weeks without shaving: "Hey, scruffy."

Buried in her arms, the phrase worked just fine.

PERCHED ON the resort's deck, we ate and drank in celebration. Had it only been a week ago that we'd done the same at Crater Lake? It seemed as if a month had passed.

Cisco insisted on buying dinner for Glenn and me, though it hardly seemed fair. We hadn't saved their trip; they'd saved ours. We laughed. Compared mosquito stories. Mentioned an array of places, from Devils Peak to Mount "Sielsen" to Summit Lake; an array of people, from Mike Jones, the fishing guide/boot wrapper, to Malto; and an array of moments, from our first meeting to—I could joke about it now—my meltdown the previous night.

Fresh clothes. Good food. Family. New friends. At some point, I looked out at the lake, beyond which Mount Bachelor rose, and thought: *I am a fortunate man.*

The sun that had draped Bachelor in orange started fading. We needed to hit the road. I shook Cisco's hand and turned to Roadrunner for a hug. "We couldn't have done it without you," I said. "Thank you guys so much."

"It was nice having you for our adopted son, Bob," she said. "Thank *you.*"

For what? I could only imagine that between duct-taped shoes, Elmer Fudd hats, and twig-splinted sunglasses, we'd somehow taken their mind off the pain of twenty-mile days.

"We'd been hiking together for 400 miles when we came across you guys," said Cisco.

"And drove right past us!" I said. "Not that I'm still bitter."

He laughed. "You lightened us up, made us laugh," he said. "We appreciate that."

So, we'd each filled a need for the other, even if those needs were different: theirs, a lighthearted distraction and a cause—keeping us from getting lost—that apparently gave them a heightened sense of purpose. Ours, guides who could keep us on track, teach us the lessons of the trail, and give me fresh fodder for jokes. And, oh yes, Roadrunner's courage to gently call me on the carpet about making light of her moving from Germany to the United States. In retrospect, I needed that.

We said our goodbyes. As the four of us drove south on Cascade Lakes Highway—strange, my first car ride in fifteen days—I wondered if we might ever see Cisco and Roadrunner again: say, off to the side of the road later that night, beneath a sky splashed in *Twilight Zone* stars, both of them hanging out hitchhikers' thumbs.

Part IV
Back on the trail

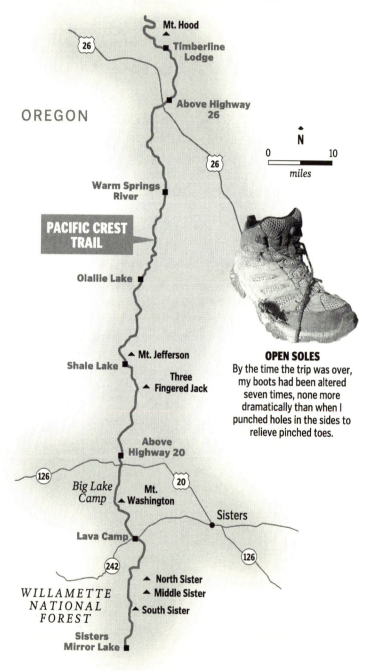

OPEN SOLES
By the time the trip was over, my boots had been altered seven times, none more dramatically than when I punched holes in the sides to relieve pinched toes.

If you can find a path with no obstacles, it probably doesn't lead anywhere.

—Frank A. Clark

17. The return

Trail log: Saturday, August 27, 2011.
PCT mile-marker: 1962.
Days on trail: 15.
Elevation: 5,250 feet.
Location: Elk Lake.
Total miles hiked Part I: 258.8.
Average miles per day: 17.2.
Portion of trip completed: 57.2%.

ABOVE THE CASCADES, thunderclouds roiled in the late afternoon sky. It was a Saturday, twenty-two days since we'd left the trail. Now we were returning to it, courtesy of Glenn's eighty-something folks, Paul and Pauline, who were pinch-hitting as drop-off drivers because Sally and Ann were at a family reunion on the coast that we'd left early.

Already, I was scrambling. I'd meant to bring a plastic garbage bag to cover my pack in case of rain. Seeing the thunderclouds—the first since the journey's start on July 22—reminded me of my oversight. Although the staff at Elk Lake Resort was preparing for a lake-side concert, a young woman happily found me a couple of bags—and refused a tip I offered in return. With that, we hit the trail about 5 P.M., hoping to get to Sisters Mirror Lake, 5.8 miles away, before dark.

Ka-boom. Thunder rumbled through the Cascades.

It was good to be back. Ahead: the Three Sisters, Three Fingered Jack, Mount Jefferson, and a stop at venerable Timberline Lodge on Mount Hood before rounding the state's highest peak and dropping off a forested shelf to the Columbia River below.

The three-week intermission had gone quickly, in part because of time spent preparing. The first thing I'd done was go in search of new boots or trail-running shoes. Wide, like my others, but another half-size larger. And without holes. I searched online and in stores, including REI, for a weekend but couldn't find just what I wanted. Instead, I took my Merrells to a Eugene shoe-repair shop and explained how I wanted lightweight patches for the two orange-slice-sized holes on the outsides of each boot. Something got lost in translation. The shop stitched on heavy leather patches that not only added unnecessary weight, but whose threads inside I could feel through my socks. Not good. I ripped them out and affixed rip-stop nylon fabric with glue. Much better, even if I could hear scoffing from Roadrunner, despite she and Rich having crossed the Columbia River on August 18 and being well into Washington.

The second modification involved food. After some analysis, I realized I needed way more. I estimated I was burning about 5,000 calories per day and eating only 3,000 to 4,000—though more than twice what I'd normally eat, not enough. I had survived Part I on Svenhard's danishes, Clif Bars, freeze-dried dinners, and trail mix. (Or GORP, as we used to call it: "Good Ol' Raisins & Peanuts.") It wasn't enough. For Part II, I added beef jerky, candy orange slices—hey, they could plug my boot holes in a pinch!—Cheez-Its, jumbo candy bars, English muffins, jam, Lifesaver Gummies, red-hot cinnamon bears, and Lays potato chips in plastic, non-crushable cups.

Natural-food fans would cringe; I understood. But my penny-pinching for weight on Part I had often left me hungry. PCT books and blogs said to suspend any thought of a balanced diet and pile up the calories. I'd resisted. Now I was a believer.

Finally, I replaced my flip-flops with Crocs and revamped my communication system. After much consternation, I decided that listening to the much-ballyhooed Oregon-LSU season-opening football game in Texas Stadium was worth bringing along my 4.5-ounce satellite radio, about the same weight as an iPhone. I knew that represented some serious weight but, then, I was a serious fan.

More importantly in the communication realm, I bought a $199, 5.2-ounce Spot Connect satellite device. (*The Register-Guard* picked up the $200 service fee.) On Part I we'd had cell coverage for less than half our 259 miles and reports from up-ahead hikers—among them, Cisco—said northern Oregon was even worse.

The plan all along was to beta-test a blog site for Part I, then tell *Register-Guard* readers about it so they could follow our progress for Part II. But without cell coverage, my iPhone wouldn't be working, meaning we couldn't get updates out nor learn, say, when Glenn's daughter, Katie, had had her baby—any day, he'd been told. To help solve the former problem I'd bought the Spot Connect, which, in no-coverage zones, could at least send our location—and a forty-one-character message—to our site. A bonus? It had an SOS button to alert rescuers in emergencies. Not, of course, that either of us would need rescuing.

In the distance, another rumble of thunder spread through the forest.

"Whoa," said Glenn.

"'Whoa' is right," I said. "Fortunately, I have my official Elk Lake garbage bag. Not to worry."

Within a half hour, I needed it and my rain pants, which I'd bought at the last minute on the advice of my *Register-Guard* colleague, Keefer, a backpacker whose thru-hiking son, Noah, was now between Mount Jefferson and Mount Hood, having passed us while we were on our three-week break.

We had only forty-two percent of our journey—193.4 miles—to go and were planning on eight days to the Bridge of the Gods. That was just over twenty miles per day, about three miles more than what we'd averaged on Part I. But two weeks on the trail had toughened us—and three weeks between sections meant all the more snow melt. We expected little of the snow that had slowed us on the first stretch. And, psychologically, we would have that horse-to-the-barn drive going for us. We were confident we could make our 20.6-miles-per-day goal and be at the Oregon-Washington border a week from Wednesday.

The day before we'd returned for Part II, I had received big news: the first thru-hikers had reached Canada—the Aussies, Ben and Kate.

"All right!" I'd shouted, then e-mailed Glenn with the news. They had arrived August 23, followed by "Marcus the German" on the 24th and Blood Bath on the 25th.

Granted, we'd had to go back to work for three weeks, but since we'd first seen them, Ben and Kate had walked nearly a thousand miles, more than three times what we had done. Good for them—and Kate with the bad leg. Incredible. Who said nice guys—and gals—finished last?

Another round of thunder rumbled through the forest. A bolt of lightning lit the distant sky. That morning, I'd read a newspaper story that said lightning the previous day had ignited a few fires that Forest Service crews were watching closely, including one on the Warm Springs Indian Reservation, through which our route would take us at week's end, though the trail was far to the west of the fire.

"Lots of lightning in them thar hills," I texted to our Web site.

THE THUNDERSHOWER didn't last long. We took off our rain gear and continued on, clearly a bounce in our steps. We were making great time, which triggered some cranial number-crunching on my part regarding whether we really needed as much time as we'd figured to make Washington.

As light began to fade, right on schedule, we arrived at Sisters Mirror Lake, a small jewel nestled in a seemingly endless forest.

"Glenny, I've been thinking," I said as we were setting up our tents. "As it is, we're getting to Timberline Lodge Sunday, right?"

"That's correct."

"I've done the math. If we add just three miles per day, we can hit Timberline Saturday in time to watch the Duck game on TV at 5 o'clock—and have time for the all-you-can-eat buffet beforehand. And the bonus for you: Instead of wasting my satellite battery on the Oregon game, we can use that to listen to your Oregon State game instead."

His response was as quick and decisive as his "count-me-in" e-mail thirteen months before.

"Let's do it."

I headed to the lake for water, all the more psyched for the trip ahead. True to its name, the still waters mirrored the dark firs ringing the lake—just as, I assumed, they mirrored the Three Sisters from the other side. Above, the day's last light powdered the clouds in tufts of pink. All was quiet. The temperature was that happy medium between hot and cold. The poet Robert Browning came to mind. "God's in his heaven. All's right with the world."

Judge Waldo knew such moments. While cowboy-camping on Deep River in south Central Oregon, he wrote on August 26, 1880: "This evening we are all here—have had a fine supper—and my blankets are spread for the night ... Think of this, my friends of the Valley, and weep."

SUNDAY MORNING was truly a religious experience: skirting the Three Sisters as the sun rose in the east. Back home, I thought, Pastor Steve Hill was readying to speak God's word at Grace Community Fellowship where my family attended; here, God was speaking to me in the grandeur of His design.

Waldo's spiritual underpinnings were more ethereal than mine. "In heaven the angels are advancing continually to the springtime of their youth, so that the oldest angels appear the youngest," he wrote on August 18, 1895, from Crater Lake.

For now, all I knew was a heavenly scene was spreading before me. The Pacific Crest Trail snaked up the pumice-dry Wickiup Plain, over which hung wisps of fog; never had I seen the trail itself snaking through the open in such graphic wonder. Beyond Wickiup rose Rock Mesa and Le Conte Crater, mere warm-up bands for the main show beyond: the 10,358-foot South Sister and, as we headed north, the 10,047-foot Middle Sister and the 10,085-foot North Sister. Three maids in a row, originally named "Faith, Hope, and Charity," by Willamette Valley missionaries in the 1830s.

On September 9, 1880—Waldo's first year in the Cascades—he summited the South Sister. "There are," he wrote, "half a dozen little summits, several with their crater-like spaces from fifty to seventy-five deep in the center. In one there is a little lake of one-third or one-fourth of an acre; deep and blue and pure out of which we filled the water bottle we had with us." He was writing of what's now known as Teardrop Lake, a tiny turquoise gem that sits atop the South Sister. "We can see thirty or forty miles to the South and East. There are fourteen lakes in sight; one very pretty in the angle between the Sisters. Davis Lake shows dimly in the South, and another large one to the Westward, which is probably O'Dell [his punctuation]Lake." Climbing historian Jeff Thomas had credited Waldo's party with the first ascent of the South Sister from Green Lake, in 1883.

I had summited the South Sister three times, once with buddies Locey and Woodman before Sally and I married in 1975; once, with Glenn, in 2008; and, finally, in 2009 with Glenn and my eldest son, Ryan. Now, two years later, Glenn and I passed the Three Sisters to the west, Wickiup Plain giving way to low trees, meadows, and creeks. A runner passed us, heading south. A father and son soon passed, too, the man telling us they were aborting a weekend trip because the boy had lost his inhaler.

"I have an inhaler," said Glenn, the ever-ready doctor. "You're welcome to have it." Trail Magic. What were the chances? Alas, the boy, for some reason, wouldn't accept it and the two returned to the trailhead from which they'd left. The incident reminded me that I was in good hands with Glenn.

We hiked on, by now the Middle Sister to our right and the North next in line. Waldo was here July 25, 1890, among his first forays back to his beloved mountains since the resounding defeat of his bill to make a reserve of Oregon's Cascades. He described "springs of pure cold water—some great ones, more of lesser magnitude" that "gush noisily over their white bottoms, wending through the meadow into the main artery which pours down through a diminutive canyon .... It is a picture of the yet free and untrodden wilderness whose only shadow is that which is cast over that future when such things are not to be."

That future when such things are not to be. Clearly, Waldo continued to burn with concern about wild places such as this. I understood. When I'd awakened at Sisters Mirror Lake that morning, I'd been less than four miles from Sparks Lake, which sat on the South Sister's front porch replete with fingers of water reaching into a grassy meadow. Beautiful. I still have the 1930s photo of my grandfather and grandmother, William and Fay Welch, looking on as my then teen-age father proudly displays a freshly caught trout from Sparks Lake. Still remember taking my eldest son, Ryan, to that lake for our first father-son camping trip, my lack of success as an angler resulting in the three-year-old's well-reasoned question: "Dad, why do we fish?" Still remember that grown-up kid waiting for me atop the South Sister in the summer of 2009, and the pride I felt that I'd made it—but more pride that he'd beaten me to the top by ten minutes. Now, putting Waldo in perspective, it hadn't escaped me that all such memories played out in his "untrodden wilderness."

If his defeat in 1889 had discouraged Waldo, his passion to preserve the Cascade carried on. "The policy of the government in establishing Reserves cannot be too highly commended," he wrote in 1890 from Odell Lake. "How splendid for this age to leave to posterity a resort and pleasure ground for the people forever!"

Nature, Waldo argued, was food to the soul, something that allowed people to live at a deeper level. "Were the whole time of man employed in getting a living, man would scarcely be superior to the cattle of his farm yards," he continued. "Does not the human intellect lose something of its charm by too close confinement to the material affairs of life? As the Mallard Drake loses the brilliancy of his plumage in domestication, so man loses the best quality of mind and soul in observing too closely the material demands of civilization."

The following year, something happened that proved integral to Waldo's goal of protecting the Cascades. On March 3, 1891, East Coast nature advocates managed to get a rider passed on a complex forest-policy bill with an amendment that abolished the sale of public domain lands and restricted the provision of the older land acts. What's more, it gave the president unprecedented power to set aside forest reserves.

Wrote Will Steel to Waldo: "Might it not be an opportune time to have the (Oregon) Alpine Club petition for the withdrawal of the summit of the Cascade Range?"

WHEN WE PASSED three guys roughly our age—the first time we'd passed anybody and, time would prove, nearly the last—Glenn and I greeted them. But it would only be later, when we saw them again, that we'd make an amazing discovery, another one of those "small-world-Oregon" moments: one of them, Ron "Fallingwater" Moak, was the founder of Portland-based Six Moon Designs. Glenn and I were both sleeping in tents made by the company he founded in 2002 because he wanted to offer a better, lighter tent than was available. Given the way I'd been sleeping, he apparently succeeded.

"Mine's working great," I said. "Love it."

By early afternoon, we'd taken in the beauty of Obsidian Falls and stopped for lunch above it at Sister Spring, whose creek babbled cold and clear through a meadow. "Thunder rumbling as we eat late lunch," I texted. Next to the creek sat a young man and woman whose dress, garb, and gear suggested day hikers heading for a heavy-metal concert. They didn't seem to fit in. A tad on the rough side.

Glenn and I walked down a ways, hung our damp tents in some brush to dry, ate, and rested.

"Excuse me." It was the young woman. "Are you hiking the PCT?"

"Yeah," I said. "Just doing Oregon."

"Cool," she said. "We did the PCT last summer. Changed our lives. You want some pop or beer or snacks?" She nodded to cans cooling in the creek.

"You're a Trail Angel," I said.

"Yep."

"Hey, thanks."

We accepted her offer, finished our lunches, and moved on, my pack slightly heavier because of the guilt I now carried for thinking angels had to conform to some sort of pristine image of my own making.

We threaded through trees, then zigzagged up steep and narrow Opie Dilldock Pass, dozens of switchbacks on a trail comprised of something we'd be facing for the next two days: Lava. Rare. Beautiful. Accented with old, bleached snags. And brutally tough on feet, boots, and the mind, I'd learned earlier during the trip.

It was near here, the year before, that we had met Helen Chou, the eighty-year-old Korean woman who was attempting the same 452-mile trip we were trying. Only alone. And with a pack another half again as heavy as mine. As our day wore on, I needed her inspiration, even if I never heard whether she made it to the Columbia River. We were closing in on the twenty-mile mark, the last few miles sometimes on rocks the size of golf balls or baseballs. In our three weeks off, I'd worked out, but I knew it'd take a few days to recover my trail legs.

The beauty of a trail, or lack thereof, could make or break me mentally. The better the views, the less I hurt—or, more precisely, the less I noticed the hurt. Conversely, I'd noticed that my spirits would often ebb in burned areas, which might have a certain haunting beauty to them but reminded me of how dead I felt.

Just north of Minnie Scott Springs, the narrow, hard-pan trail ran arrow-straight through a meadow painted purple with wildflowers. The North Sister watched from behind us, creating a scene as beautiful as I remembered it from the year before. I stopped and breathed in a panorama so rare and pure that I sensed it somehow changed me for the better for my having occupied it for only a moment.

But it was only a few minutes later, from a high perch on the edge of Yapoah Crater, that I spotted something that reminded me the trail was not only beauty, but beast as well:

Smoke.

AT LAVA CAMP that night—just before arriving, we'd encountered the same runner we'd seen that morning as he completed a forty-five mile loop of the Three Sisters—a Trail Angel named Lost and Found assured us we had nothing to worry about; the fire wasn't threatening the PCT.

Lost and Found was a fifty-something thru-hiker who was taking the summer off to sit in a dusty camp, pop up a mosquito-net canopy, and offer food, drink, and fellowship to people like us. She was the PCT's Statue of Liberty, offering this oasis in the lava as if to say, "Give me your tired, your poor, your huddled masses yearning to eat for free."

We were more than happy to oblige. Regarding the fire, though, Glenn and I weren't so sure. From our vantage point, the smoke from the fire was billowing from just north of Mount Washington, about six miles away as the crow flies. The PCT skirted the mountain's western edge, then the eastern edge of Big Lake Camp, where resupplies were to be waiting for us. It didn't look good.

"Not to worry," she said. "Have some more food. Come on, eat up!"

Her lack of worry worried me. Because it was obvious she wasn't basing her assumption on anything but blind faith, sort of the reverse corollary of the pre-trip ranger who'd told us we wouldn't get within twelve miles of the PCT at the Oregon-California border because of snow. Obviously, he didn't know the truth and defaulted to a worst-case scenario; now, she seemed to be defaulting to a best-case scenario. Maybe it was the reporter in me but where was the substantiation? Where was the "according to?"

We walked up Highway 242 to the Dee Wright Observatory, a rock lookout amid a sea of lava, where Glenn connected with Ann to ask if Katie and David's baby had arrived. No. Nor was there any word on trail closures related to the fires. Mount Washington was midway between two east-west highways: Highway 242 to the south and Highway 20 to the north. If the trail were to close, 242 was undoubtedly where they'd post the notice for north-bound hikers.

By now, I couldn't imagine *not* continuing, even if I was wiped at the end of each day. After we'd completed the first part of the trip, people back home had asked me if I fished in the evenings. Fished? I barely had the energy to set up a tent, fix a freeze-dried dinner, and slip into my sleeping bag. PCT hikers, I was beginning to realize, were either imbued with vision clearer than Glacier Creek or were certified nuts. Perhaps both.

We returned to the camp. Glenn, uncharacteristically, wasn't interested in gathering around the campfire with other PCT hikers who'd arrived. He was beat, but I talked him into it. About ten of them were gathered around the campfire, looking to be in their twenties or early thirties. People from Australia, Germany, New Hampshire, and Georgia. Tired but spirited.

They roasted marshmallows, talked, laughed, drank beer, and drank more beer. One of the joys of being a journalist is learning about people different from you. Being on the trail afforded the same opportunity. One of the main threads of conversation involved a hiker from Australia who went on and on about the number of kangaroos—"'roos," as she called them—she had accidentally hit with her car over the years. Who knew? But as the night deepened, nobody seemed particularly concerned about the forest fire. Maybe I was worrying too much.

A definite difference in approach divided the trail's young people from us less-than-young people. We got up early, over-thought everything, and were constantly buried in maps. They slept in, hiked by instincts, and looked at stops like this as chances to drink with great gusto.

Perhaps it was time to cast off my fuddy-duddy ways and live on the edge as they did. Somebody offered me a marshmallow for s'mores. I couldn't resist. With unchecked bravado I said it loud and proud: "Make mine a double."

18. Above the clouds

Trail log: Monday, August 29, 2011.
PCT mile-marker: 1991.6.
Days on trail: 17.
Elevation: 5300 feet.
Total miles hiked: 288.4.

Location: Lava Camp.
Miles hiked Sunday: 23.8.
Average miles per day: 18.0.
Portion of trip completed: 63.4%.

The words, in the quiet of the lava lands, came moments after Glenn had looked at his cell phone.

"Hey, it's a boy!"

I knew when Glenn heard he was a grandfather that he wasn't going to go act like some NFL receiver who'd just scored a touchdown—get all jitter-buggy on me—even if we were alone in the middle of miles of moonscape-like lava rock. He was brought up as a Lutheran and, as Garrison Keillor writes, "Lutherans, generally speaking, are not the ones up on stage." Glenn's father's favorite part of Disneyland, his daughter Carrie once told me, was the Tiki Room, which featured singing and talking birds; in other words, excitement did not run thick in the Petersen blood.

But if the news didn't trigger a yelp and a fist pump, Glenn exuded a quiet pride that manifested itself in a slightly silly grin. "All right," he said. "Jeremiah Walker Black."

"Congratulations, old man," I said. "And everything went well?"

"I guess so," he said, staring down at his cell phone to read the message.

It was about 7 A.M. and, on rough rock, the path twisted and turned like Mister Toad's Wild Ride. At times we were literally heading due south, from whence we'd come. Finally, we got enough north traction to reach Highway 242. I was relieved to find no "Trail-closed-by-fire" sign. The day was young and we'd already received two gifts of good news. We proceeded through the rock, the sky to the north tinted with the hazy aftermath of fire.

Waldo encountered fires from time to time; even though most forest fires now were man-caused, lightning hadn't exactly been a twenty-first century phenomenon. He also mentioned lava beds, though none of his entries suggested he and his party had ventured too deeply into the rugged terrain, presumably because of the lack of trails or roads through the treacherous rock.

I soon stopped at a wooden sign that said "Little Belknap" with an arrow pointing east. "You gotta get a photo of me here," I said when Glenn arrived.

"Why here?"

"Because this, my friend, is where it all began," I said. "Remember that day back in the late nineties when we did Little Belknap and we saw that woman who was doing the PCT right at this spot?"

He nodded. "Laura Buhl. I wrote a column about her. How she made it the whole way from Mexico to Canada, celebrated for a day in Seattle, and made it to class on time to start fall term at U of O the next morning. That's when I was first introduced to the PCT. That's where I got the inspiration for this. Right here."

I paused, feeling ever so small and far from the Columbia River amid this seemingly non-ending sea of rock. "So blame her."

With my iPhone, Glenn took a few photos. "Here's to Laura Buhl," I said, and drank lustily from my CamelBak squeeze tube in her honor. A few miles ahead, I would not even note another spot on the trail that we should have celebrated: the 300-mile mark of our 452-mile journey.

IN THE MID-1960s, NASA thought this mass of lava—more than forty square miles of it in this patch alone—might resemble the surface of the moon so closely that the space organization sent astronauts to Central Oregon to familiarize them with the rocky, jagged basalt. Between 1964 and 1966, no fewer than forty-six astronauts walked the same area we were walking now, including the two men who would ultimately step foot on the moon July 20, 1969: Neil Armstrong and Buzz Aldrin. (Michael Collins, meanwhile, orbited the moon in the Columbia module.)

The astronauts' lava-lands visits made national news. Central Oregon was dubbed "Moon Country." Tourism increased. Years later, in 1971, NASA commemorated the testing when astronaut James B. Irwin delivered a rock from one of Oregon's lava flows to the lunar surface during the Apollo 15 mission.

Back on earth forty years later, Glenn and I wound our way through the bleak yet beautiful fields of rock. He led. I followed, though soon lost sight of him. Maybe it was the grandfather news pumping him up, maybe it was the increasing blister pain slowing me down. For whatever reason, Glenn stretched the distance between us to at least a half mile.

The lava rock finally transitioned into forest—burned forest. This area near Mount Washington had always been a tinder box, though smoke from the fire that had started the previous afternoon had seemingly dissipated. When we reached Big Lake Youth Camp in the early afternoon, we learned the fire was two miles to the east—our predictions of its location were fairly close—but winds were blowing it away from us. The Forest Service had put the camp "on alert" but obviously hadn't evacuated the staff.

As with most stops on the PCT, the people at Big Lake treated us with far more respect than we deserved. It was a transition day at the Seventh-Day Adventists camp—no campers—and we had the place to ourselves. We showered, found our mailed-to-here resupply packages in an upstairs room, ate on a building's wooden deck, and reconfigured our packs.

For me, it was like trying to fit a gallon of pop into a sixteen-ounce bottle. "This," I said, "is pathetic."

"I know what you mean," said Glenn.

"I must have forty pounds," I said, remembering preparation days when I didn't want an ounce over twenty-five.

Because we had 110 miles between here and our next—and last—resupply stop, Timberline Lodge, we had figured on carrying food for six days. That was at least twelve pounds to add to our packs. However, because we'd already shortened the trip a day to reach Timberline by 5 P.M. Saturday, we could afford to give up a little food. But even after compensating for that, my pack was unmanageable.

"I need to jettison a bunch of stuff," I said.

Leaving behind food when you were often famished was hard to do, akin to shopping when you were hungry. Emotions got in the way of your making a logical decision. Impulses took over. Mine said: *Take it, take it.* But I couldn't. Clif Bars. Cheez-Its. Oatmeal. I was about to toss such items into the hiker box for those behind us when a trio of thru-hikers showed up. A hungry trio. They welcomed our discards. And discarding it that way somehow felt better. It was a little like an open adoption; we weren't giving our valuable stuff to faceless others, but to real people who needed it badly and thanked us profusely.

Whether it was food, gear, or information, the trail was a help-each-other-out place, as it seemed to be in Waldo's day, too. On August 2, 1895, he wrote about getting information from a "homesteader" about trails. "We compensated him," wrote Waldo, "by giving him yesterday's *Oregonian*."

Now, at Big Lake Youth Camp, I repacked and repacked. Almost there. Finally, I pulled out a small nylon bundle whose bulk, not so much weight, had been bugging me.

"Who needs rain pants?"

Despite leaving them for a hiker who might covet them more than I did, my pack must have been close to forty pounds, embarrassingly heavy for a long-distance hiker. We crossed Highway 20, the major east-west route through the Cascades for the state's mid-section and the last paved road we would see for about ninety trail miles. From here north, beyond some asphalt in the Timberline Lodge area, we would be in the wildest section of the Oregon PCT since the Crater-Lake-to-Summit-Lake stretch. To our west the Cascade foothills stretched down to the farm-sprinkled Willamette Valley, Oregon's "wet side." To our east forests gave way to high desert juniper and scrub brush, Oregon's "dry side."

Looking left, I saw Hoodoo Ski Bowl, where I'd learned to ski as a boy; where fire had once whipped through, taking the hangar-like 1940-built wooden lodge with it; and where, atop the butte's summit, now rose a glorious cell-phone tower. We weren't expecting much coverage from here north, so I called Sally and, later, my eighty-four-year-old mother, Marolyn Tarrant, who lived in Corvallis, an hour north of Eugene.

"Where are you in relation to that fire?" my mother asked.

"We just passed it to the east," I said. "It was a few miles from the trail."

"Well I'm glad you're beyond it," she said. "I'm enjoying following your blogs."

Hearing the word "blogs" in a sentence spoken by someone eighty-four wasn't common, but, then, my mother wasn't one to rock away her days watching *Jeopardy*. At sixty-nine she had been part of an all-woman sailboat crew, at seventy-nine snorkeled at Cabos San Lucas, and now, still swam laps three times a week.

"I'm glad you're having a good time," she said. "Your father would be proud of you."

What was it about this father-son relationship that, even at fifty-seven, even after our fathers had been gone for fifteen years, even when we were fathers and grandfathers ourselves—even after all that, reached into our souls and touched us so deeply?

"And I'm proud of you, too," she said.

"Thanks, mom," I said. "We're having a great time."

With Glenn on up ahead, I said goodbye and headed up a rise north of Highway 20. Later, when I'd rejoined Glenn, we passed a seventy-seven year-old hiker, Turtle Don, who was biting off chunks of the PCT here and there—slowly but surely. He was the male counterpart to my mom, someone who was, in essence, leaving it all on the trail. And, beyond Cisco and the "Six Moon" trio back in the lava, the only hiker on the entire trip who appeared older than us.

After twenty-one miles under our (getting looser) belts, we found a level shelf—a rarity on terrain not only sloped but so thick with brush and blow-down that we could hardly find a spot to plunk down our tents. It had been a good day. Glenn had become a grandfather. And we had missed what would become known as the Shadow Lake Fire, a blaze that, with shifting winds, would soon spread so quickly that, five days hence, it would close the Pacific Crest Trail.

WHEN WE AWOKE, the world had changed. As the forest came to light, a mist settled over the mostly dead trees, shading it with eeriness. I tugged on some light gloves. It was August 30 and the chill was, from childhood days, that first back-to-school reminder, the subtle hint of a shift from summer to fall.

"Brrrrr," I said before stuffing in a third and final Svenhard's danish, by now as routine as morning teeth-brushing back home.

"Really," said Glenn. "It's cold."

By now, we'd entered the Mount Jefferson Wilderness Area. After stowing our headlamps, we headed north on a spine that arched up toward 7,841-foot Three Fingered Jack. (Though, particularly from the north, it looked like three distinct spires, *Oregon Geographic Names* suggests the name may have come from a three-fingered trapper in the area named Jack. Waldo called it "Trident.") As we broke out of the forest, a view unfolded to the east that literally stopped us in our tracks.

A preface to sunrise lined the horizon, its soft orange hue contrasted by a dark pyramid, the nearly symmetrical Black Butte, in the foreground. Further south, low clouds shrouded the forest in low spots. Soon, the rising sun painted us in a hue of pinkish-orange light. It was a wonderful start to a Tuesday morning on the PCT.

As the trail twisted to the other edge of the ridge, an even more dramatic view opened to the west and south: between us and Mount Washington, thick clouds filled the basin. The peak jutted out like a shark fin in a frothy white sea.

"Unbelievable," said Glenn.

"Look at the valley," I said, nodding farther west. "Totally socked in."

We continued the trek north as if clambering up the neck of a dinosaur. The forest itself was mainly charred trees from long-ago fires—I was surprised at how much "burn" we'd walked through since the trip's start—but the views beyond were incredible. To our right, Three Fingered Jack's steep slope of scree swept up into its distinctive three peaks.

Glenn took advantage of what we expected to be our last cell coverage for awhile by calling his daughter, Katie, to congratulate her on the arrival of Jeremiah. We followed the rocky trail, then wrapped eastward where another gorgeous view greeted us far below: Canyon Meadows, carpeted in green through which Canyon Creek twisted. Tucked beneath Jack, the view had the feel of the Alps.

In late July, 1895, Waldo had camped in the area below us. "This day we left the Big Meadows and crossed the summit just North of the Peak heretofore called Three Fingered Jack—which we call 'Trident Peak.' We camped in the Valley making down from the Peak, on the East." A dangerous climb, it wouldn't be until 1923 that six Bend youths made the first documented summit of Three Fingered Jack.

Fingers of fog reached for the sloping forest below like slow-motion beach waves. The trail zigzagged down, but not to the meadow. Instead, it took us northeast into the worst-kept stretch of PCT trail we would see on the entire trip. Clearly, a trail crew hadn't worked this deeply into the woods after the year's slow snow melt. Blow-down was strewn across whatever trail we could see. Some we went around, some we climbed over, some we crawled under—the hard part getting to our feet again with thirty-five pounds on our backs and nearly sixty years on our respective knees.

"That's hard," said Glenn, getting up after crawling under a log. "One of these times I'm not going to be able to get up."

"Not to worry, I'll call Life Flight or Ann," I said.
I let the hook set, then yanked on the line. "And then hike on."

ON THE TRAIL, imagination could be friend or foe. If all you imagined was food you didn't have and weariness you *did*, every step was more difficult. But if you could get your mind off the trail, miles clipped by more quickly. A trio of experiences had disciplined me to use my imagination to my advantage:

First, working mindless jobs as a kid. I mowed a large fraternity lawn every week for three summers. And for a couple of summers raked beans onto a conveyor belt at a cannery. The only way I could survive, I realized, was to get my mind off grass and beans, so I'd figure, over and over, what my quarter-mile splits would need to be to run a sub-five-minute mile. Or try to remember every book I'd read, beginning, of course, with the Hardy Boys series.

Second, running long distances. I started as a high school sophomore. I'd imagine myself in races. Add up my total miles for the year. Or, shifting gears, try to list every Crosby, Stills & Nash song I knew. Every one of my teachers since kindergarten. The sites of summer and winter Olympic Games.

Finally, being a writer. To write you have to be curious. "You have to be like a grown-up three-year old, always saying, 'Why? Why? Why?'" I'd tell my Beachside Writers Workshop students. "You have to want to know the story behind everything."

North of Three Fingered Jack, on a PCT section that was completed in 1930, I saw a fire-charred sign that said "Oregon Skyline Trail No. 2000," with mileage to such places as Minto Pass (½ mile), Rockpile Lake (3), and Pamelia Lake F.S. Station (16). Immediately, my mind was off to Portland. Specifically, to the eighth-floor apartment of Lewis L. McArthur. It was there, in June 2008, that I interviewed the man who had nurtured four editions of the *Oregon Geographic Names* book that his father had started in 1928, the bible of state place-names. In its 1,073 pages were the answers to questions about how, say, Minto, Pamelia and 6,250 other Oregon places got their names. (Rockpile, we'd soon learn, was self-explanatory.)

Already, on the PCT, Glenn and I had passed such curiosities as Moon Prairie Road, Tipsoo Peak, and my all-time favorite, Opie Dilldock Pass. (Named, in 1932, by U.S. Forest Service personnel Dee Wright, for whom the observatory in the lava fields was named, and Ralph Engels.

"They had had difficulty finding a good way down into White Branch Canyon but finally found one small, practical passage," said the book. "They were both reminded of a comic strip character of the early 1900s named Opie Dilldock who always found some way out of impossible situations, so they decided to honor the pass with his name.")

This stuff fascinated me. And I wasn't alone. "I get letters about places daily," said McArthur, ninety-one at the time. "It never stops."

Pamelia Creek was named for Pamelia Ann Berry, a cook for the Marion County road locating party, whom John Minto lauded for her "unfailing cheerfulness." Waldo himself likely named the lake after the creek, according to McArthur's book. And Minto Pass was named for Minto, who'd come west on the Oregon Trail in 1844 and was a leading authority on Oregon history who spearheaded road-building on the North Santiam Pass.

Lanky and white-haired, McArthur resembled Oregon's lightning-rod governor, Tom McCall, in his later years. He had hiked all across the state, including numerous trips on the precursor to the PCT, the Skyline Trail, and summits of Mount Hood. He loved Oregon in the same way I did, not so much for the cities but for the open country. And he loved the names that helped give the state its unique identity.

"We're fortunate," McArthur told me. "Because we're such a young state there are still links to the stories about how something got named. In places like Massachusetts and Connecticut, too many generations have passed."

BY THE TIME Glenn and I reached Rockpile Lake for lunch, the wind had picked up so fiercely that, when drying our tents, we had to literally tie them to trees. The good news? We had hardly seen a mosquito on the second part of our trip. As we ate, I realized the rip-stock nylon patches on my boots were starting to fray because of scraping rocks and branches. Somewhere up north, I figured, Roadrunner was smirking. I wasn't. My feet were fraying, too. I popped off my boots, aired out my feet—brrr—and put on a few more Second Skin patches.

By now, food was losing whatever luster it might have had earlier in Part II of our trip. The highlights were jerky and potato chips. Waldo, on the other hand, was forever extolling the great food he and his boys were eating. "Adolph and I lunched to-day off of fried beef, Swiss cheese, and bread baked at breakfast, and then a cup of water out of the cool stream at our elbows," he wrote from Elk Mountain on August 20, 1880. And on August 2, 1883: "Dinner is just over. Bread and beans, such baked in the reflector, mustard for the beans, milk (Mrs. Cottingham's recipe, prepared by me), tea, coffee, mountain trout (29) and honey … " Not to mention the game the men killed and ate, including deer, antelope, bear, grouse, and ducks. These were, of course, different times, before conservation extended to animals, and Waldo didn't hunt nearly as much as the other men on his trips. Still, the men shot essentially anything that moved. Among the prey: chipmunks, bear cubs, and eagles.

As Glenn and I finished up lunch, a north-bound hiker arrived. He was young, lanky, neat, and fast. His trail name was Garfunkel. He was an Austrian and, en route to Canada from Mexico, had 2,024 miles of the 2,650-mile trip behind him. We talked for a bit and he bid us farewell. As we returned to the trail, I did the math: counting Ben and Kate, eight Mexico-to-Canada hikers had passed us—frankly, not that many, considering a few hundred usually do the entire stretch each year. But on the PCT in 2011, the snow was laughing last; far more hikers were quitting than usual.

If the trashed trail, my tender feet, and a tedious wind had way-laid my once-high spirits, Mount Jefferson soon came to the rescue. It appeared before us about six miles to the north, beyond the burned area we'd been in and punctuated by a land formation called The Tables. We planned to spend the night at Shale Lake, just southwest of Jeff.

In 1806, Meriwether Lewis and William Clark had first seen Jefferson from a much different vantage point, far north, at the Columbia River, and named it after the president who had commissioned them to explore the Oregon country. In 1913, two climbers on a ridge called Red Saddle near the summit of Jefferson found a whiskey bottle inside that contained this note:

> Within less than 100 feet of the summit of Mount Jefferson, Oregon, Wednesday, August 13, 1879. On this date, about noon, we, J.B. Waldo and E.W. Bingham of Portland, Oregon, climbed to this spot and deposited this record. We have found the record of Preston Looney, July 11, 1854, on the pinnacle immediately south of this, and of others later. As we consider this spot the greatest elevation we have ever attained we prefer to deposit ours here. August 13, 1879, (signed) J.B. Waldo and E. W. Bingham.

If Waldo reveled in conquering mountains, he desired the same kind of victory in protecting the Cascades. By 1892, momentum was beginning to shift for the establishment of the Cascade Forest Reserve. Two years earlier, Congress had passed the National Park bill that John Muir had championed. In California, the Sierra Club formed in 1892 with Muir as the first president. *The Oregonian,* Portland's largest newspaper, published an interview with R.G. Savery, an agent from the General Land Office, suggesting a Cascade Reserve wasn't just pie-in-the-sky stuff. It was quite doable.

Meanwhile, Will Steel's Alpine Club had created a formal committee to advocate for the protection of the Cascades. But Steel wasn't advocating for the entire range as was Waldo, who singled out the lakes region of Central Oregon as examples of places that needed protecting. "To wit, the Twin Lakes at the head of the West Fork of the Deschutes; Trout Lake; Crane Prairie & its fine streams; Davis River & Davis Lake; Diamond Lake lies further South & I think you have included it. It has no fish. Last summer there were three, I think, possibly four bands of sheep in this whole region and they were desolating it to an extent that would please the Evil One himself."

NOW, MOUNT JEFFERSON dropped out of view as we returned into the forest canopy—the wind had ended—and started a gradual twisting down to Shale Lake. "Arriving on Jeff's stately front porch," I texted at 3:24 P.M.

By this point in our journey, two patterns had emerged regarding time and terrain on the trail: I was strong and energetic in the morning, then faded in the afternoon like a spent marathoner who had gone out too fast. Glenn started slowly but grinded through the afternoons with a gusto I couldn't match. I usually stretched into a good lead going uphill; Glenn did the same on downhill. The latter put more pressure on my battered toes and I compensated by easing up.

Because of our different paces, we sometimes hiked apart. When we hiked together, it was often in silences broken only by the sound of boots, trekking poles, and the subtle groans of our packs—and by mentions of what we were seeing, how far we had to go, and how we were feeling. On occasion we'd banter about more significant things—our adult children, a few theological topics, football—but most of the time we were comfortable being quiet.

As we neared Shale Lake, Glenn was, as usual, somewhere up ahead of me. Suddenly, on a stretch notched into a steep, forested slope, a slightly disturbing sight confronted me: a man on a horse, a rifle tucked in his saddle's scabbard, a Bud Light in his hand. Coming toward me. I'd seen a bow hunter the previous night just above Highway 20, and the sight of his weapon had, like the rifle, flashed concern in my mind. These guys weren't doing anything illegal, I assumed. They had every right to be on the trail. And having gone on two elk-hunting trips in recent years for *Register-Guard* columns had whittled away most of my anti-hunter bias. That said, when you've been brought up in a family without such weapons—and have been on a trail where hunters were clearly the exception, not the rule—your mind easily gravitates to the newspaper headline: *Hunter mistakes hiker for deer.* The beer/rifle combination only deepened my concern, and as I stepped off trail so man and horse could pass, I confess: I was glad we were going opposite ways.

I caught up to Glenn just before our 20.2-mile day ended at Shale Lake. As if on cue, fog and darkness soon rolled in with a wintry one-two punch. My REI thermometer hovered near forty degrees, roughly half what the temperature had been the previous day. I tugged on my stocking cap to complement a light down Patagonia jacket. We set up our tents south of the lake, got a fire going, then—famished, as usual—ate. By now, the lake was shrouded in chowder-thick fog.

Later, I doctored my feet. By now, beyond the blisters on my little toes, I had developed a problem on the right side of my left heel, weirdly as much on the side as on the bottom of the foot. It stretched two fingers in size. My heel looked like a rounded chunk of feta cheese. Waldo never mentioned problems with boots, but said his pal, Ed, suffered from them. "After soaking one night I believe they are getting set to his feet, and no longer press on his toenails," he wrote on August 2, 1883, near Oakridge.

Meanwhile, realizing that my nylon patches weren't going to cut it much longer, I wrapped true "Duck tape" around my Merrell boots. While I did so, Glenn, of course, perused the map. That was how the trail worked: you worked your plan during the day, then planned your work in the evening. Originally, we'd planned on camping where we'd eaten lunch: Rockpile Lake. But we were 8.8 miles ahead of that pace. A twenty-one-mile day would take us to Upper Lake, leaving us three days to Timberline Lodge.

"How much farther beyond Upper Lake to Olallie?" I asked as Glenn prepared a fire.

"Two-point-four miles," he said.

Olallie Lake was the largest lake on the entire northern section of the trail, reachable by a long, sometimes treacherous road. Though its campground store no longer accepted PCT resupply boxes, it was, nevertheless, a store. In the middle of nowhere. Right on our route.

"I wonder if that Olallie store would have hot dogs," I said.

"An interesting possibility," said Glenn, whose fire now flamed to life. "Probably would."

A 23.6-mile day, after a steep climb out of Jefferson Park, would get us there the next night. That was a piece of cake for the trail's generational saplings—the Garfunkels of the PCT—but a killer for old-growth firs like Glenn and me. Still, if my feet said no, my stomach argued yes. The flames of the fire fanned my imagination.

"Can you see us tomorrow night, feasting on hot dogs around a campfire?" I said. "I mean, real meat. Sort of."

"You talking about going all the day to Olallie?" Glenn asked.

By now, my stomach was more than arguing yes. It was Jimmy Stewart filibustering on the Senate floor in *Mr. Smith Goes to Washington.*

"Yes, let's go to Olallie," I said. "Why not? The store might even have mustard packets. Relish. We could split an entire pack of dogs."

Glenn poked the fire and flames leapt up. "Count me in," he said.

My spirits soared. From afar, I'm sure it would have seemed odd to an outsider that a cholesterol-packed tube of beef, salt, fat, and preservatives could inspire such joy. But, as Ken Kesey wrote in *Sometimes a Great Notion* about Oregon's rain: "You must go through a winter to understand." Indeed, you had to go through a PCT experience to understand how a simple hot dog could suddenly become more than a bad-for-your-cholesterol food item but a beacon of hope on a distant hill.

Perhaps Waldo and his boys had lighthearted moments like this, though, with their hunting skills, meat didn't seem to be much of a problem. His journal certainly didn't suggest rollicking laughter and incessant one-liners. "Everything is going well," he wrote August 27, 1889, from Rigdon Station. "Daley has laid up anecdotes about Johnson that will last him the remainder of his life." It was one of the few times his journal made reference—if even subtle—to any sort of lightheartedness, and it was telling that Waldo was neither the one dishing out the humor nor the one taking it. His role on these trips seemed to be as the chronicler, the historian, the one who noticed huckleberries along the trail but not the life of the party.

The campfire—intentionally built small by Glenn lest we set the entire forest aflame—started to die. It was about 9 P.M., known on the trail as "hiker midnight." In the darkness to the west something caught my eye. A light. The rifle-and-Bud-Lite guy? Wait, two lights. They gyrated like fireflies, coming toward us, accompanied by footsteps. In a moment, two hikers emerged from the darkness: a young man and woman. Both slim. Both clearly spent. His mouth framed by a dark brown beard, a black earring in his left ear. Her light brown hair pulled back. A handsome pair, olive skinned.

"Greetings," said Glenn.

"Hello," I said.

The man stepped forward. "Hello, I am Bugs," he said with a foreign accent accompanied by unnecessary formality. "And this is Bunny. May we camp here with you?"

We welcomed them to the Shale Lake Sheraton.

"Where you from?" I asked.

"Israel," he said.

They had both completed mandatory military stints in their homeland, then traveled here to hike the trail they'd heard so much about. Bugs was thru-hiking from somewhere in southern California, not necessarily the border. Bunny, his girlfriend, had joined him at Crater Lake. They busied themselves setting up a tent.

If Waldo didn't pursue handshakes with strangers, he wasn't rude either. "A Warm Springs Indian came to our camp at dusk last night—a hunter—with his Henry rifle and blanket," he wrote from Pamelia Lake, less than two miles from where we were now. "We gave him his supper and breakfast and he now stands at our camp fire as we are packing. Silent and apparently uninquisitive … but he was taking it all in."

When Lewis and Clark arrived at the mouth of the Columbia River in 1805, some 50,000 to 100,000 Indians were living in what would become Oregon. However, because of "Old World" diseases brought by white settlers, far fewer inhabited the region by the time Waldo headed for the woods seventy-five years later. By 1880, the Indian population was confined to five reservations, tribes having been paid only a few cents per acre for their land.

On September 16, 1892, Waldo recorded another gathering of Indians around his campfire at Waldo Lake, expressing admiration that one of the women had been to New York and Washington, D.C., and fear of the men "because [they] are great hunters" and would make it harder for Waldo and his men to bag fresh venison.

I had witnessed no such competitiveness on the PCT. Turf wasn't the issue, tiredness was. The battles were hiker vs. trail and, more deeply, hiker vs. self, not hiker vs. other hikers. From the fire, I listened to the conversation between Bugs and Bunny in their native tongue. Later, we said goodnight and headed for our tents. It would, by far, be our coldest night of the trip. Outside, Bugs had, in only a few moments, piled on wood to turn our small fire into something of an inferno. As I lay there, listening to them talk, it was with a sense of wonder—and no longer simply because of the prospects of eating a hot dog. It was because of moments like these that would arrive out of nowhere, moments like finding yourself chatting with Ben, the Aussie, about sailing around the world or with Cisco about star patterns in the sky.

"Every journey has a secret destination of which the traveler is unaware," said Martin Buber, an Austrian-born Jewish philosopher. I presumed I knew where this trail was leading us: to Cascade Locks, to the Columbia River, to the Oregon-Washington border. But perhaps I was being too simple in my expectations. Perhaps it was leading to a destination that I hadn't chosen but needed to find nevertheless.

For now, I drifted toward sleep, thinking how wonderful it was to be snug in a small tent high in the Oregon mountains while listening to the sound of an Israeli couple, around a campfire, speaking soft words in Hebrew.

19. Waldo's triumph

Trail log: Wednesday, August 31.
PCT mile-marker: 2032.8.
Days on trail: 19.
Elevation: 5900 feet.
Total miles hiked: 329.6.

Location: Shale Lake.
Miles hiked Monday: 21.0.
Miles hiked Tuesday: 20.2.
Average miles per day: 18.3.
Portion of trip completed: 72.9%.

WEDNESDAY DAWNED with a wintry bite. "Leave camp 556 am in fog and cold," I texted. "Fall!"

"How do you get ready so fast?" said Glenn as we headed up the trail with our headlamps on. "I can never get going as fast as you."

I didn't dare share my dirty secret. "Two words," I said. "Hot dogs."

About three miles into our hike, I saw it to my left, cradled about a thousand feet below in a bed of seemingly endless firs: Pamelia Lake. I had camped there a couple of times in my college days. More importantly, Waldo had camped there scores of times. In August 1905, he began an entry from Pamelia by pointing out that it was being written by "boiled huckleberry juice."

That same year, Waldo spent virtually his entire mountain time on or near its shores, from August 9 to September 25. Leafing through Waldo's journal always sparked something special when I'd see a notation for a place I'd been, such as the entry of August 11, 1905: "Heideck and I started with the horses for Hunt's Cove." I'd fished Hunt's Cove back in my early twenties.

"Trail making to-day," he wrote the next day. "Getting logs out of the trail along the South shore of Pamela Lake." (He spelled it "Pamela," without the "i," but had, in journal entries two years later, corrected it to "Pamelia.")

On August 13, he reported weather not unlike ours: "Clouds were about halfway down the side of Jefferson." And four days later: "The commercial view of the forest is not the whole view, nor the correct view, any more than it is of most things. We do not 'live by bread alone.' A wise compromise is probably the end to be attained."

On the 19th, the group climbed to what Waldo estimated to be less than a thousand feet from Mount Jefferson's summit. They came upon a camp they had established the previous year. "Here at our old camp," he wrote, "we find things we left amazingly fresh. Everything ages very slow here, even the trees live and look young for a thousand years, I believe. The same applies to the human mind. 'In the woods,' says Emerson, 'is perpetual youth.' "

> The air is pure and refreshing here—a delight to breathe—and it is quite a wilderness still. We have seen or heard no one until just after finishing dinner a while ago, when two stout-looking, youngish men with guns in their hands and packs on their backs came up the trail into camp. They are out of Portland on a general outing through the mountains; have been in Alaska, and can pack on their backs. One is an architect, the other a builder, I believe, and they seem well pleased to be out away from crowded thoroughfares."

Near the trail junction to Pamelia Lake, the forest gave way to a v-shaped flume of heavy rock. Down the steep ravine pounded Milk Creek, a silty flow from a crease in Mount Jefferson. This was not California, where PCT river crossings could mean wading through waist-high water and missteps could be life-threatening. Still, what *Pacific Crest Trail: Oregon and Washington,* in an oxymoron, calls a "minor torrent" was no easy crossing. My concern wasn't drowning but soaked sleeping bags, dead iPhones, and wrecked solar battery chargers.

The water coursed down, as if on a steep staircase, from Mount Jefferson. On this mountain, in September 1966, a former *Register-Guard* colleague of mine, Gary Kirk, had been heading up Jeff when he saw what appeared to be a climber sleeping on a glacier. Kirk and two climbing pals approached him. The young man was not sleeping. He was dead. Later, he was identified as a seventeen-year-old New Jersey youth who'd fallen 400 feet off Eagle Rock, a kid whose wanderlust—and lack of experience—had led to a poor choice of a first mountain to climb. I was glad I was down below, even if I took each step along the pulsating creek with a touch of uncertainty.

Before the trip, I'd read in *The Pacific Crest Trailside Reader; Oregon & Washington* of a seventy-two year-old PCT section hiker, Jim Rea, who'd been not far from here when struck by an intestinal blockage. Because he hiked alone, his wife had talked him into taking a satellite phone. It may have saved his life. He was airlifted out by a National Guard Blackhawk helicopter to a hospital, where surgeons removed nearly a yard of his intestines. I didn't have a satellite phone. I *did* have a satellite device that could send an SOS message. But I'd bought it to communicate our positions and send short messages to *Register-Guard* readers when we were out of cell range, with no intention of ever needing that button.

I scouted the best place to cross Milk Creek. In a different area, Glenn did the same. We carefully hopped rocks and stayed dry.

WE BROKE for lunch in Jeff Park. Despite clouds shrouding the mountain, the area was like nothing we'd seen thus far: not a wisp of a meadow like most, but a far-reaching splay of grass that stretched more than a square mile in size, thick with multi-color wildflowers and dotted with lakes, islands of trees, and rocks. We had the place entirely to ourselves.

Even in this odd late-summer chill and with clouds hiding the mountain—even with our heads covered in stocking caps—Jefferson Park felt like a place of privilege, as if you were miles up in the sky and part of a fictional fantasy land. But in Frostian terms, we had miles to go before we slept—and, of course, before we ate hot dogs. Time to move on.

We were just readying to begin a steep climb out of the meadow when two hikers greeted us heading the opposite way: Theresa O'Brien, perhaps a little younger than us, and her college-aged daughter, Lana. And, ironically, from Eugene, where Lana was a University of Oregon student and where Theresa told me she'd heard me give a book talk at the Central Presbyterian Church she used to attend. (Another "Only in Oregon" moment.) Lana was going from Cascade Locks to Crater Lake with various family members joining her for segments along the way. The two had spent the previous night at Breitenbush Lake, a Waldo favorite, and had just descended some one thousand feet from Park Butte.

"It's really cold up there," said Theresa. "Snowfields. Ice pellets coming out of the trees. Do you have gloves?" The two were bundled; Glenn and I only semi-bundled. Lana had wool socks over her gloves. Theresa wore gloves, a windbreaker over fleece, a neck bandanna and some sort of buff around her ears, beneath a nylon hat.

They were right. By the time a rocky trail took us to an "Entering

Mount Hood National Forest" sign at 7,010 feet, the conditions had changed dramatically. It was like going from autumn to winter in an hour. The wind howled. The temperature plummeted to the mid-thirties. Ice that had formed on high branches of pines was, as they'd warned, falling on us.

Elevation could change everything in a hurry. Even though Thoreau was hardly Jeremiah Johnson—Walden Pond was a mile from his home in Concord and a train ran close to its shore—he did scramble up Maine's highest peak, 5,269-foot Mount Katahdin in September 1846. (John Waldo was two years old at the time.) Even without snow, Thoreau was unsettled at best—and frightened to his core at worst—by the windswept, barren summit rising high above dense forests: "Here was no man's garden," he wrote, "but the unhandselled glove. It was not lawn, nor pasture, nor mead, nor woodland, nor lea, nor arable, nor wasteland." Despite his gentlemanly demeanor, Waldo might have scoffed at Thoreau if he weren't so smitten with Henry David's transcendental philosophizing. To Waldo, a mountain was simply beauty with a rugged soul. And came with a reward: a view, a sense of satisfaction, a memory.

The reward was a sign that bolstered my confidence: If we were now in the Mount Hood National Forest, Oregon's highest mountain must be out there somewhere. And once we reached that mountain, we were only two or three days from finishing.

We boot-skied across a shale ridge covered in snow, then made our way through a rocky saddle as desolate and colorless as Jeff Park had been the opposite. Soon, we were back in the trees. The wind died. We were more than halfway home for the day.

By now, the trail, after three weeks of hiking, had become more friend than foe. To be sure, it had a mind of its own. You might think, "Surely, the trail can't go across this steep-pitched mass of shale" and, moments later, you were trying to negotiate a steep-pitched mass of shale. But if in the beginning the trail had been something to overcome, it was now something to take us home. A means to an end. A companion, not a combatant.

"Getting closer to our three-dog night," I said to Glenn, my trekking poles tat-tat-tatting the rock trail.

"Why stop at only three?" said Glenn.

"You're right. Let's not limit ourselves. Eight to a pack, right?"

"Right," he said.

"So, that's perfect." I said. "You have a pack, I'll have a pack."

As Waldo tramped the Cascades, hot dogs were in their American infancy, Coney Island having begun selling them in 1870, about ten years before Waldo took to the Oregon woods. But meat itself was a huge part of his high Cascades diet, thanks to plentiful game, little competition, and—unlike us—no need to hurry along the trail to make deadlines. Near Black Butte, on July 28, 1895, he wrote: "Fifty-one (rather small sized) trout constituted our first meal." That paled compared to a report a decade later from Pamelia: "The boys report 1,013 fish caught to this time."

Late in the afternoon, we spotted Breitenbush Lake, at which Waldo had once written: "I have read Thoreau's *Maine Woods* through at this camp and am going over some of it a second time. He reads well far off in the boughy and aromatic forest of the Cascade Mountains where the foot of the lumberer he detested so much has never trod."

Glenn and I climbed again—this time in a recently burned area—and, when reaching the top of a west-facing ridge, were buffeted by winds even stronger than those just north of Jefferson Park. From here, it was a gradual, if rocky, downhill stretch to Olallie Lake. Over the last two miles, my feet ached with each step but my mind was firmly fixed on the tubular reward for what would be a twenty-three-mile day.

We'd been hiking for fourteen hours. Light would soon fade. My body desperately needed sustenance. And, suddenly, there it was, nailed to a trail-side tree: a brown paper bag upon which was hand-written with a thick, red marker: "Olallie Lake Store Open." An arrow pointed east, to our right. If the discovery all but triggered a heavenly chorus, the fine print immediately worried me. Yes, it had said open. But in smaller writing, it also said: "7 a.m. 8 p.m. ish."

In particular, it was the "ish" part that worried me. It was 7:15 P.M. We were perhaps ten or fifteen minutes away. But "ish" changed everything. "Ish" could mean 7:15 or 8:30. "Ish" was the opposite of a promise. It was wiggle room for the resort's young staff, which, I presumed, having not had many customers this late in the day, might feel justified in locking up early to go play video games in their cabins. I picked up my step.

"If it's closed I'm gonna howl like a coyote," I said.

We broke out of the forest and onto a dirt road. The lake appeared between the trees, large and chilly looking on the cool summer eve. Soon we saw the "resort," a simple wooden, peaked-roofed store accented with log railings. Its front deck looked out on a great view of the docks, rental boats, the lake, and Mount Jefferson beyond.

"It's open!"

"All right!" said Glenn.

I picked up my pace—to heck with blisters—with Glenn close on my heels. Up six steps. Across the wooden porch. Through the door. A young woman was alone at the counter. Flames flickered inside a wood stove in the back corner. My stomach felt a pang of promise. *Perspective*, I reminded myself. *Don't seem too anxious. Make some small talk first.*

"Hello," I said.

"Welcome."

"Doyouhavehotdogs?" The words leapt forth like a mad dog yanking a leash.

"I'm sor—"

No, no, no, stop, I wanted to say. *My sanity depends on your not having to say you're sorry. Because if you don't say it, maybe what I presume to be true may not be. Don't say you're sorry because even if you are, "sorry" doesn't cut it. "Sorry" isn't going to curb this insatiable hunger that I promised I would satiate with a hot dog—or eight. Instead, "sorry" will suggest that Trail Magic is somehow conditional, that it comes and goes with the fickleness of a shorting-out light switch.*

Maybe, as if I were editing an iMovie video, I could stop the film right here and import an alternative ending. The one that includes a freezer stuffed full of Ball Park Wieners, flanked by a rack of hot dog buns, instead of the bitter truth I learned when her sentence unfroze.

"Sorry," she said, "but the only cold stuff we have is beer and pop."

THE PCT is about resiliency. About getting up when you've been knocked down, taking another step when you don't want to, moving forward when dreams shatter with the suddenness of a lightning bolt splintering a towering pine.

By mid-morning the next day, I had recovered. Sort of.

"I'm over it," I told Glenn, then fetched a line from *Home Alone*, the part where a polka-band member (John Candy) was trying to reassure Kevin's mother that everything was going to be OK. To do so, he told her about having once left his son in a funeral parlor with a corpse, but how the kid had bounced right back: "After six, seven weeks, he came around, started talking again."

"With a little therapy," I told Glenn, "I'll be talking again."

If humor was a sign of resiliency, the increasing pain in my feet was a sign of regret. Regret that twenty days into this trip, I still couldn't shake this nagging blister problem. Glenn, on the other hand, was doing great. In fact, though, he, too, had initially taken the hot dog news hard—we'd drowned our sorrows in a family-sized bag of Lay's barbecue potato chips, sitting on the store's front deck and watching the lake—he was positively giddy the next morning as we headed north on a dirt trail that felt like a freeway compared to the rocky travails of the previous day.

"Where did she say we could get cell coverage out here?" he asked.

"In the bathroom at the Equestrian Center two miles down the trail," I said, "and beneath the power lines, depending on our provider."

"Men's or women's bathroom?"

"There's only one," I said. "But I think that's AT&T. We're Verizon. So, power lines."

Obviously, cell coverage didn't come easily to these parts. It was Thursday morning. We hadn't been able to connect with home—or to send full-length blog posts—since the northwest spur of Three Fingered Jack two days before. Our only communication out had been our Spot Connect locations and a few 41-character updates each day, accompanied by a GPS-precise map of where, precisely, we were at that moment.

"You go on ahead," I said to Glenn. "I've got some feet issues."

The salt in my (blistered) wound was that the trail was smooth, flat, and gradually downhill. I should have been gobbling up miles en route to our Thursday night destination, the Warm Springs River, twenty-one miles away and, at 3,300 feet, our lowest point since taking our first step. Instead, I was sitting on a log, trying to find some sort of combination of tape, moleskin, Body Glide—even Monkey Butt—that would ease the friction and stop the pain.

It wasn't working. After another couple of miles, I again pulled over for repairs. When that didn't do much good, my frustration deepened. In life, I'd learned, the problem wasn't the problem; the problem was not finding a solution to the problem. That's where I was now. I hadn't seen Glenn for almost an hour. I limped on. Looked far up the trail. And there he was, sitting on a log. He read my body language from 100 feet.

"Not good?" he said when I arrived.

"Not good."

"Let me take a look."

What happened next was humbling and heartwarming: He fixed my feet. As if he were the doctor and I were some Haitian kid who'd stepped on the coals of a fire—a fairly common problem in Haiti, by the way—he did what needed doing. In this case, slapped on some Second Skin and wrapped on the same blue Kinesio Tex tape that he was using.

"Try that, Bob," he said.

I did. I walked for about twenty-five feet. "I'm healed! I'm healed! Thanks, doc."

I joked about it then. That's what men usually do when something tugs at their hearts. We take a subconscious detour around the deeper elements of the story. It's a pride thing. But as Glenn and I continued on—me with renewed vigor—I was touched by what he had done. I wouldn't have blamed him if he hadn't even waited for me, much less taken the time and effort to fix my feet.

Only later would Glenn tell me the real reason he had stopped. "I hadn't seen you in quite a while, and I heard some thrashing around in the woods," he said. "I thought maybe a bear had gotten you. Seriously."

IF WALDO NEVER complained about blisters—or, with a personality much like Glenn's, about much of anything—he did find himself sick enough on occasion that he couldn't go on. Apparently, it was often due to his allergy problems, which led to killer headaches and sinus drainage. "I had a relapse or two," he wrote on July 20, 1886, near Pamelia Lake, "and as a consequence, was not well enough to start."

The next year, from Davis Lake, he wrote on August 8 how "my general health is extremely good—can endure fatigue and do labor admirably; but the pain in my head still lingers, feebly .... I hope to be quite rid of it in another month, but I cannot be perfectly confident of it. It certainly had a strong hold, and I didn't come to the mountains any too soon."

In years to come, the sting of his 1889 defeat at the hands of the Oregon State Senate gave way to renewed efforts to win in some other way. Four years later, Waldo, Steel, and other leaders of the Cascade preservation movement were able to convinced the state senate to unanimously pass a joint resolution preserving Oregon's entire Cascade Range. Steel exploited the momentum by taking the train to Washington, D.C., where he lobbied Secretary of Interior John Noble and Congressman Binger Hermann. President William Harrison's administration was cool to the idea, but Grover Cleveland had won the November election and would assume office in March. There was hope.

It was a lesson from the trail: At the moment, you might not be where you wanted to be. But if you kept grinding, you might get where you needed to be. And grind Waldo and Steel did. Finally, six months after he took office, on September 28, 1893—and having heard plenty from the duo and a third Oregonian, R.G. Savery—President Grover Cleveland made a decision: He proclaimed the establishment of the Cascade Range Forest Reserve, the fulfillment of Waldo's dream. It would be 4.9 million acres in size, the largest such reserve in the nation.

"The reservation will be known as the 'Cascade forest reservation,'" reported *The Oregonian* in a small story. "It extends from the Columbia River 200 miles southward, about 20 miles in width, taking in the Cascade Range. Hereafter no settlement will be allowed within its boundaries."

Initially, the effort was credited to Will Steel and Savery, an agent from the General Land Office. And Steel, in a letter to *The Oregonian* written from Mount Hood's Government Camp, did nothing to dispute that. It wasn't for another couple months that the paper explained just how the reserve had come to be. "Judge Waldo Did It" was the paper's headline on November 27, 1893.

> The credit of originating the idea of a reserve along the summit of the Cascade range is due to John B. Waldo, ex-chief justice of the supreme court of Oregon. He made the first move toward this end when he was a member of the legislature, about six years ago [actually, four years ago, 1889] by introducing a memorial, which was [not] adopted, asking congress to set aside the summit of the range as a reservation. He has favored the scheme ever since, and favors it yet, which relieves the [forest reserve] movement entirely of any suspicion of fraud or self-seeking. The idea was a good one, and it is a very proper thing to have these lands reserved.
>
> That is what John Forster, an old settler and trapper ... had to say yesterday about the Cascade reserve. "I do not know," he continued, "any of these Johnny-come-latelys who claim to have originated the idea of the reserve, but I do know that Judge Waldo has spent every summer for many years exploring the summit of the Cascade range from the Columbia to the California line, and I believe that he is more familiar with the summit of the range as a whole than any other man. One of the largest and most beautiful lakes on the range has been named for him, an honor he is well entitled to for his explorations.

"Despite a measure of statewide fame from his political activities, Waldo never sought the public limelight during his career as a preservationist, preferring to work quietly but tenaciously for forest conservation issues," wrote Jeff LaLande in *Oregon Historical Quarterly*. Not surprisingly, Waldo did nothing to set the "credit-due" record straight, even if the words of a backwoods trapper weren't necessarily packed with much political punch. But Steel took care of that. On November 25, he wrote to *The Oregonian*, claiming that the newspaper had excluded a portion of a previous letter he'd sent it, making it appear that he was taking full credit for the movement's beginnings.

> The fact of the matter is, Hon. John B. Waldo, of Marion County, suggested the idea long before entering the legislature, and we have continually worked in harmony on this subject. He not only originated this idea, but has been one of its staunchest supporters and has been prominently identified with the movement from the first ... ."

Meanwhile, those opposed to the new reserve couldn't care less where it originated. They just wanted it to go away. And, quietly, behind the scenes, they hatched plans to speed its demise. Waldo's journey to save his mountains wasn't over.

THE WARM SPRINGS RIVER was another one of those "it-must-look-like-this" images in my mind that turned out to be nothing like I expected. By now, we'd spent most of the day on Warm Springs Indian Reservation land, in increasingly lush forest accented with a touch of smoke. We'd heard about a Warm Springs fire, but, as expected, it was far east of us.

Having been on the reservation years ago to do interviews for a story, I knew it to be a rocky, sage-and-juniper mix of land. I had combined that image with my image of a river—a wide, smooth-flowing body of water—to picture us sleeping among prairie scrub while a 100-foot-wide river meandered by. Instead, the Warm Springs River was a fifteen-foot-wide creek that trickled through a deep, lush forest thick with Douglas firs.

Two perfect camp sites flanked either side of the trail, just beyond a wooden bridge crossing the "river." Glenn built a small fire on the one to the west. "I don't want my name in headlines for setting the entire Warm Springs Indian Reservation on fire," he said. We popped up our tents, ate, and were battening things down for sleep when another hiker arrived and dropped his pack at the other camp site. Glenn, ever the social butterfly, invited him to come join our fire.

"No, thanks," he said, if not rude then business-like. The newcomer started piling huge chunks of wood on his own fire pit. Within moments, the flames leapt skyward. Whoa, this guy was serious about his fires. Later, we found out why. His name was Mike, thirty-ish, and a civilian bean-counter for the Coast Guard in Seattle. He was hiking a chunk of the PCT to Timberline Lodge. I listened from our fire as, across the trail, he and Glenn talked.

"So, late Wednesday, I come through Jeff Park and it's cold and windy but I decide to go on," Coast Guard Mike said beyond the high-licking flames.

"We must have come through just a few hours before you," said Glenn.

"I climb up, cross that snowfield in the dark"—a harrowing thought, I considered as I listened from afar—"and then came to all that shale. Pitch black. I'm dead tired. Thirty miles on me. Wind blowing like crazy. I realize I can't make it to Olallie, I'm going to have to camp right here."

I took a few steps closer to hear better.

"So, I'm in my tent, right, and I heard this noise, something scratching around out on the rocks," he said. "So I pull out my hunting knife."

I joined the two of them by the fire. "You had me at 'pulled out my knife,'" I said. "Then what?"

"And I wait. And the noise continues. It's like whatever's out there was stalking me, circling me."

"Bear?" I ask.

"That's what I'm thinking." Better be a sharp knife, I thought; even a black bear, I knew, could hit speeds of thirty-five mph. "But I don't know. And yet I'm not going to spend the whole night cowering in my tent, so I put on my headlamp, zip open the flap and"—now I'm thinking cougar—"nothing was there."

The story collapsed like a crumpled ultra light that falls from the sky, but I liked it anyway. I had spent a few hundred nights in the woods and had never seen a bear or cougar. Then again, I had interviewed dozens of people over the years convinced that they had had Bigfoot encounters. The fact that one such siting was in a Burger King parking lot and another on the back deck of a suburban home didn't do much to raise the believability of the reports. And yet, I had to admit, I loved a good close-encounter story, even if such tales tended to make the person sound a bit more heroic than what they might have been. At night around a campfire, the story was never told by a guy who heard a noise outside his tent, imagined a 500-pound grizzly bear that could squish his head like a seedless grape—and promptly cowered into the fetal position while peeing his pants.

Still, I liked Coast Guard Mike's story, and honored him for telling it. Though lacking a killer ending, it left the door of possibility open just a crack. And even if a century-plus survey showed more people died in a grizzly-rich place like Yellowstone National Park from lightning, falling trees, and accidental shootings, the idea of a bear attack could settle in your gut like battery acid.

Up the trail, we heard footsteps. Saw headlamps. Out of the semi-darkness they came: Bugs and Bunny once again arriving fashionably late. Later, when I crawled into my tent, I had trouble getting to sleep. Coast Guard Mike's story had me thinking of cougars and bears. On October 28, 1892, Waldo wrote of a "formidable looking cougar" that stared down a tramping buddy, Andrew. And on July 22, 1881, Waldo was on the northwest side of Mount Jefferson, when "remote from human intrusion, I saw a grizzly bear—genuine; such a monster of a bear could be nothing else but a grizzly. There have been two or three seen before at long intervals in these mountains … . He was about two hundred yards distant, feeding, unconscious of my presence. I took one look at him through the glass and at once looked around for some safe retreat."

By now, a grizzly bear had not been killed in Oregon since the 1930s nor one *seen* since 1979 (Hells Canyon Wilderness) but black bear prowled the Cascades. As the night deepened, I occasionally drifted off, then heard a snap or crack from Coast Guard Mike's fire, and felt an emotional jolt.

In the night woods, it always lessened your fears to consider the odds, which favored a continual safe journey. What increased those fears was remembering that the forest paid no regard to such odds and, as Cisco liked to say, the trail went wherever it wanted to go.

20. The perfect day

Trail log: Friday, September 2.
PCT mile-marker: 2077.4.
Days on trail: 21.
Elevation: 3300 feet.
Total miles hiked: 374.2.

Location: Warm Springs River.
Miles hiked Wednesday: 23.6.
Miles hiked Thursday: 21.0.
Average miles per day: 18.7.
Portion of trip completed: 82.8%.

AS WE NEARED Timberline Lodge, our pace was as crisp as the morning air. In fact, by mid-morning I announced our milestone achievement. "Ten by ten, Glenny. The Colorado Boys would be proud of us."

"Bob, the two-by-four days are long gone," he said. "We are *good*."

The trees got larger, the green foliage thicker, the anticipation keener. A forest floor that had been sparse with vegetation was now carpeted in ferns, vine maples, rhododendrons, Oregon grape, huckleberries, moss, and growing anticipation of reaching the river. Glenn couldn't get over Douglas firs as wide as mini-vans.

"Take my picture by this one," he'd say. A quarter-mile later: "Bob, can you get a shot of me with this one?" Then, with more childlike awe: "Whoa. Look at this monster! These trees are huge! Here, take my camera." He was a sixteen-year-old Boy Scout in the body of a fifty-nine year-old man.

By evening, the plan was to be just below Mount Hood's front steps, leaving eight uphill miles remaining for a mid-day arrival at the famed lodge dedicated by President Franklin Roosevelt himself in 1937. More significantly, at least from my narrow perspective, the lodge in which there would not only be at least one large-screen tuned to the Oregon-LSU football opener, but food, glorious food.

"They have this all-you-can-eat buffet," said Glenn, referencing some PCT book extolling the virtues of the lodge.

"We can eat, listen to the Beavers on the satellite radio—they're not on TV—and then watch the Ducks at 5 P.M.," I said. "The perfect day."

After a week and nearly 150 miles on Part II of the trail, it all sounded, if not like heaven itself, then at least the outer gates. Gates that would swing open with a two-day, forty-five mile push to the river around Hood's western shoulder. We hoped to be celebrating Labor Day night in Cascade Locks with Sally and Ann.

By mid-day, we were just beyond Timothy Lake, a much-photographed spot as a foreground for majestic Mount Hood to the north. About fifteen miles to the southwest lay Bagby Hot Springs, where I'd once hiked with my family as a youngster—and where Waldo encountered a couple of families with "children ... as lively as crickets. They deserve to enjoy themselves here. The Springs and the wilderness all to themselves, and nothing to annoy, unless a few gnats."

The day deepened, the air warmed. We lunched next to a Forest Service road, Glenn's Elmer Fudd hat pulled over his face to shade the sun. Frankly, we looked a mess. I hadn't shaved since hitting the California border nearly six weeks before and iPhone photos suggested I'd starting to look like a psychotic 1800s fur trapper. Dirt was so enmeshed in my once-khaki-colored pants that they had taken on a camo look. Though I had clothes to sleep in, I felt like the living embodiment of Waldo's reference to "an old Spaniard, who wrote the account of Cortez's conquest of Mexico, how for ... at least months together never took off his clothes." My boots—I'd shifted from green and yellow duct tape to gray—looked as if part of the earth itself, a couple of organic dirt clods with laces. Glenn's cobalt blue shirt was so encrusted with salt-tinged sweat that I imagined it scaring off wild animals; no wonder we hadn't seen anything beyond squirrels and a few deer. (Waldo reported seeing forty-one deer on one trip alone.)

"Hey, I brush my teeth every other day," deadpanned Glenn, "whether I need to or not."

I rewarded him with laughter; his one-liners arrived with the frequency of Halley's Comet, but when they did, they were often good.

"We're gonna have to clean up a little before stepping into that lodge," I said. "I mean, will they even let us into a bar to watch the game if we look like this?"

"We'll be fine," he said.

"Hey, there's going to be tourists from around the world there. Neat, clean, well-dressed tourists wearing Dockers and loafers. And we stink worse than we look, which is pretty bad."

"Don't worry, Bob."

It was Classic Glenn, the guy who, at some posh golf course we might play once a year—a place with an actual dress code—would show up in a red, hoody sweatshirt.

"OK," I said, "but promise me one thing."

"What's that?"

"Lose the Elmer Fudd look. At least flip down the bill on your cap. You look bad enough as it is. Why make things worse?"

He laughed. I thought briefly of Mike Jones, the Shelter Cove fishing guide, and his comment about the least likely doctor among the four of us, which got me thinking about how long we'd been on this trail and where Cisco and Roadrunner were—probably midway through Washington, I figured. Then, like Glenn had before me, I promptly fell asleep in the mid-day sun.

THREE MONTHS after the government created the Cascade Forest Reserve, the sheep men came seeking a compromise. Could they be granted permits to graze their flocks on the reservation? Waldo was a naturalist but also a realist. Better to have the sheep men's support for the reserve rewarded with carefully controlled limited rights than to have them amass their considerable political clout and try to quash the reserve altogether.

But in April 1894 the General Land Office made it a moot point. "The agency was embarrassed by the blatant disregard for its authority on the part of lumbermen, settlers, and sheepherders who were abusing the forest reserves in other parts of the country," wrote Bobbie Snead in *Judge John B. Waldo: Oregon's John Muir*. Instead of a compromise, the office chose to play hard ball—not Waldo's first choice.

Notices were tacked to trees on borders of such reserves, including Oregon's: "ALL PERSONS ARE HEREBY WARNED not to settle upon, occupy, or use any of the lands for agricultural, prospecting, mining, or other business purposes; not to cut, remove, or use any of the timber, grass or other natural product thereof ... DRIVING, FEEDING, GRAZING, PASTURING, OR HERDING OF CATTLE OR SHEEP, OR OTHER LIVESTOCK WITHIN THIS RESERVATION,

IS STRICTLY PROHIBITED ... ANY PERSON VIOLATING THESE REGULATIONS WILL BE PROSECUTED FOR TRESPASS."

"The attorney general," wrote Snead, "reinforced the notice in Oregon with pointed instructions to the state to 'vigorously prosecute' trespass of sheepherders."

The backlash from sheep men was predictable. In their minds, this meant war. In California, wrote Snead, half the notices posted along the western border of the Sierra Forest Reserve were ripped down. "In Oregon," she wrote, "sheep owners began a bold campaign to have the Cascade Forest Reserve greatly reduced, if not eliminated completely."

In the next two years, they did so by pressuring the state's U.S. congressional members at a time when such members could be easily persuaded. The sheep lobby had money, power, and little respect for ethical boundaries. This was a time when all U.S. senators were selected by the state legislature rather than by voters. Corruption came with the territory.

"Oregon enjoyed the unenviable reputation of having one of the most corrupt and inefficient governments to be found north of Mexico and west of Pennsylvania," wrote Walter Pierce, a fledgling politician at the time who later rose to be Oregon's governor (1923 to 1927).

Oswald West, who as governor in 1911 would protect the Oregon Coast from wanton private development, said positions were routinely bought with bribes. "The prevailing prices were four and three—four thousand for Republicans ... and three thousand for Democrats," he wrote.

Waldo and Steel, it appeared, had clearly stirred a hornet's nest. But neither was backing down. In 1886, three years after they thought they'd already won this battle, Waldo and other reserve backers convinced Steel to go to Washington, D.C. What he found was predictable: Oregon's congressional delegation had told President Grover Cleveland that most Oregonians wanted the Cascade Forest Reserve abolished. In fact, a proclamation had been offered "to wipe the Cascade reserve off the map" and, said Steel, it was expected to be signed by Cleveland by week's end.

Steel managed to get a thirty-day delay. While he went nose-to-nose with policymakers in D.C., Waldo mounted a furious letter- and telegram-writing campaign back home. He understood the need for political posturing and greatly respected Steel's ability to do it well. "The 'Sheep Men'," he wrote to Steel, "forgot one thing before they started to murder the Cascade Mountains—they should have dispatched a man East, to assassinate you." But he also believed in the power of the written word. Soon, he had convinced some powerful people of his own, including a number of judges, to write Cleveland in defense of the reserve.

In the end, the most powerful letter may have come from Waldo's pen. Its passion was equaled by its length: about 4,000 words. It was vintage Waldo: a small portion political, a large portion a heartfelt defense of why Americans would be better off for preserving such beauty than exploiting it. He ended it thusly:

> "The wilderness is near as well as dear to every man," says Thoreau. "Our lives need the relief of such a background, where the pine flourishes and the jay still screams."
>
> Why should not Americans, with a continent in their hands to fashion as they would, have provided broadly for all the wants of men which can be supplied by human institutions? Not only fields to toil in, but mountains and wilderness to camp in, to hunt and fish in, and where, in communion with untrammeled nature and the free air, the narrowing tendencies of an artificial and petty existence might be perceived and corrected, and the spirit enlarged and strengthened.
>
> The wisdom of such a policy, certainly cannot be disproved by pointing to the results we see around us.
>
> Very truly yours,
>
> *John Breckenridge Waldo*

In 1896, President Cleveland reached a decision: he would *not* revoke his proclamation. The Cascade Forest Reserve would remain just that: a place to remain wild. The issue was settled; no appeals were to be allowed.

Over the decades, the reserve would evolve into the Mount Hood National Forest that Glenn and I were now in—and five other national forests: Willamette, Deschutes, Umpqua, Rogue River, and Winema. Within them: nineteen protected wilderness areas ultimately would encompass more than a million acres, all linked by the Pacific Crest Trail, whose earliest renditions were traveled by Waldo and his men. Wrote Jeff LaLande in *Oregon Historical Quarterly*: "As the state's first advocate for wilderness preservation, the self-effacing John Waldo deserves recognition as the 'Father of Oregon's Wilderness.'"

BECAUSE GLENN and I had no realistic alternative, we would be "dry-camping" Friday night—only the second time the entire trip we would not bed down next to available water. To compensate, we stopped at a last-gas-for-500-miles spring twelve miles from the next available water.

Besides filling my pack's bladder and Glenn's bottles, we needed to carry additional water for our freeze-dried dinners and Saturday morning's eight-mile final stretch. But how? Never mind that the spring turned out to be little more than a tree-ringed mud puddle, we had no choice but to pull out the water filter and go for it. Alas, we also had no additional containers beyond my 100-ounce bladder and Glenn's two one-liter bottles.

"I have that heavy garbage bag I got at Elk Lake," I said. "We could put a little water in it and I could carry it at the bottom of my pack."

Glenn was skeptical. But, though no engineer, I reasoned that my pack would absorb much of the force, leaving little strain on the garbage bag itself. Ten minutes later, the water was secured, atop which I'd placed my other items, crowned by my sleeping bag, the thing I could least afford to get wet. Which was good, because I hadn't walked more than ten feet when my pack started dripping water from its bottom. The garbage bag was leaking as if made of mosquito netting.

"Hey, I went to a liberal arts school at the UO," I said to Glenn. "I can't tell you how to carry water in a garbage bag like an engineering student from OSU might, but I can tell you how it feels when that garbage bag leaks: Bad. Really bad."

"So," said Glenn, "we're just going to have to go light on water."

We did. But less than an hour later, something so splendid happened that we forgot all about our water shortage: While we were high on a north-facing slope, 11,240-foot Mount Hood—the state's highest peak—suddenly appeared from amid the trees as a symbolic welcome to the Oregon PCT's homestretch. It was named in 1791 for British admiral Samuel Hood; never mind that, during the Revolutionary War, he had fought against the country that would so honor him one day. "The mountains are great restorers," Waldo wrote September 16, 1891, from Odell Lake. "Thoreau says ... 'they are great poets.'"

The mountain was reach-out-and-touch close—or so it seemed after two days in thick forests. We hadn't had a view of anything since Olallie Lake two days before. Despite the new sense of hope, the next few minutes turned into an odd frenzy of activity. With cell coverage suddenly available for the first time in two days, I called Sally. I realized my blog feeds—for reasons beyond me—weren't getting through so called a Web-savvy colleague at *The Register-Guard,* Micky Hulse, who with precious little to go on, had the problem solved in minutes. I called another newspaper colleague, designer Tom Penix, to celebrate the Mount Hood milestone.

A thru-hiker from Japan swept by—we chatted briefly—and then I heard the strangest thing of the entire trip: what I assumed was Israeli rock music. Could it be? Yep, there he was: Bugs, of Bugs and Bunny fame, with an iPod plugged into two hand-size speakers affixed to the top of his pack. A very un-PC(T) scene—and hardly the soothing sound Waldo heard from across Fish Lake in 1901, probably by guitar or harmonica: *Auld Lang Syne.* "Oh music," wrote Waldo. "I could sit in my door of summer evenings and listen forever to thy strains."

"Hello, Bugs," I said.

"Hey, Bob," he said. "Where are you camping tonight?" It looked as if the American-Israeli contingent might be joining forces with us for a third straight night.

"We're dry-camping above Highway 26, about eight miles short of Timberline," I said. "And you?"

"We are hitchhiking around the mountain to Cascade Locks," he said.

They planned to attend a big Labor Day PCT festival there. We bid the two farewell, then again an hour later when we reached the east-west Highway 26, where they had their thumbs out.

"Stay safe," I said after posing for a few farewell photos with them.

Glenn and I headed up Timberline's front steps. Just a few miles beyond us lay remnants of Barlow Road, built in 1845-46—just after Waldo's birth—so emigrants on the Oregon Trail could avoid the wild Columbia River, which had drowned countless pioneers just short of the Promised Land. (Dams have since tamed the once-wild river.) When we finally pulled off the trail and carved out a couple of spots for tents, we'd put in 25.1 miles, our longest day on the trail—and just 1.1 miles short of a marathon. Which fit because my hunger was like the hunger I'd experienced the three times I'd finished such events. Huge. For the first time on the PCT, freeze-dried spaghetti did little for me as an end-of-the-day reward. I'd been thinking too much about the food at Timberline.

THE TRIP UP to the lodge proved to be a gut fight: a 1,500-foot climb, the steepest stretch coming near the end of the 8.3 miles. Once we hit the timberline, the last few miles were on a cinder trail. Winds from the east—gusting to perhaps thirty mph—scattered sandy whirlwinds. The footing was like soft-sand beach.

Glenn's shirt and pants whipped in the wind. He kept his head down to protect his eyes from the cinder dust, but as I watched him I had an epiphany of sorts: He now had what's known on the PCT as "the look." A certain confidence. A hunger. A machine-like resolve, as if, after twenty-three days on the trail, he had found a groove and nothing could stop him—even if I knew the trail might beg to differ.

"We have come thus far without any serious mishap, and, may indeed, congratulate ourselves on our good fortune," wrote Waldo on July 18, 1888. "A loaded wagon that preceded us a couple of days turned over twice. We had two or three narrow escapes at a place where such an accident would have been attended with most serious consequences to the team, wagon, and contents."

Another time, one of Waldo's travel mates, "Davey," sliced open his leg with a hatchet while splitting wood. "The cut seemed to be doing very well until last night when it took a turn for the worse," wrote Waldo, "and for hours it seemed to me it might end fatally."

We hit the parking lot of Timberline Lodge at mid-morning. First, we cleaned up in a more spartan ski lodge, Wy'East Day Lodge; I basically bathed in a sink and put on my non-hiking long-sleeved shirt. We picked up our resupplies at a post office built into a ski shop. Originally, we were expecting to take three days from Timberline to Cascade Locks so, with plans altered for just two, we had an oversupply of food. We diverted some of our shipments to the hiker's box for others who would follow, then headed for the main lodge.

Snowboarders walked by with their slabs on their shoulders; the idea of Labor Day weekend skiing was weird, but, then, we *were* at 6,000 feet and the slopes above still had snow. Just before the main lodge, we ran into Coast Guard Mike. The previous day he had met a young woman roughly his age—not uncommon on the trail, I'd learned— and was now hiking with her.

"Instead of calling it quits here," he said, "I'm heading around the mountain to Bridge of the Gods. Leaving after we eat."

"Need any food to take?" I asked.

His eyes widened. "Got some?"

"We just left a ton in the hiker's box," I said. "Hustle and it's yours."

"Thanks, man."

"Safe travels," I said. "And, hey, watch out for those bears."

BLUEBERRY WAFFLES. Sausage. Scrambled eggs. Doughnuts. Orange juice. Fruit. As I finished up my brunch in Timberline Lodge's upstairs dining room late Saturday morning, the only question was what was I going to have in Round II. And Round III. The answer was pancakes, bacon, more orange juice, and more fruit, whereupon I fast-forwarded to lunch: rice, gravy, salmon, dinner salad with blue cheese dressing, and a roll. Oh, and then dessert: vanilla ice cream with fudge topping crowned with a squirt of whip cream, and chocolate-chip cookies. I may have never, in my life, packed more calories into a meal. Nor done so within such a clash of styles: the lodge's food lavishly heaped on silver trays upon white linen cloth—and I looking like something out of *Tales of the Crypt*. Around us, a few tourists dabbled the corners of their mouths with their napkins.

"It's Caddy Day at the country club pool," I told Glenn. "I feel like we don't really belong."

"I feel like more pancakes," said Glenn, who, blessedly, had lost the Elmer Fudd look.

"Hey, look, it's that hiker from Japan," I said. Mij had left the Mexican border on May 5. He was thirty-one and a wood stove salesman in Japan. He was scarfing down food with the "all in" pace of the PCT hiker that he was. We said hello, talked a bit, and posed for a quick photo—the kind of picture you think is kind of cheesy at the moment but later you're glad you had. He then left to continue on around Mount Hood's western edge.

TIMBERLINE LODGE is 55,000 square-feet of rough-hewn mountain charm: peeled logs, artisan craftsmanship, and a walk-in fireplace whose grate is made from railroad rails. Six hand-hewn firs anchor the ceiling. Earthy art decorates the walls. Volcanic-stone walls accent the wood, giving it all the feel of an "indoor outdoors."

The lodge exudes history. A photo shows skiers whose pole's baskets are roughly the size of Frisbees. Another depicts the polio-stricken president, Roosevelt, being helped from his car, a rare shot given that the press was discouraged from showing such. Because Timberline was part of his Works Projects Administration (WPA), he had come for the 1937 dedication to bask in a bit of back-to-work glory.

Now, as we poked around, I couldn't help but notice the international makeup of the tourists. The lodge was much like the trail. Thus far, we'd seen more foreign hikers than we had Oregon hikers. We walked out to a sunny, second-floor deck and tried to find, without success, the Oregon State game on my satellite radio. The view was startling: hundreds of miles of Oregon, the Cascade spine clearly the star of the show. Jefferson, Three Fingered Jack and—barely visible—Mount Washington and the Three Sisters.

"I can't believe we've hiked through all that," I said. "I mean, there's Jeff. We were there just—what?—four days ago. It looks a thousand miles away." Earlier on this Saturday, with a few-hundred yard lead on Glenn, I'd stopped to spell out "400" in fir cones to mark our new mileage milestone. Officially, we had 407 miles down and forty-five to go.

"Hey, look there, by Jeff—smoke," said Glenn.

"And more near Washington," I said. "That must be the same fire we just missed, the one that broke out Sunday. Looks bigger."

"Way bigger," said Glenn. "We dodged a bullet."

High on the south side of Hood, I felt like a sparrow on the front perch of a tree-side birdhouse. In two days, we had climbed 2,650 feet from the Warm Springs River.

We had left our packs tucked to the side of the lodge's entrance, but a gangly, bearded, and PCT-looking young man recognized us as hikers anyway.

"Where you headed?" he asked.

"Bridge of the Gods," I said. "We're just doing Oregon."

He was a thru-hiker, doing the whole enchilada, but frowned with my response.

"Hey, man, never say 'just,'" he said. "You're doing Oregon. Dude, that's a fair piece of trail. Don't minimize it."

"Yeah," I said. "I suppose it is. Thanks."

It felt good to just sit in the sun amid a light breeze. We never were able to find the OSU game on my satellite radio—I'd lugged 4.5 ounces for nothing—but we followed the game on my iPhone. Later that afternoon, as we set up our tents in a windy PCT-hiker perch a few hundred feet above the lodge, the iPhone relayed the bad news that the Beavers had lost to lowly Sacramento State. That evening, in the lodge's recreation/movie room, we watched an equally lackluster effort by my Oregon Ducks in losing to LSU as we ate club sandwiches that Glenn rounded up from an upstairs grill.

Weirdly, though, as we returned to our campsite that night—a few other PCT tents had popped up while we were watching the game—I wasn't particularly devastated. Bummed, sure. But the PCT had opened up a wider world. In some ways—and I felt a touch guilty for this—the game had almost seemed an intrusion on that world, on the purity of the trip, on a poetic rhythm that suddenly had a line that didn't rhyme.

I felt a little as I had the previous day when hearing Bugs' rock music on the trail. It was as if I'd been tainted by the very cultural clatter that I'd intentionally unplugged from—and, yes, I would have felt that way had the Ducks won, too. Oh, sure, I knew that even some of the back-to-nature purists had skeletons in their closets, too; Thoreau, his biographers say, routinely took his laundry home from Walden Pond to his mother in Concord. Some PCT thru-hikers, mainly in California, hitchhiked into towns to sleep in motels and go to movies, breaking up the back-to-nature theme.

Still, I was slightly bothered by the game's ripple on the glass-smooth sanctity of the journey. I mean, really. What would Waldo think?

MOUNT HOOD is the second most-climbed mountain in the world—true *mountain*, not, say New Hampshire's 3,165-foot Mount Monadnock, the Emerson and Thoreau writing subject so often touted for its present-day popularity. Only Japan's Mount Fuji is more popular. Some 10,000 people attempt to summit Mount Hood each year, more than a few enjoying the expensive pampering at Timberline Lodge along the way. In the early 2000s, in fact, I got an early morning phone call from a Portland friend who was standing atop the tennis-court-sized summit. In 1891, when Waldo arrived here, however, he and his men would have seen few others, even at a mid-level base camp.

In July that year he and his party had gone from Salem to Clackamas to the Columbia Gorge, where they had headed east. They explored Eagle Creek, then swung south at Hood River at what was now Highway 35 to Government Camp. Waldo wrote little about the mountain, only that two of his friends would summit Mount Hood in a few days, but he would not be among them.

"Sick to-day," he wrote. "Was taken with a violent pain in my right lung early last night. Hunter put on a mustard plaster which relieved it by morning, but leaves me to-day in a condition that prevents any mountain climbing for the present. Was in bed nearly all day."

THE WIND HOWLED Saturday night, but I felt a certain peace as sleep neared. If our journey were a 1,500-meter race, we had rounded the final turn and were coming down the straightaway. Two hard days and we'd be, in essence, home, with a cross-state walk neatly sealed in our memories. Glenn was as pumped as I was; we'd agreed on leaving fifteen minutes earlier than usual. To him, that meant rising at 4:45 A.M. I set my alarm for 4:35 A.M.

The wind died in the night. When I awoke all was still. A touch of pink colored the eastern horizon; otherwise, we might as well have been getting ready in my father's old basement darkroom.

"Bob, I still don't see how you can get going so quickly," he said.

"What can I say?" A small victory, yes, and some would say an insidious one, but I took a certain fiendish pleasure in being ready before Mr. Eagle Scout.

I looked at my watch. "Hitting the trail at 5:31 A.M. That, my friend, is a record."

"All right," he said. "To the Columbia River."

"To the Columbia," I said.

Headlamps on, we headed west into the darkness on a wide, sandy trail cut into a semi-steep pitch. Glenn led. Above us, to the right, Mount Hood loomed somewhere in the night.

The quiet cadence of boots on trail. The feel of bones and muscles awakening to the challenge ahead. The look of the bordered-in-rock trail, only a small swath of it awash in the light from my headlamp—the headlamp that now brought into view a wooden Pacific Crest Trail sign. We'd seen dozens of such signs at trail junctions and this one looked no different than all the rest except—

Except for the 8½-by-11-inch red sign below it, flagged by pink "notice-me!" tape.

"Glenny, hold on!" I called ahead.

I bent over and shined my light on the red sign:

> PACIFIC CREST TRAIL CLOSED
> FROM RUSHING WATER CREEK
> SOUTH OF RAMONA FALLS TO
> WAHTUM LAKE DUE TO WILDFIRE
> A PCT WALK AROUND ROUTE WILL BE POSTED SUNDAY, SEPT. 4TH.
> THANK YOU FOR YOUR COOPERATION!

My gut dropped like Disneyland's Tower of Terror. Beneath the sign was an official order, the fine print as it were. But big, red type or small black-on-white type, it all added up to the same thing: Disaster. I looked off to the east, to the thin strip of red, as if looking away would make the reality go away.

I am, by nature, an optimist. When my computer crashes or a key source for a column isn't available as my deadline approaches, I despair momentarily then shift into "Plan B." But a quick cell phone call to a local ranger station—I found the number in the fine print—connected me with a night-shift ranger who only made the situation bleaker. With my iPhone on speaker so Glenn could hear, the ranger painted the PCT fire danger as extreme, the alternative route as iffy at best—and of little priority. "It could be three or four days before we come up with some sort of alternative route," he said.

Conversation over. Glenn and I needed to be back at work Wednesday; we couldn't be waiting around for days for a detour route.

"Doesn't look good," said Glenn.

I didn't say anything. What could I say? Ninety percent of the trail done; ten percent left. This was the Pacific Crest Trail version of having the brass ring firmly in hand, then feeling it slip away.

Without speaking, we trudged toward the Timberline Lodge parking lot. I didn't know what Glenn was thinking; disappointment for sure, but probably not laced with the poor-me self pity that I'd already started sliding toward. Glenn was steadier, less emotional, more stoic. A bus in Haiti crashes. You don't freak out. You work overtime, then, while everyone is eating, start setting up the makeshift clinic back into a church for that night's service.

Me? All I could think of was how the two of us, for more than a year, had planned, trained for, dumped a couple thousand dollars into, and dreamed about this border-to-border trek; had overcome an array of obstacles to get this far; had even brought along some of *The Register-Guard's* 65,000 readers for the second half of the journey.

And now, because of something we had no control over, it was over.

Part V
The foreboding trail

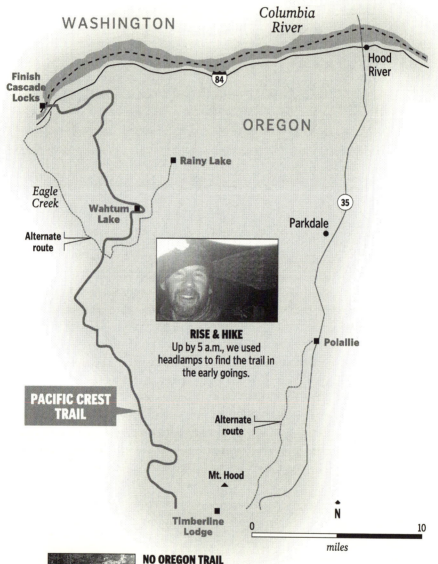

RISE & HIKE
Up by 5 a.m., we used headlamps to find the trail in the early goings.

PACIFIC CREST TRAIL

NO OREGON TRAIL
Bugs, right, and Bunny, of Israel, camped two nights with us, among nine foreign hikers we encountered. Only ten thru- or section-hikers we met were from Oregon, thirty-eight from other states.

Every journey has a secret destination of which the traveler is unaware.

—Martin Buber

21. Dreams deferred

Trail log: Sunday, September 4.
PCT mile-marker: 2110.8.
Days on trail: 23.
Elevation: 5950 feet.
Total miles hiked: 407.6.

Location: Timberline Lodge.
Miles hiked Friday: 25.1.
Miles hiked Saturday: 8.3.
Average miles per day: 18.5.
Portion of trip completed: 90.1%.

THE BREAKFAST BUFFET was no consolation at all. As good as the Timberline food was, that's how badly we felt. Nobody at the lodge had additional information. A second phone call to another Forest Service office elicited no more hope than the first. The trail was closed by fire six miles from Timberline Lodge for a twenty-mile stretch wrapping around to Wahtum Lake, north of the mountain.

"We'd better call Ann and Sally," said Glenn. I could read between the lines. He was the surgeon looking up at the clock, turning to a nurse and saying. "Time of death: 7:53 A.M." He was the woman at Olallie Lake saying, "Sorry, the only thing we have that's cold is beer and pop." He was the game's final out, the guy at the Oregon Book Awards—where the winners of each category were revealed by the reading of a paragraph from the triumphant entry—starting a passage from a book about the bubonic plague in Hawaii in 1900, and my mother next to me whispering, "Is that yours?" and me shaking my head no, that's not. I'm a runner-up again. The close-but-no-cigar king.

I called Sally.

"Hey, babe," I said.

"Morning, sorry about your Ducks."

"No problem, but a fire has closed the trail."

"Oh, no."

"Yeah, so we're going to need a ride home from Timberline."

"I am *so* sorry."

And I knew she truly was. For fourteen months, she and Ann had been the ultimate team players through all of this, patiently supporting our "little adventure." A defeat for us was a defeat for them. In particular, Sally, as an author's spouse, knew the routine: feast or famine. From researching it to writing it to getting it sold to marketing it, an author's book was an emotional Space Mountain ride. A high-risk, high-reward stock. Mountain top glory and Hell's Canyon despair, as when a subject bails on a project, wasting a year's worth of work.

Sometimes we laugh so we don't cry. "On the bright side," I told her, "we can all have the lunch buffet at Timberline Lodge. So, we've got that going for us, which is nice!"

Her understanding words, short but sweet, took away the sting, grounding me in the reminder that life was wider than a hiking trail. I was still a fortunate man. But if her support was a swab of emotional novocaine, it numbed the disappointment for only a little while, then started to fade. As we waited to be picked up, Glenn and I bumped around the lodge like people leaf through magazines in hospital waiting rooms—trying to act interested but *not*, their minds on bigger things than "Ten Ways to Be a Happier You." We talked, without much conviction, of coming back in a few weeks if we could clear a weekend, but even that was iffy given our schedules.

"I'm going to check out that store down at the day lodge," Glenn said.

I stayed at the main lodge, scrolling through Saturday football scores on my iPhone as the place slowly came to life with people. Most likely the trail-closed sign had been posted in the middle of the night, I figured. If we'd been Coast Guard Mike or Mij, the hiker from Japan, or if we hadn't stayed for the football games but had pressed on, we'd have slipped through before the closure. Or, conversely, I realized, might be heading blindly into a dangerous forest fire zone.

In my state of mind, I self-selected "slipped through," imagining the fire presenting the two hikers no problems at all; after all, such closures were often as much about precaution and potential danger as they were about actual danger. Nobody was saying the PCT itself was engulfed in flames; the fire could be miles from the actual trail.

In Oregon's lightning-prone Cascades, fires and the PCT were like a really long, skinny game of musical chairs. Everything depended on where you were when the music stopped. And unlike the fire near Mount Washington, where we'd been fortunate, this time Glenn and I had been caught with no place to sit.

I wandered up to the second-floor deck and looked back at the Cascades that had seemed so glorious the previous day. Now, the view was tinged with regret. Better make a final Spot Satellite post for readers, I thought. Forty-one characters to sum up the sour end of a fourteen-month story. With cell coverage, I could have posted a longer message—and would later. For now, my thumbs tapped out a final message:

> 4 Sept 8:49 a
> Fire closes PCT.Going home w/hopes 2 rtrn

Wishful thinking, that hoping-to-return stuff. I was no forest fire expert but knew that such blazes didn't behave like the twenty-four-hour flu. Most such fires smoldered for weeks, sometimes months. The Dollar Lake Fire, located just north of Mount Hood, was named for a lake even smaller than my beloved Comma. It had begun, I would later learn, with a lightning bolt that struck on the day before we had returned to Elk Lake for Part II, nine days before it would ultimately force the trail closure.

In the lodge, PCT hikers, including the young man who'd told me never to say "just" when talking of walking across Oregon, were hanging around, like me, lost in limbo. Nobody had any news. Just blank expressions. I looked around at us, nearly a dozen bearded and blistered ragamuffins amid the rustic opulence of the lodge. Twenty-something "kids" and me, two disparate parties who would seemingly have little in common other than a twisting trail that we sometimes cursed when our weary bodies were on it but now were lost without. The trail, I realized, had created a certain oneness that transcended our differences, the specifics of which I could only assume. And, unfortunately, nothing said "we're in this together" like defeat.

Shortly after 10 o'clock, I realized my iPhone battery was getting low and decided to get the charger in my pack. I walked out the lodge, down the steps, and was just reaching into the lower reaches of the outer netting when she startled me.

"You a PCT hiker?"

I turned around to see a woman in Forest Service green and khaki, heading up the steps with purpose. Her badge said "MaryEllen."

"I am," I said, momentarily surprised that she would even consider the possibility.

"Grab any other hikers and meet me in the lodge in ten minutes," she said. "We've got an alternative route for you. We're sending you around the east side."

JOY. PANIC. UNCERTAINTY. The Forest Service's defibrillation paddles had jolted our journey back to life but Glenn, our navigator who needed to hear the re-route instructions, was still at the day lodge. I raced as fast as my blistered feet would allow.

"Follow me, quick," I said when finding him. "We're back in business."

"What?"

"Just come on, man," I said. "They have a re-route for the east side of the mountain, and they're showing us where it goes in five minutes."

Glenn then did a very Glenn-ish thing. He turned and hustled back toward the store from where he'd been.

"What are you—"

"Getting a map," he said. "Ours won't have Hood's east side."

Something, of course, that I hadn't even considered. That was the difference between us. He was the calm, practical, let's-plan-this-thing guy. I was the meteoric, emotional, let's-do-this-thing guy.

In minutes, he was out of breath but on time for the impromptu meeting in the lobby, where MaryEllen Fitzgerald, a special-uses permit administrator with Mount Hood National Forest, had spread her map on a rough-hewn coffee table. She handed the nearly dozen hikers each a four-page handout—one page of trail-by-trail instructions and three pages of marked, photocopied maps, a re-route that had been approved by the U.S. Forest Service and the Pacific Crest Trail Association. To me, it looked no less confusing than, say, the guts of my MacBook Air.

"Got it, Glenn?" I said, hoping for a quick affirmation.

He didn't seem to hear me. He was listening to the conversation, asking questions, then making notes on his handout. Of course he was getting it. Meanwhile, I slipped off with my iPhone and called Sally and Ann, who, I discovered, were on I-5, midway between the Petersen's house in Albany and Salem. The two were glad to hear the news—and even as I babbled on, began making plans for some craft-store shopping in Salem to not waste the miles they'd already put in.

"It's lengthening the trip considerably," I said. "We're looking at getting to Cascade Locks Tuesday instead of Monday. We've already lost half a day hiking."

Not that I was complaining. I was ecstatic we'd been de-fibbed back to life. We would hug Hood's south and southeast flanks for a few hours, then fall off to the east to hit Highway 35, where we had a couple of options to the river from there.

"Oh, and you'll be happy to know," said Fitzgerald, "that there are three major water crossings. Have fun, guys!"

"Sweet," said the young man next to me with a burgundy bandanna tied over his head and a new smile creasing his face. I made a furtive glance at Glenn.

In a few minutes, hikers were tying laces, topping off water bottles, and stuffing into their packs cinnamon rolls and breadsticks they'd grabbed while going through the buffet line. It all had the slight feel of an episode of TV's *The Amazing Race*, folks challenged with racing around the world looking for clues that might help them finish first and win big bucks. A few tourists stopped, puzzled, I presumed, by this rejuvenated collection of trail wanderers.

But that's how it was when you'd lost something and then found it again, in this case, a trail, even if it wasn't the actual PCT. Other hikers may have seen it differently. For me, our getting to continue was grace, pure and simple. We once were blind but now we saw. *Thank you, God. Thank you, Forest Service.*

IN MORE THAN 400 miles on the trail, this was the first time we'd seen a warning sign. It was nailed to a tree in regard to crossing the White River, which fed from the 1.5-mile-long White River Glacier due south from the summit of the mountain. The river had gouged a wide, twisting route out of the rocky moraine. In November 2006, after more than a foot of rain fell on Mount Hood, debris dammed the river high up, then broke loose. More than a million cubic yards of mud and boulders and a million gallons of water roared down the valley, burying a river bed that would later remake itself.

This late in the season, with much of the snow melted, the river's milky-white waters wound down more like a bull snake than a python. But as we watched a party trying to cross it coming toward us, it was clear White River was not to be taken lightly. As we descended steep switchbacks to the river bed, I reminded myself that pride might feel good for a moment but humility could save your life.

"So," I said to the young man in front of me, a twenty-something kid from Michigan hiking with a girl from Texas, "I assume you did a few of these river crossings in California. What's the key?"

"Face upstream. Use your trekking poles to steady yourself. Keep your pack on your back."

The advice proved unnecessary. Though the White was swift and deep in pockets, we were able to cross with a few well-executed leaps from rock to rock. We then scrambled up and over another ridge. As the day wore on, the pattern continued. Up, down, stream; up, down, stream. It was as if Mount Hood were a giant orange squeezer and our challenge was to round a quarter-portion of it: up a slope, down a slope, cross a stream. Repeat.

By now, Glenn and I were on our own; The Young Ones had left us behind. In Waldo's journeys, he mentioned a few times when his party had to split up; because of illness or injury or whatever, some went on while others stayed behind. The most chilling instant I remembered, though, involved a horse whose backbone injury turned into paralysis. "We let her look her last upon her companions, packed and ready for the march," Judge Waldo wrote from Lake of the Woods on September 7, 1888, "and, as I started off, a friendly bullet ended her suffering."

WE HIKED BENEATH four chairlift cables of Mount Hood Ski Meadows, its once-snowy runs now filled with grassy splays of wildflowers; crossed a creek in Heather Canyon with no problem while a waterfall above misted the trail; and then faced Newton Creek, similar in its rocky, pounding nature, to the White River.

To even get down to water level on a steep trail required shinnying down a rope some Trail Angel had rigged; without it, the task would have been like trying to hike down the side of a two-story building. I remember reading that PCT trails weren't supposed to exceed a fifteen-percent gradient. A nice idea, but on the PCT nature clearly batted last.

Newton Creek was to be our final water crossing. Again, a Trail Angel had come to the rescue, having strung a waist-high rope, horizontally, above a six-to-ten-inch log that had either fallen across the stream or been positioned there. The idea was to grab hold of the rope—attached to vertical snags on either end of the creek—to steady yourself while tip-toeing the fifteen feet across.

With a constant roar, the water cascaded down in a rhythm of pools and falls. Though swift and steep, the creek was so pocked with rocks that anyone who fell wasn't going to get swept down to Highway 35. The fear, at least in my mind, was falling and hitting your head on a rock, or breaking an ankle, or the rapids pinning you underwater against a boulder as your pack served as an anchor. One slip and the trip could be over for at least one person. The closer we inched our way to the Columbia—at times quite literally—the more concerned I became about a mis-step sabotaging our success. I remembered World War II books I'd written about how soldiers started "thinking too much" just before they were to be shipped home.

"Me or you?" asked Glenn over the roar of the creek.

"I'll go," I said.

As with Devils Peak, I remembered the one-rung-at-a-time lesson I'd learned while climbing the crane tower above UO's Autzen Stadium: *concentrate on the steps on the log, nothing else.* To do that would be to ignore a larger context that would only invite fear. Instead of boots on a log, I'd be thinking of how narrow the log, how fast-moving the water, how unforgiving the rocks might be. In some situations, imagination was your friend; here, it was not. Here, what mattered was not *imagination* but *concentration*.

I prayed a quick prayer and inched my way out. *Baby steps, baby steps.* At the midway point, I already felt home free but reminded myself to stay patient. *Boots. Log. Boots. Log.* Finally, success. Glenn, too, made it without a problem.

As fit our styles, I mentally fist-pumped the small victory while he pulled out the directions for the revised route and compared them to his map. "Turn right (east) on Gnarl Ridge Trail #652," he said, "to Elk Meadows Trail #645. Turn left (north) on Elk Meadows Trail #645 (north) to Polallie Trailhead on Highway 35."

"Whatever you say."

"I think," he said, "that's where we need to stay tonight, Bob. Polallie Campground."

Given that it was on the main road between Hood River and Timberline, I imagined a fairly large campground. Nice restrooms. Running water. The works. Sure, it was Labor Day weekend and spots might be hard to find, but we were PCT hikers. In a worst-case scenario, some accommodating soul would probably give us nook of dirt to throw our tents on.

"Sounds good."

At the junction where we were to leave the No. 600 trail, one of The Young Ones had stopped for a rest. He, too, was headed for Polallie, he told us, but he and some others planned to keep going beyond the campground.

"When we hit the highway, we're going to have someone hitchhike ahead for some beer," he said. "We're going to do some 'night drunk-walking.'"

"Hmmm," I said, having never heard the term before—and thankful for that.

It sounded, at best, stupid and, at worst, *really* stupid, particularly on the shoulder of a highway with a 55-mph speed limit—at night. Like the sleepover back in my teenage years when a friend and I had lit fire crackers in empty beer bottles, then inhaled the smoke to pretend we were smoking. I had wound up puking my guts out and, if that were not humiliating enough, having to call my mother to bring me home.

"Hey, you're welcome to join us," he said.

It was, of course, tempting, like being invited into an exclusive club whose initiation was, say, crossing a freeway during the evening commute. Not that I hadn't been flattered that he'd asked.

"Thanks," I said, "but I think we're going to stay at Polallie."

"Sounds good," he said, then started picking up the pace to leave us.

"Hey," I said, "stay safe with your, uh, night-walking."

"Oh, yeah."

I looked back at Glenn, who'd heard the whole thing.

"What was I thinking?" I said. "I didn't even check with you. How rude of me."

Dr. Dull was too busy laughing to respond.

BY NOW, late afternoon, the trail paralleling Bluegrass Ridge to Polallie was like a soap-box derby ramp: smooth, gradually downhill, and fast. It paralleled Cold Springs Creek, which made for a fun and frothy companion. All in all, it was a nice way to finish a hike that had begun with a stretch as pitched and rocky as anything we'd encountered, the water crossings only adding to the challenge.

Soon I saw The Young Ones sitting in a gravel turnout fronting Polallie, which, naturally, was nothing like what I expected. Through the trees, I realized it was not a campground but a picnic area consisting of a single picnic table. Not a single camper anywhere. I poked around and wished I hadn't: Empty beer bottles. Fast-food wrappers. Shotgun shells. The place left me uneasy. It wasn't just the realization that we were clearly out of the wilderness. It was something else, something I couldn't quite pinpoint, but *there*.

Waldo would have been perturbed by the garbage alone. In his final years he continued to defend the Cascades as wilds that needed protecting. But, even then, he lamented an increasing disregard for the purity of what he saw as sacred places. From more than a century beyond, we might puzzle over his hand wringing, but it was all relative. In the twenty years he'd been tramping these mountains, Oregon's population had nearly tripled to 413,536 in 1900. The car had been invented. By 1907, the Oregon Auto Association was pressuring counties to put up road signs "so that auto-tourists might be able to find their way anywhere in Oregon." More people were in the mountains. And many lacked his concern for the purity of the places or for the experiences. Wrote Waldo:

> Here I am after the lapse of so many years, sitting on the bank of the [North] Santiam at our old crossing. Then the freshness of an almost untrodden wilderness was around me; now, one hears the rattle of wagons, and sees the evidences of a habitation on every hand. Even the river has a tamer look. How altered—not only the scene, but the thought and feeling of the beholder.
> I am not now entering upon new adventures.

The Young Ones—six of them, one having made the beer run—were finishing up dinner with their jet-boil stoves while sitting in the gravel turnout along Highway 35. Waldo had crossed this route in 1891, though north-to-south after having checked out Eagle Creek, while preparing for the party's attempt to summit Hood.

Glenn scooted close to The Young Ones and, map in hand, was talking "where-do-we-go-from-here?" routes. Meanwhile, I searched for cell service. Nothing. I widened my search. Still nothing. My only hope: Because of the highway cutting a swath in the trees, I'd have enough of a shot to the southern sky that I could send a Spot Connect satellite message. And I did:

4Sept 7:24p
Cmpd@Polallie ne of Hood,rerouted by fire

Soon, The Young Ones started north, alongside Highway 35. Darkness descended. We got water—later, I noticed an oil sheen in an eddy—from Hood River's north fork, set up the tents, and began eating our freeze-dried dinners at the picnic table. It was just us, the sound of the river, and an occasional car on the highway.

"So, Bob, we have two choices," said Glenn, with a serious edge to his voice that immediately worried me, an edge I hadn't heard since he'd offered "The Great Compromise at Grouse Hill" regarding Carrie and Molly. "We can go straight into Hood River, along the highway, about twenty-five miles to the Columbia, and call it good. Or go back into the woods near Parkdale, wind our way up to the west, then catch the PCT near something called Chinidere Mountain, and on down to Bridge of the Gods. Much longer. You're climbing way up, then coming way down."

I had no context for what either of these solutions looked like, only that the first one was on a road—and I hated walking on, or along, roads—and the second one was back in the forest, where we belonged.

A car stopped on the highway and idled not just for seconds, but for minutes, then proceeded. I realized that traffic, because of construction, was being narrowed to a single lane and cars were having to wait for a green light to proceed.

"So, what option do you like?" I said.

"Neither," he said, "but I think following the highway into Hood River is the most practical."

Ouch. "So, instead of going down Eagle Creek as planned, we'd end the trip on a major highway that hits Interstate-84?"

He nodded his head, almost sheepishly.

I shook my head sideways. I was weary. My feet were trashed. My spirits sagged.

"What?" he said.

"That's just not how I imagined us ending our PCT, going 400 miles through wilderness then finishing it by spending twenty-five miles on a major highway with cars whooshing by."

He didn't say anything. I didn't say anything. Another car idled beyond. Then, like that mass of debris that had dammed up the White River broken free, my emotional dam gave way.

"I just—" I tried to talk but the words were stuck. "I just thought it would be cool to finish the trip where our friendship really started, on Eagle Creek. That's all."

That I'd gotten choked up had surprised me as much as it had probably surprised Glenn. Part of it was frayed nerves from too many days on the trail. Part of it was wanting to finish strong, the way we intended to: coming down Eagle Creek. And part of it, honestly, was the uneasiness I felt about this place where we were camping.

"OK, let's check it out tomorrow," he said. "Maybe we can make that work."

I pursed my lips and nodded in agreement but sensed no peace at all about what was to come.

WE CRAWLED into our tents; a Forest Service ranger who'd driven by when The Young Ones were here had told us we were welcome to camp. For twenty-three nights, I'd gone to sleep to the sounds of silence, the only exception being at Deer Lake, on the night before hitting Devils Peak, when seemingly a million bullfrogs serenaded me to sleep with bar songs. Now, even though the traffic was light, I heard every car stop at that red light, idle, then proceed. Finally, after what seemed like agonizingly hours but was probably forty-five minutes, I drifted away.

I awoke at the sound of a snapping twig. I tensed up, the fear magnified by little sense of time or place. *Where was I? What time was it?* When that lens focused—Polallie Picnic Area and, after a glance at my watch, 4:58 A.M.—I relaxed. Just a deer, I assumed. But I heard more crunching, as if someone, or something, was walking. A groan of sorts, like a man who'd been shot or kicked in the gut.

Slowly, I unzipped my tent flap and poked my head out. In the distance: a single light in the darkness. A motorcycle idling up on the highway? Something closer? Of course, I figured: Glenn's headlamp. He must be taking a morning leak. Mystery solved.

But the light started gyrating, like a firefly, up, down, sideways.

"Glenny?" I said.

No response. Another soft groan, a guttural heave. Was someone throwing up?

"Glenn, is that you?"

A weak, "Yeah."

"What's up? What's going on?"

I slipped on my headlamp and walked out of the tent in my long johns. In the headlamp's beam there was Glenn: on all fours, some 20 feet beyond his tent, puking.

"You OK?" I asked.

"No, I'm sick," he said. "Vertigo."

22. The dilemma

Trail log: Monday, September 5.
PCT mile-marker *: Off trail.
Days hiking: 24.
Elevation: 2900 feet.
Total miles hiked: 423.6.
* — *Not valid since we were forced off trail.*

Location: Polallie Picnic Area; driven to Rainy Lake trailhead.
Miles hiked Sunday: 16.0.
Average miles per day: 18.5.
Portion of trip completed **: 92.7%.
** — *Based on mileage only.*

THIS WASN'T SUPPOSED to happen. If anyone got sick, it was supposed to be me with a mastocytosis attack or planter fasciitis feet that just couldn't take another step or a bee sting that erupted on my skin like Mount St. Helens. Glenn was a doctor. Doctors don't get sick. They make people well. Especially my invincible brother-in-law, the Haiti hero.

He heaved again. "I get it every now and then," he said. "I'll be OK." Another involuntary jerk, more vomit spewed forth.

"So, tell me, Glenny," I said, trying to sound calm, "what do I need to do here?"

"I'm OK, just give me a little time."

He returned to his tent, kicked off his boots, lay on his side and slept for fifteen minutes. He then stuck his head out the tent flap and threw up again, scraping the vomit into a hole he'd gouged by using his boot in his hand like a trowel.

"Glenny, really, do we need to get you into Hood River? Do you need me to call 911? Talk to me."

"I just need to sleep, then I'll be good to go."

His illness had nothing to do with altitude, I would learn, a common misconception likely based on the Alfred Hitchcock movie, *Vertigo*, about a detective who suffers from acrophobia, the fear of heights. Ironically, though people linked vertigo to heights, we were at 2,900 feet, the lowest point on the trail since we'd left July 22. Instead, vertigo was a type of dizziness caused by a disturbance in the inner ear.

"Glenn, do I need to call Ann?"

"No, don't call Ann."

He fell back asleep. Puked. Fell asleep. Puked.

Then it dawned on me. Here I was, asking if I needed to call 911 or his wife and I yet hadn't been able to scare up a cell connection the previous night. If he needed medical attention, what were my options? As dawn broke, a car hadn't been by in the fifteen minutes since I'd discovered him getting sick. And even if a north-bound car—Hood River, population 7,000, was our best option—did come by, what were the chances of the driver—in near darkness no less—being willing to take us a half hour to a hospital emergency room or Doc-in-a-Box?

To an outsider with little context, we looked and smelled homeless, like vagabonds. And one of us was puking every five minutes—yeah, that one I would keep telling the driver was actually a doctor. "Yeah, right," I could hear the guy saying. "And I'm Bubba Watson. Just won the Masters." More likely, he'd think Glenn was some I-84 off-ramp beggar who got flipped a $10 bill and overdid it last night on malt liquor. *Sure, I'd love to have you in my backseat. Climb in. Throw up all you want.*

I was over-thinking this. *Don't get lost in the emotions; don't be a Bob. Be a Glenn. Ask: What was happening and what needed to happen?* What was happening, I believed, was that my brother-in-law was trying to be heroic. And what needed to happen was a conversation with Ann. She knew Glenn. She knew this condition. And she would know what to do. But could I find a connection?

I went back to the tent and grabbed my cell phone. Glenn leaned out and puked again.

"I'm calling Ann," I said.

"No, don't," he said. "It's not necess—" And retched again.

In a moment of clarity, I realized why he didn't want me to call Ann: because to do so meant his PCT trip was over. To wave the white flag. To quit. And after fourteen months in the mindset of reaching the Bridge of the Gods, who could blame him? In his position, I probably would be just as obstinate. No, *more*.

"I'll be right back," I said, "and, don't worry, I'm not calling Ann."

I started running beyond the canopy of trees, up to the graveled wide spot on the highway, some 200 feet away. No bars rose on the phone to indicate available cell phone service. *Please, Lord, please. A connection, please.* (Did God really respond to cell-service concerns? I mean, in a world racked by hunger and strife and war, didn't he have bigger fish to fry? But the Scriptures speak of praying in all things, and pray I did.) Nothing. No bars. I walked south. I walked north. I walked east. I walked west. No bars.

OK, *think*. With no phone option, two choices remained. The area was open enough to the southern sky that I'd been able to get a Spot connection the previous night. With a touch of the finger, I could send an SOS message. But do you call for the cavalry—at who knows what expense?—when you're on a major road a half hour from at least a small-town hospital? When your brother-in-law suggests it is no big deal even though, from your perspective, it seemed to be? It was like the Devils Peak situation. I wanted the choices to be black or white, either simple to move forward or impossible.

Likewise, I wanted this decision to be decisive: if his condition really was serious, I needed to ignore his "I'm OK" stuff and either hit SOS on the Spot Connect or drag him up to the road and flag down a Good Samaritan. If his condition was *not* that serious, I needed to trust his judgment that he just needed to sleep. Make sure he stayed warm. Get water if he needed it. And, meanwhile, with the day getting light, flag down a driver who, with phone service in Hood River, could get instructions to Ann about where we were and what was happening—even though I'd have no way of knowing whether the person had relayed such instructions.

The idea of hunkering down in this campsite for a day or two while his vertigo ran its course seemed foolhardy; even if he got better, he would be in no condition to walk twenty-five miles in two days. And not allowing Ann to weigh in on the decision seemed unfair to her—and flat-out negligent on my part.

Frankly, I didn't like either option: SOS or hunkering down until he got well. For now, I needed to get back and check on him. I took one last glance at the phone when I saw them: two tiny bars next to my phone's "Verizon 3G." *Praise God.* I punched her speed dial number.

One ring. Two rings.
Pick up, pick up.
Three rings.
Pick up, please.

Four rings. Another problem, I realized while waiting: my phone's battery was down to twenty percent, getting close to the "low battery" level.

"Hello?"

"Sally, it's me." Obviously, I'd awakened her. It was around 6:30 A.M.

"Is everything all right?"

"Glenn is sick," I said. "Vertigo. I want to give you our location right now. Can you get a pen?"

"Getting one." She sounded half asleep, which, of course, she was. "OK."

"We're on Highway 35, about twenty-five miles south of Hood River, at Polallie Campground. P-O-L-A-L-L-I-E. East side of the road. By some road construction. Got that?"

"Got it."

"He didn't want me calling Ann, but she needs to come pick up Glenn. Nothing life threatening; he's had this before."

"Yeah, he has."

"But he's too sick to go on. He's being stubborn, but she needs to come."

"OK."

"So you call her, then have her call me, OK? I need to go because I'm low on battery and I need some for her phone call."

"Got it."

Ten minutes later, my phone buzzed. I explained the situation to Ann. As I expected, she was cool, calm, and convinced that picking him up was the right thing to do, regardless of what he said. She would be on her way in fifteen minutes—and said she'd bring food and drink for me.

"Don't worry about that," I said.

"I assume you'll be continuing on," she said. "No reason not to. You're so close."

When I got back to Glenn, he was fast asleep. Later, when he awakened so he could puke again, I broke the news. "I talked to Ann," I said. "She'll be here in about three hours."

At first he didn't say anything. Technically, I hadn't called her, but he didn't know that. Was he mad?

"Good," he said. "That's good. Thanks, Bob."

He seemed relieved. I was relieved. Like the prodigal son in Luke, he'd finally gotten over his pride and "come to his senses." He realized he needed to return home.

"Bob," he said while still lying on his side in his sleeping bag, "call her back and tell her to make sure she fills up with gas in Hood River."

"OK, but why?"

"Because she needs to get you up to Rainy Lake, and it's a long way up there."

"Why Rainy Lake?"

He took a swig of water. "I've been thinking of a route for you that might let you finish by going down Eagle Creek."

"Glenn, I don't need to—"

"No, no, no, this will work," he said. "And it's in line with the Forest Service's new route; just a little variation. Get me my map. It's in my backpack."

I handed it to him.

"You start at Rainy. You go south on the Rainy-Wahtum Trail Number 409 to Anthill Trail Number 406B. Yes, *away* from the Columbia River." He paused. Dry heaves.

"Glenny, you don't have to do this. Just sleep. Really."

"You'll then have two choices. Go left to the Wahtum Lake Campground. There, you'll see the Pacific Crest Trail—Number 2000. If you take that down, you'll come to Cascade Locks and the Bridge of the Gods, but if you want to take Eagle Creek you need to take 440, it'll take you to 433, the Eagle Creek Trail. And you're home free."

I had only the vaguest idea of what he was telling me; having not hiked this area, I had no starting-point context. For now, there was only one thing to say.

"Glenny," I said. "Thanks."

He went back to sleep.

ANN MADE good time. She arrived three hours after she'd hung up the phone—and came with food, drink, and, yes, a full tank of gas. By then, Glenn was outside, sitting with his back to a log. He had all the pizazz of a store-front mannequin.

"So, here's the patient, huh?" said Ann, getting out of the Izusu Trooper. She didn't rush to him with open arms. Instead, she knelt to take a photo.

"OK, Bob, now one with you in there, too."

How could she be so calm? I reluctantly bent onto one knee and put my arm around Glenn and forced a smile.

"Bob, get the other maps out of my pack," Glenn said. "They'll help."

I did so, feeling like a soldier might feel taking ammo off a wounded buddy's body. This was not right.

I headed for the car to plug in my iPhone to get as much GPS juice as possible before hitting the trail. Meanwhile, Ann's more compassionate side came out as she went to Glenn, asked how he was doing, got him water, and prepared to get him into the car. Once we were ready to go, Glenn gave her driving instructions.

"There's a park in this place called Parkdale," he said. "You're going to drop me there. I'll sleep. Then you take Bob up to Rainy Lake. It's going to take a while. You have to go up all these Forest Service roads. Steep stuff."

When we arrived at the park, Glenn greeted it by throwing up again. Finished with that, he went over the map with us both, best he could, so we knew where we were heading, then reclined against a tree trunk. I didn't like leaving him like this. Ann got him his water, his sleeping bag, some soda crackers.

Meanwhile, I called Sally, and told her the plan. Glenn was coming home with Ann. I was finishing the final twenty-four miles this afternoon and tomorrow. I was coming down Eagle Creek, would then walk east along I-84 for a few miles, and meet Sally at the Bridge of the Gods about 3 P.M.

"Be safe," she said. "I love you."

"Love you, too," I said. "I'm ready for this to be finished. Anxious to get home."

I turned back to Glenn, who was stretched out on his side, glasses off. He looked pale.

"Shouldn't we tell the campers across the road what's going on?" I said to Ann. "I mean, really—I'm not trying to be funny—but he looks like a homeless drunk. It'd be good for someone to know what's going on, just in case you get delayed getting back or something."

Ann vetoed that idea without checking with Glenn. "He'll be fine," she said. For a final time, Glenn turned to her to double check that she understood the convoluted route to Rainy Lake. She said she did.

The gravity of the moment suddenly hit me. Unlike the Oregon Boys' parting at the Diamond Lake cutoff, this time there wouldn't be a reunion. More than a year of planning and nearly a month together on the trail together, of overcoming snow, mosquitoes, rocks, rivers, and too many bad jokes to count was now all for naught in terms of us standing together on the Bridge of the Gods and posing for that photo by the "Entering Washington" sign. I blinked back tears and instinctively turned away from Glenn to Ann, which seemed the safer refuge.

I looked back at Glenn, wiping my eyes, and bending onto a knee. "It just doesn't seem fair that I get to go on and you don't."

I put my hand on his shoulder. "Take care" was all I could manage.

Glenn was his usual stoic self—or at least looked it. In sickness or in health, his face did little to reveal the deeper feelings. "Finish strong, Bob," he said.

And, with that, the Oregon Boys parted ways again.

23. 'Evacuate'

AFTER MORE THAN an hour's drive on gravel roads that snaked high into the Hatfield Wilderness Area, we saw a Rainy-Lake-ahead sign.

"You can just drop me off here," I said. "I can get to the trailhead."

"Nuh-uh," said Ann. "I can't go back and tell him I got you *almost* there. Glenn doesn't want you getting lost."

She smiled. I smiled. I felt twelve years old. At the trailhead, I hugged her goodbye, said thanks, and started down a trail I never expected to be on. By myself. And heading *away* from my final destination, the Columbia River and the Bridge of the Gods. Everything about this new scenario seemed wrong.

I understood the method to the madness of hiking southwest. Unlike city streets, forests, usually because of slopes, weren't neat north-south grids where you could often get to where you wanted to go by heading the general direction. The only way I could come down the Eagle Creek Trail was to backtrack southwest to Wahtum Lake, head west, then catch the Eagle Creek Trail for the steepest drop of the trip, 3,500 feet in a fifteen-mile plunge.

What was harder to understand was the idea of hiking by myself. Going solo wasn't uncommon on the PCT; Laura Buhl, my inspiration, did the entire trail in 1999 by herself. Going solo when you've had a partner through all the planning, training, and nearly a month on the trail—therein lay the dissonance within me.

Lonely wasn't the best way to describe my feelings, at least at first; I'd hiked some 200 miles by myself in preparation for the trip, and, frankly, enjoyed it. I often sailed alone and have enjoyed golfing alone, too.

Incomplete. Maybe that was it. Incomplete with a side order of survivor's guilt. Never mind that before the trip Glenn and I had agree that, when practical, if one of us had to quit, the other should feel free to continue if the can't-go-on guy was OK. Still, as I'd told Ann and Glenn back at the park, it didn't seem fair.

Did I want to continue? Sure, I couldn't deny that. The fire-mandated alternative route—going east around Hood rather than west—had tainted the purity of my complete border-to-border trip on the Pacific Crest Trail. But I still yearned to, in essence, complete the PCT—and to finish it on the same trail where Glenn, Ann, Sally, and I had forged our friendships nearly four decades earlier. Now I had that chance, thanks to Glenn not only expecting me to continue, but giving me the directions—and encouragement—to make it possible.

The trail was smooth, the afternoon mild, the view of Mount Hood's north face inspiring. The only thing even mildly disconcerting about the conditions was the low feathering of smoke at the base of the mountain, obviously from the Dollar Lake Fire that had diverted us the previous morning. Two ridges separated me from the fire, which was much farther east than I'd imagined, considering it had closed the west side of the mountain. Still, there was something eerie about being alone in a forest and seeing that smoke.

After five miles of easy hiking, I noticed, through the trees, Wahtum, a good-sized lake my father used to fish as a young man. While popular for hikers starting from the Columbia Gorge, it was also accessible by a twisting gravel road from the south. That's why as I neared the campground area—a well-developed, well-maintained campground—I expected to find gobs of campers; after all, it was Labor Day and two hours from Oregon's largest city, Portland.

Not a single person was at Wahtum Lake and only one vehicle. It was a white SUV with a flier under its windshield whose bold warning gave me the shivers: "EVACUATE. Because of a nearby fire … ." Nearby, at a trail junction, a sign was posted: "Wahtum Lake Campground is closed due to fire activity in the area." I looked around, the quiet tinged with subtle trepidation, the kind Hitchcock employed so often in his films. The kind that left the viewer feeling fear though nothing in the scene screamed fear.

Now I felt lonely.

EARLY ON, I'd been high on perches with far-ranging views to the south and southeast, and seen that the fire was far, far away. Later, I'd been on ridges with views to the south-southwest. No fires at all. But perceptions of the forest were one thing, perceptions of one's self were another. I couldn't shake the spooky feel of Wahtum Lake.

In more ways than one, I was in unfamiliar territory. Normally, to feel as if you're the only person in a forest might carry with it a sense of wonder, honor, privilege—*something*. And, yes, I felt a touch of that. But I also felt uncertainty. After checking my map and heading down a bazillion wooden steps toward the lake, such feelings gave way to concern, like a concerto in which the kettle drums get louder and louder until they drown out whatever melody the other instruments are playing.

At lake's edge, I started around the trail, toward the west, but it seemed surprisingly small and untraveled. Could this really be the connector I wanted to get to the Eagle Creek Trail? In Glenn's explanations of where to go, I'd jotted notes on the Forest Service's "Dollar Lake Fire Detour" handout and looked at the map, but somehow this final part was still fuzzy in my mind.

I stopped, reminded myself not to panic, and pulled out my iPhone to check my GPS. I then checked my map. Yes, probably, this was what I wanted. This must be Trail No. 440, which would zigzag down to Eagle Creek. But I wasn't completely sure. On the map, I also saw where the actual PCT came right by the Wahtum Campground up above, where I'd just been. And I could see clearly that this route would connect me with the Eagle Creek trail. What's more, the PCT paralleled a road, meaning yet another landmark to help me know exactly where I was.

If someone were around, their answer to my question probably would have solved my dilemma. If Glenn were around, there wouldn't *be* any dilemma. But nobody was around. I chose to return to the security of the actual PCT.

The trip back up the wooden campground steps melded my shirt to me in sweat. My heart pounded. I looked at the white SUV with its "EVACUATE" sign on the windshield. If this were truly an off-limits area, why did the Forest Service's "Dollar Lake Fire Detour" handout—

as part of the alternative route Fitzgerald had given to PCT hikers—say, at one point: " …. or you can go left on Anthill Trail #406B to the Wahtum Lake Campground?" Clearly, Wahtum Lake was "fair territory" for PCT hikers going east around Mount Hood on the re-route. But, why, then, wasn't it fair territory for campers? Too many questions, not enough answers.

By now, it was late afternoon. With my iPhone GPS on, I got on the road and headed southwest, anxious to find the cutoff that would take me north-northwest, to my right, down the mountain to Eagle Creek, where I planned to camp. For the first time in hours, I allowed a little whimsy to poke its head over the fence and comment on what was happening here: For nearly a month, Glenn's trail guiding—and, for a week, Cisco's and Roadrunner's—had kept me on course. Now, a mere two hours after starting out by myself, I'd already willfully strayed from that course. And why? Because a trail hadn't *felt* right. I could see the headlines now: *Lost Hiker Said Trail Didn't 'Feel' Right; OSU Friends Blame UO's Liberal Arts Education*. This newspaper account, of course, assumed that I would be found.

I mentally shook my head and moved on. The view from the ridge was incredible. To my left, Hood rose proudly above the skirt of smoke below. Ahead, ridge after ridge and millions of trees stretched west to Portland, the only blight an occasional clearcut, among the first I'd seen on the trip. The blue dot on my GPS kept getting closer to a campground marked "Indian Springs." That's where I was to find the junction to a spur that would take me to Eagle Creek: Trail 435, according to the map.

I kept following the road, kept checking my GPS, kept sipping water and throwing back trail mix. I was hiking Waucoma Ridge, on which three things bothered me: First, that I was still walking *away* from my ultimate destination, the Columbia River—heading southwest; second, that although the eventual idea was to "fall off the shelf"—head down to the river—I was climbing *up* with each step I took, by now far above and beyond Wahtum Lake; and, third, that the sun was getting low in the southwestern sky.

It was a mind game, really. Intellect vs. imagination. The map, the blue dot on my GPS closing in on the junction, the estimated eight to ten miles between me and the fire, the still-shining sun—all suggested safety. But the imagination was a double-edged sword, able to help the artist create beauty—or a lone hiker create doubt. Miss this junction, I realized, and darkness would be on me like a blanket.

By now, I'd left the road and was on the clearly marked PCT that had twisted from the south side of Waucoma Ridge to the north. I was going the opposite direction that north-bound PCT hikers would be on right now—that Glenn and I would have taken if the fire hadn't closed the trail and he hadn't gotten sick.

I checked my map: The little camping symbol—white tepee on a black background—was only about a quarter-mile away. But maps, I'd learned, could be deceptive. Inaccurate. Like on Day Three, in southern Oregon, when we'd gotten off on a trail that wasn't actually the PCT but our non-updated maps suggested was.

I hoped the junction would be as well-marked as a freeway exit. But I wasn't taking any chances. For all I knew, this spur to Eagle Creek could be used so little that overgrowth had all but obscured it. I began looking for anything that resembled a trail heading off to my right.

Perhaps there would be a few campers at this Indian Springs Campground who could confirm where Trail 435 was. On September 19, 1888, Waldo was in southern Oregon and suspected, but wasn't sure, that he and the boys needed to get off a wagon road and back in the woods en route down to Mount Shasta. "A wagon came by with a man, two women, sisters from their looks, two babies, and a small boy. The man was Mr. Humphrey of Pelican Bay, Klamath Falls. He confirmed our impression we had gone far enough on the Wagon Road; so we turned into the woods again, toward the Southeast."

I could use a Mr. Humphrey about now. But as a lone picnic table came into view, I realized that the campground was nothing more: just one picnic table and a few flat spots for tents. No people. No trail junction. No end to this sense that I was alone and, if not lost, then not completely found either. It was an odd sense: Knowing exactly where I was, but not knowing the whereabouts of the path I needed to take.

I continued west on the PCT, cautioning myself not to panic because the map actually showed the cutoff being just west of the little black tepee. After a few hundred feet, however, I was surprised to find no junction. Ahead I saw what looked like a trail-side pyramid of rocks. That must be it. As I rose higher and higher on the trail, a view to the north now opened up of Mount St. Helens and Mount Adams to the north. But when I reached the junction, I realized it was the junction for the Indian Mountain trail heading up to my left, not down to my right.

My pulse quickened. Clearly, I'd come too far. My iPhone was nearing the "low battery" level, but I turned it on, the blue dot of my GPS confirming that I must have overshot the trail. I picked up my pace and headed downhill, back to Indian Springs. I walked to the back of the clearing on which the picnic table sat and worked my way around its edge, right to left. Finally, far to the left, there it was: Trail 435, small, overgrown and easily missed from the PCT. At last, after thirty-six hours of discombobulation—after the trail closure and re-routing at Timberline; after Glenn's illness and our splitting; after my uncertainty with the route to Eagle Creek—I felt back on track.

IT PROVED TO BE a steep, twisting track, a virtual giant-slalom course for hikers: Switchback after switchback on which a slip could send you tumbling down a tree-studded slope. I needed to slow down, dig in my boots. I remembered Waldo's entry about a horse, Gyp, that had slid seventy-five feet to its death in the river. Since hitting the Eagle Creek area, I'd been like the proverbial horse seeing the barn—even if I had only another day of hiking beyond tonight. My thoughts: *Don't be a Gyp.*

If now hiking with more caution, it was also with increased enthusiasm, knowing that each step, finally, was getting me closer to the Bridge of the Gods. As darkness began swallowing the day, I found—just in time–the first flat spot for a tent I'd seen since dropping off the edge toward Eagle Creek.

I popped up my tent, got water from a nearby creek, ate, and did something I hadn't done enough on this trip: just sat there in the forest and let the quiet soak in like a hot bath. I had not seen another soul since I'd said goodbye to Ann; if my aloneness earlier had come with an eerie edge, it now seemed a cozy fit for my final night on the PCT. I thought of Glenn, by now, probably home. I thought of Sally, with whom I'd be reunited the next day. And I thought of Judge John Waldo.

"You can hardly imagine," he once wrote from the shores of Odell Lake, "how I enjoy my 'silent hours' on Otter Point."

> Had Emerson had such a study there might have been beauties not now found in his works ... The noise of a waterfall across the Lake, and the occasional splash of a trout as he leaped after a fly, projected the harmony of their sounds into the morning stillness. Three white gulls were flying slowly along the Northern shore, and a fish hawk came out of Trappers Bay and passed around the point. 'The face of nature,' says Emerson, 'remains irresistibly alluring.'"

Likewise, on this last night of the trip, I enjoyed my silent hours on Eagle Creek.

24. The one-handed clap

Trail log: Tuesday, September 6.
PCT mile-marker *: Off trail.
Days hiking: 25.
Elevation: 2,800 feet.
Total miles hiked: 435.6.
* — Not valid since we were forced off trail.

Location: Eagle Creek.
Miles hiked Monday: 12.0.
Average miles per day: 18.1.
Portion of trip completed **: 96.4%.
** — Based on mileage only.

THE YEARS BEGAN taking their toll on Waldo and his health. Edith, the little girl whom he'd once returned from the mountains to greet with a gift pony, was now a grown woman. One of his tramping buddies, Bert Potter, died in 1901.

While the Cascades, officially, had been set off as a wilderness reserve, the federal regulations were often ignored. On September 3, 1903, Waldo wrote from Fish Lake: "The sheep are everywhere and spoil the mountain pastures for campers. Many thousand are in the mountains this year, above the number last year, I suppose, from the new flocks I hear of. I trust they will keep clear of Waldo Lake next year. These mountains belong to all the people and are being monopolized for business purposes by a few."

At the end of each journey, Waldo lamented the coming of fall and winter. "Summer departs lingeringly," he wrote in 1887 from Diamond Lake, "as if loath to leave such a magnificent dwelling place." In September 1905, from Pamelia Lake, he offered this: "To-morrow we leave the lake to the kingfishers, the blue cranes, and solitude. Our stay is drawing to a close. Homeward bound in the morning. This trip with its events will soon in its narrow cell be forever laid."

The next year, also from Pamelia, he told of a horse, Job, that went missing. Waldo found his body in a sink hole. "He had lived evidently quite a while after falling in, and made many efforts to get out. There his bones will lie, and ages hence may be discovered long after we have gone to dust."

In 1906, Waldo turned sixty-two. By then, his battles had been fought, his trips had gotten shorter, and his body was getting weaker. What remained staunchly Waldo was his love for the Cascades and his sense that, despite the reserve he'd helped create, the purity of nature was somehow fading.

"The years roll away and here I am again on my way to the mountains," he wrote from along the North Santiam River soon thereafter. "The almost unbroken wilderness is no longer here. The changes made only by time are probably not very great. The river still flows as of old, and the noise of its rushing waters must be the same, but the waters do not issue out of the old unbroken solitudes and hence there is something missing."

In August of 1907, he returned to his beloved Pamelia Lake beneath Mount Jefferson. In retrospect, perhaps to say goodbye. One day, he hiked alone to Hunt's Cove 1.5 miles away, ostensibly to check on the party's horses. He was due back at 4 P.M. After sundown, two buddies found him walking the shores of Pamelia, not particularly concerned about his late return. "I was tired and hungry, but alright," he wrote, "and to-day feeling better for the tramp."

Sometime between August 14 and 17, he wrote:

> The high wild hills about here, totally unfenced and uncultivated, are good for the eyes that would not have the world altogether cut up into cabbage patches.

After twenty-six years of journaling, they were the last words he would write from the Cascades.

Some of the younger men along on this trip were pining to summit Mount Jefferson. Waldo volunteered to be their guide. A friend, George Downing, intervened to persuade the judge to stay at the base camp. Waldo was tired. He'd seemed disoriented a few days before. But he insisted on going.

On August 17, the party left Pamelia Lake and camped on a ridge at timberline, not far from what would one day be known as Waldo Glacier. In the morning, the others awakened to find Waldo sick, as I had with Glenn just that morning. Though reluctant, Waldo realized he needed to return home. Before going, however, he had unfinished business: He gave the young men specific instructions on what route they needed to take to get to the top, making sure they understood; it was as if their triumph at the top would be his own. He then walked slowly down toward Pamelia Lake.

Downing found Waldo standing on a trail near the lake. His condition had worsened. It would be impossible for him to ride out on horseback; the men would need a stretcher to carry him out of his beloved woods. The slow journey began. It was eighteen miles to Detroit, the nearest town of any size between Pamelia and his home in Salem. It took twenty-four hours to get the judge to Detroit.

Meanwhile, someone in the party rode ahead to get word to Clara Waldo in Salem. She arrived in Detroit, presumably by train, soon after her husband did. She accompanied him back to the family farm in the Waldo Hills. Two weeks later, on September 2, 1907, Judge John Breckenridge Waldo died. He was sixty-three.

A headline in Salem's *Capitol Journal* read: DEATH CLAIMS NOBLE MAN. Part of the editorial below it read:

> He grew up in touch with nature, and he grew great and strong and firm; a man such as nature's teaching molds. To him the mountains with their purpling canyons and glittering snow peaks were a book to which there was no end. The beauty of the hills was a sermon, the whispering trees a prayer, the mountain streams songs of gladness and hymns of peace. The forest was his temple, and there he worshiped. He was of a retiring disposition, almost to shyness, but once known, he was a most delightful companion … .

ON MY FINAL day on the trail, I threw caution to the wind and slept in. I had to hike only nine miles to the Eagle Creek trailhead and a few miles to the Bridge of the Gods. Thus, I rolled out of my bag at 6:30 A.M. instead of the usual 4:50 A.M. There was no Glenn to wake up ten minutes after I did, then listen to him decry his inability to get ready as fast I could. I never did confess to my daily delay in awakening him.

I ate the last of sixty Svenhard's danishes that had started each of my twenty-six days on the PCT and headed down the twisting trail. For the most part, the trip down Eagle Creek—and memory lane—was light, enjoyable, and as beautiful a part of the journey as I would experience.

The Eagle Creek stretch, an approved alternative to the actual PCT trail a few miles east, was like no other part of the PCT I had seen: A dozen waterfalls, some as high as 150-foot Tunnel Falls, pounded their way down the narrow gorge, many interspersed by deep, clear pools.

The path hugged the creek for the most part, sometimes chiseled so narrowly into vertical-wall basalt that trail crews had long ago installed cables for hikers to hold onto. At aptly named Tunnel Falls, I followed a narrow route that had been bored through solid rock *behind* the cascading plume of water.

It was amazing, I mulled, how different the very composition of the trail had been over these twenty-six days: Tunnels. Bridges. Switchbacks. Up. Down. And, every now and then, the rare arrow-straight stretch, though not for long. I'd walked on dirt, rock, sand, scree, gravel, asphalt, shale, lava, cinder, creek beds, mud, pine needles, fir needles, horse dung, and snow—more than fifty miles of it, I figured, roughly ten percent of the trail.

In the higher reaches of Eagle Creek I felt as if I were on my own private path; I hadn't seen another hiker on the trail for nearly two days. The pace, the beauty, the aloneness—soon I was lost in the past. The memories flowed with the ease and beauty of the waterfalls themselves.

Memorial Day weekend 1974. Four college-age kids. Three days. We had come in Glenn's 1952 Chevrolet—if he was a throwback now, he was a throwback then—fueled by wanderlust, each other, and a sack of Arctic Circle fifteen-cent hamburgers we'd picked up in Portland. At the trailhead, we posed for a group photo. (See Page 8.) We were all slimmer. My shaggy hair popped out from my Corvallis High ball cap with the size and whimsy of Mr. Potato Head's oversized ears. With my elbow bent on Sally's shoulder, I exuded cool and casual, my Turkey Bowl jersey untucked. At the other end of the photo, Glenn stood with a certain impish earnestness. Shirt tucked in. Jeans rolled up at the bottom. With his round-rimmed glasses, he exuded a blend of John Denver and Dudley Do-Right.

Nobody stopped to think that Memorial Day weekend might be a tad crowded. By late afternoon, we were scrambling for even a semi-flat place to pitch our tents in the steep canyon.

"Follow me," said Glenn, who led us across a thick log bridging water that was tumbling down at a heart-pounding pace. We followed. I'm not sure anything I've done on the PCT was as foolhardy, given that a single slip and our packs might have anchored us to the deep creek's bottom. As it turned out, the only casualty was my Corvallis High baseball hat, which blew off in the tight-rope-walk across and floated out of my life.

We burrowed in on the other side, spent Sunday day-hiking, and hiked out Monday, the day of the infamous Bob-vs.-Glenn wrestling match in the creek. The weekend galvanized our friendships. Two weddings followed, ours in 1975 and the Petersens' in 1976. The four of us have been great friends ever since. Now, I was glad for a chance to return to where it had all begun and sad that I wasn't hearing Glenn's footsteps along with mine. He had been, as the Salem paper said of Waldo, "a most delightful companion."

SO INTENT WAS I to get to the Bridge of the Gods that I didn't stop for lunch. I did scramble down a steep trail to get a pool-level photo of Punch Bowl Falls because it was beautiful and because my father, as a young man, had taken photos of it from the same spot. Beyond that, my pace picked up as the day deepened—not my usual style.

The nearer I got to the trailhead, the more people I started seeing. First, a day-hiker here or there. Then a trickle of school kids. And, within a mile of the trailhead, a wide assortment of humanity coming at me, including a six-month-old baby in a stroller, which, given the narrow, chiseled-in-rock sections of trail, seemed an invitation to disaster.

Soon I was having to step aside as gaggles of giggly kids marched by in running shoes, Crocs, and flip-flops. Locals. Oregonians, I presumed, on a trail on which there had been so few. Looking back, I could remember only one Oregonian we had encountered—a guy named Rusty, near Hyatt Lake—who was doing the complete state like us. Beyond, of course, the couple who'd turned around south of Devils Peak, the couple who'd hoped to do Oregon.

Now, with the parade of people coming at me, I found myself swept up in a clash of cross-purposes, feeling as if I, not they, were intruding. As if I were that California football player, in "The Play," the famous 1982 game that ends with five laterals and a Bears player crossing the end zone only to run straight into the Stanford band that's heading onto the field to celebrate.

Oddly, the influx of people ushered in a feeling not of assimilation, as if I were now part of something to which I belonged, but of loneliness, as if I were now part of something to which I did not. In 1937, a Coquille, Oregon, service station attendant, Buzz Holmstrom, became the first person to navigate the Colorado River and Green Rivers, through the Grand Canyon, alone. More than a thousand miles. Afterward, when touring the East Coast, he told a reporter: "I felt more lonely in New York than I ever did in the depths of the Grand Canyon." In the smallest of ways, I understood.

Finally, a polite young teenager said hello and asked if I could tell him something.

"Sure," I said.

"How far is it?"

The question took me aback. "How far is what?" I said. "There are lots of places you could hike to—or from. Lots of 'its.'"

"Well, I don't know," he said. "Where did you hike from?"

"You mean today or in the beginning?"

"The beginning, I guess."

"California," I said.

"Whoa," he said. "And where are you hiking *to*?"

The questions sounded like those I'd asked Laura Buhl when first seeing her at Little Belknap Crater twelve years before.

"Just doing Ore—"

I caught myself. "I'm hiking the state of Oregon. Finishing today, in fact."

His eyes widened and he offered what I took as a cross-generational compliment. "Dude!"

AFTER THE Eagle Creek trailhead, I juiced-up my nearly-dead iPhone at a parking lot restroom and called Sally. Traffic from I-84 whirred beyond. Given as much, the scene lacked the ambiance of Waldo's letter to Clara from October 14, 1881: "I shall follow so close on the heels of this letter (if I do not reach home before it) that you can hear all the rest by word of mouth. My tongue will need unloosing after so many days passed without any conversation whatsoever."

Still, the two-mile walk along I-84 to Cascade Locks was far nicer than I expected because I was on the old Columbia Gorge Highway: cool, shrouded in shade, and buffered from much of the traffic noise. I crossed beneath the freeway through a culvert—I preferred the passage behind Tunnel Falls—and soon saw it before me: the Bridge of the Gods, a striking contrast to the naturalness of the trail, all concrete and metal, perched high above the river so ships could pass beneath. A virtual Erector Set that, after twenty-six days of nature, grated against my trail-worn grain of more natural elements.

It was just before 2 P.M. Across the road, in a restaurant parking lot, I saw her: Sally Jean. *She Who Waits.* If there was beauty in Waldo's high mountains, there was beauty at home, too, and I knew which I would choose if I had to choose. For all his love for the Cascades, Waldo, too understood the broader life. On September 5, 1890, he wrote about how there were "other beauties around me: a beautiful, sweet wife, a wise little daughter, and a home of light. My forest life is fitting me to enjoy the treasures awaiting me—a wife, the sweetest of the earth—daughter, the wisest, and a home whose beauties are not so apparent to the mere physical eye in the sketch my little daughter has sent me, but which, to the minds eye, is, in that sketch, the fairest spot on the globe."

Sally and I hugged. "Thanks for being here," I said.

"Wouldn't have missed it."

With permission from the bridge keeper—pedestrians weren't normally allowed on the bridge but exceptions were made for PCT hikers—we ventured forth to the official Oregon-Washington border. Here, the Mexico-to-Canada PCT reached its lowest elevation: 200 feet. I looked down through the grated metal, to the vast waters of the Columbia, a grand river—the 1,200-mile "River of the West" that flowed to the U.S. from farther north than any other river outside Alaska. After weeks of streams and creeks, its breadth was startling; more water coursed through its veins than Oregon's next ten largest rivers combined.

"Oh, my gosh," I told Sally, "this is much scarier than anything on the PCT."

I hadn't thought about how I would react when reaching this bridge, but my emotions did not explode. Satisfaction? Sure. Relief? Definitely. But I'd processed the deeper stuff regarding Glenn, my father, Laura Buhl, Waldo, and the like on the trail itself, and it seemed unnecessary to reconvene with them at journey's end. Oddly, what I remembered on the bridge were the words from the lanky PCT kid at Timberline from two days earlier: "Hey, man, that's a fair piece of trail. Don't minimize it."

I would not. With my piecemeal finish, I'd gone 447 miles, five short of what a true PCT route would have required. I'd taken just over an estimated one million steps, a few, amazingly, while free of blisters. But when I got to the "Entering Washington" sign for the proverbial end-of-journey photo, any sense of the milestone was muted by the one who was missing, the one whose absence precluded a true "Oregon Boys" triumph. The moment had all the energy of a one-handed clap.

I handed the iPhone to Sally for a photo. I put my arm around an imaginary Glenn, thinking of how he would be smiling big beneath that Elmer Fudd hat. And smiled with him.

AFTER FRESH clothes, a huge lunch, and a chocolate malt to go, I sat in the passenger seat as Sally drove. I learned that she had given a couple of PCT hikers a ride to Wal-Mart in Hood River, only to discover they were Bugs and Bunny. The Second Coming of Cisco and Roadrunner, always popping up in the middle of nowhere.

Sally heard tales of the trail. I heard updates of "the fam." At age six, grandson Cade was starting first-grade that week, four-year-old Avin debuting in preschool, and Keaton had not only started walking, but running a bit.

"And Glenny's a grandfather," I said. "Who woulda thunk?"

As the scenery passed, as civilization returned, as time on the trail faded, the question naturally emerged: Was I any different from when I first stepped foot on the trail?

Waldo believed every such wanderer was changed by the endeavor. On September 7, 1896, from Odell Lake, he quoted Emerson: "Is it not true that every landscape I behold, every friend I meet, every act I perform, every pain I suffer, leaves me a different being from that they found me?"

If I was changed, however, it was not in some sweeping, life-altering way, but in rediscovering nuances that had often been lost in my pre-trip life of deadlines, busy-ness, and suburban existence. Beyond renewed confidence in what I could accomplish, it was in the realization that, after shelving my time in the woods, I *could* go home again, both to a place, the Cascades, and to a time, Emerson's "perpetual youth." It was in the discovery that Waldo's wilderness—in essence, my father's end-of-his-movie hope for me—was, for the most part, just that: wilderness so deep and quiet and clean that I hope my father and Waldo would be pleased to see how well it had aged over the decades. Finally, it was in the reminder of the goodness of strangers-become-friends such as Roadrunner and Cisco. And of the selflessness of a brother-in-law who, though forced from the mountains, first showed me the way forward—just as Waldo had done for the young men on Mount Jefferson.

Which reminded me: I needed to call Glenn. Never mind that we were now on a stretch of I-5 just north of Albany that sometimes offered dicey cell coverage, I phoned.

"Way to go, Bob, you made it," he said, sounding far more chipper than the day before.

"Yeah, thanks. How you doing?"

"Much better."

"Good," I said. "I missed your navigational skills."

I told him how I'd nearly become lost. How Wahtum Lake was posted for evacuation. And how I hadn't seen another hiker until late that morning.

He was his usual understated, unemotional self.

"Hey, I haven't puked since Parkdale," he said, then laughed.

"Proud of you, man."

A pause ensued. "Bob," he said, "I just wanna than—"

Then nothing. Dead air.

"Glenny, you there? I think we lost cell service."

"Wanna thank you," he said.

Another pause.

"Glenn?"

We hadn't lost cell service, I realized. He had broken down.

" … for inviting me."

The words weren't coming easily for him. This from a guy whose emotions ran like Thielsen Creek, swift and deep, but, for the most part, hidden beneath the snow.

"It was," he said, "the trip—the trip of a lifetime."

Now it was my words that were log-jammed. "You're right," I finally managed. "It was. It really was."

Epilogue

ON SEPTEMBER 18, Cisco (Rich Combs), after 1,370 miles on the trail from northern California, reached Manning Park in Canada. Roadrunner (Baerbel Steffestun) was not with him. Because of a leg injury, she had been forced to stop August 31—the day Glenn and I had arrived at Olallie Lake. In November 2013, the two planned to watch a total eclipse of the sun in Australia, then go to New Zealand to hike Te Araroa ("The Long Pathway"), a new 3000-kilometer trail stretching from Cape Reinga in north New Zealand to Bluff in the south.

BEN AND KATE, the Australian hikers we'd met within moments of arriving near the Oregon-California border and were the first to complete the entire PCT in 2011, worked for awhile in Canada before returning to Australia. Ben did not kayak the Amazon River or sail around the world; those dreams are still in the blueprint stage. But he did plan to hike the Bicentennial National Trail up the east coast of Australia in January 2013. And he and Kate were toying with the idea of bicycling through Southeast Asia.

IN JUNE 2012, I got an e-mail from a Rob Widmer, the founder, with brother Kurt, of Widmer Brothers Brewery in Portland. He'd come across some online reports I'd posted from the trail in 2011. That same summer, he and his wife, Barb, had been hiking south near Highway 140 in southern Oregon after aborting an attempt to get beyond Devils Peak. They'd warned a guy and his brother-in-law of the dangers. By any chance, was that me and my brother-in-law? And so began a number of e-mail exchanges between Rob and me as he and Barb readied to climb back on the PCT horse and ride again. They started July 22. With Oregon experiencing a rare rash of triple-digit temperatures, Barb was forced off the trail August 13 after showing signs of heat exhaustion. She had made it to Timothy Lake, just south of Mt. Hood. And, when completing an earlier section near Mt. Washington, had now hiked every section of the Oregon PCT at some point in her life. Rob continued on, arriving at the Bridge of the Gods August 16.

BECAUSE of the Internet, I was able to track down Natsuki "Mij" Tsuboi, the Japanese hiker we met the day before reaching Timberline and saw the next day at the lodge. Though I assumed he and Coast Guard Mike made it around Mount Hood before the trail was closed because of the Dollar Lake fire, I was wrong. He told me he was forced to leave the PCT about ten trail miles from Timberline and hitchhiked around to Cascade Locks to continue. He reached Canada on October 5. Ten days later the Dollar Lake Fire on Mount Hood was finally contained. Tsuboi returned to his job as a wood stove salesman in Gunma, Japan.

FOR THE 2011 season, the Pacific Crest Trail Association issued 673 thru-hiker permits for those hoping to hike from Mexico to Canada. In most years, estimates the PCTA, 60 percent who start make the entire distance. However, because of the unusually heavy snow, PCTA Trail Information Specialist Jack Haskelt said 40 percent, at best, did so in 2011.

FIGURING IN my piecemeal last three days, I finished with 447 trail miles, five short of Oregon's PCT's mileage. I averaged 17.2 miles per day for the twenty-six days, 18.6 per day discounting partial days. From February 2011 when I started serious training to the end of the hike I had lost twenty-seven pounds, Glenn about the same amount.
    Unlike some long-distance hikers, I had little difficulty resuming my non-trail life, picking up with column writing, book writing, and, with the arrival of fall, college football watching. The only oddity: nightly dreams of the trail. Weird dreams of trying to follow a never-ending

PCT confined to a frustratingly small area. But, eventually, the dreams went away.

However, the lost weight returned—most of it. Beyond my day job as a columnist, I wound up tending to three books at various points in their life cycles; putting on my annual writers workshop on the Oregon coast; and helping launch a marriage coaching program at our church. In the spring, during a three-month period, I contracted shingles and experienced an eighteen-day mastocytosis attack, my worst ever.

In other words, by July 2012, I was hardly the well-conditioned hiker I'd been the previous summer, nor was Glenn. What's more, emotionally, he had just withstood the unexpected death of his eighty-five year-old father, Paul, who I'd last spoken to on the August afternoon he and his wife, Pauline, had bid us farewell at the Elk Lake Trailhead.

But Glenn and I had promises to keep—promises we'd made each other soon after our PCT journeys had ended. So, in July we threw ourselves into better-late-than-never training for a return to Mount Hood, where we believed we had some unfinished business.

On Friday, August 19, we started for the Columbia River from Timberline Lodge, west around Mount Hood as we had started to do the previous year before the fire and Glenn's illness struck. On the first day it was hot. On the second day we were so whipped after twenty-two miles that we were asleep long before the forest swallowed the last light of day. Meanwhile, we added four extraneous miles by taking two wrong trails, though we still were able to laugh when my GPS indicated we were in McMinnville, a town nearly a hundred miles away. And when Glenn pulled his GPS out of his pocket and its screen was coated with a white, moist, chalky substance indicative of age.

"Aleve tablets," he said. "Guess they got a little sweaty."

But after forty-eight hours, after forty-five miles, and after nearly forty years of growing a friendship on the same Eagle Creek Trail that now became our homestretch, we finally finished walking every step of Oregon's Pacific Crest Trail.

Just after noon on Sunday we reached the Columbia River. There, at the same spot midway across the Bridge of the Gods where I'd half-heartedly done the same by myself the summer before, we smiled for a triumphant photo.

The Oregon Boys: Together at the Oregon-California border nearly thirteen months before. And together at the end.

September 6, 2011: At the Oregon-Washington border on the Bridge of the Gods, Bob celebrates the end of his 447-mile journey with an imaginary Glenn. (Sally Welch.)

August 19, 2012: At the Oregon-Washington border on the Bridge of the Gods, Bob celebrates the completion of their 452-mile Oregon PCT journey with the real Glenn. (Anonymous guy, a drifter, to whom Bob paid $20 to take photo.)

Author's note

AFTER THE trip was over, I thought a lot about the experience. In some cases, I second-guessed some situations, three in particular:

♦ **My blister dilemma.** Though it wasn't a constant problem, I never completely solved the footwear challenge. The irony was that in preparation for the trip I'd read an entire book on care of the feet for long-distance running and hiking and had bought and tested two pairs of boots. And yet in the end I don't blame my Merrells. I blame myself for underestimating how much your feet swell when you're walking day after day. (I'd had few serious blisters while training.) In the end I went with size-10 extra wide boots. I should have gone with 11s.

♦ **The Rainy-Lake-to-Eagle-Creek stretch when, having left Glenn behind, I chose not to take the "connector" trail he recommended.** In retrospect, I should have taken it. But I got spooked, plain and simple. The "evacuate" sign, the lack of people at Wahtum Lake, the sun getting lower in the sky—I let fear influence the decision. And because of it, instead of heading down toward Eagle Creek, I wound up climbing nearly 500 feet in elevation—and away from the creek—before finding another connector trail. All because I wanted the security of the Pacific Crest Trail and a dirt road. The lesson: Don't let emotions override information, which, in this case, would have guided me far more easily to my

Monday night camping spot.

As for why the Wahtum Lake Campground was, because of the fire, posted as off-limits when it was on the recommended PCT alternative hiking route, the Forest Service explained it thusly: The fire was to the south of Wahtum, near the road up to the campground. It seemed wise to close the road and campground to car campers. Hikers, however, wouldn't be any farther south than the lake and, thus, were considered safe to pass through en route to the Columbia.

- **Glenn getting sick.** Given that he was up and around the next day, is it possible he could have continued? Yes, but given how sick he'd been, it's also possible that when faced with the rigors of twenty-four more miles of up-down hiking, he would have struggled mightily—in a far more remote area than we'd just been.

Sally posed the more intriguing question: Had the Dollar Lake Fire not re-routed us, where might we have been that Labor Day morning when Glenn got sick and how accessible would we have been?

In short, in a far worse location than the Polallie Picnic Area.

Beyond our stay at Callahans Mountain Lodge on I-5 and at Lava Camp on Highway 242, Polallie on Highway 35 was the most accessible-to-a-major-road stay of the entire trip. Had we gone west around Hood on the PCT, the plan was to stay at Salvation Spring Camp above Bull Run Lake that Sunday night. There is no cell-phone coverage anywhere in that area. And to reach the nearest accessible Forest Service road would have meant backtracking four miles to Lolo Pass. In short, getting Glenn out of there in his condition would have been nearly impossible.

Later, I realized that had I never gotten cell coverage at Polallie, I could have sent Ann a personal 41-character e-mail message via the Spot Connect satellite, though because it was one-way communication, there would have been no way for her to confirm she'd even received it.

In the end, given the circumstances, Ann's "retrieval" of Glenn was efficient, fast, and—all things considered—best for us all. Adventure necessarily requires the unknown. Rather than bemoan what went wrong at the trip's conclusion, I'd rather celebrate all that went right as Glenn and I experienced one special summer in Waldo's "still woods."

Afterword

By Glenn Petersen

"TRIP OF A LIFETIME," I replied with tears in my eyes and a lump in my throat. Bob was on the phone. He had finished the trek and was calling to check on me. After twenty-four days backpacking on the Pacific Crest Trail, I had pulled off two days short of our destination. Vertigo and vomiting had done me in. When Bob called, I was overwhelmed with a flood of emotions regarding the great summer adventure we'd had.

More than a year earlier Bob had floated the idea of backpacking the Oregon section of the PCT. It wasn't a difficult decision to say, "yes, count me in." I knew Bob would be a great hiking partner. His preparation and unbridled enthusiasm would exceed my own, and I knew he wouldn't easily fade if the going got tough. This was an opportunity to have some fun. I have known Bob for almost forty years. While playing golf with him, I have literally rolled on the ground weeping with laughter, like when he hooked one onto Highway 34 at Trysting Tree Golf Club in Corvallis. Surely, the trip would include such Bob-like moments.

I joined the Boy Scouts at age thirteen. I will always carry a warm place in my heart for my years in scouting. My friends and I went on many weekend camping trips and to many week-long summer camps. Some of the older Scouts had hiked a long portion of the Skyline Trail, parts of which would later become the PCT. Rumor had it they had a terrific time, and I had been envious of their experience. Here was a chance to live a childhood dream.

I checked my Webster's. It defined "adventure" as "a bold undertaking in which hazards are to be met and the issue hangs on unforeseen events." Bob's idea didn't sound dangerous, but to be sure, it had all the elements of a great summer adventure. Would my middle-age body hold up to backpacking 452 miles? I knew how to point a compass north, but could we find and stay on a trail the length of Oregon? What if we packed too little or too much? How would we resupply? How would we get into physical condition? These and a dozen more questions would be answered in the next year and on the trail.

In preparation I ran four nights a week, dieted and lost twenty-five pounds, the equivalent of my fully loaded backpack. I scoured the Internet for insights and advice. I put together a homemade alcohol cooking stove and discarded it. More than one lightweight shelter emerged in the backyard, replaced by the next better idea.

As the departure date approached I was worried. This was a near record year for the level of high Cascade snow pack. The trail was likely to be buried for long stretches. I spent hours researching the right GPS to buy and hours more walking the neighborhood learning how to use it. Dreaming about hordes of blood-thirsty mosquitoes lurking to drive us insane, I absorbed considerable ridicule for my full-length mosquito net suit.

Finally we were off. Along the way I enjoyed it all—spectacular scenery, long miles of solitude, new acquaintances and friends. I enjoyed the satisfaction of backpacking more than twenty miles a day, evening campfires, and sleeping soundly with a boot for a pillow. I had four special days when two of my daughters, Carrie and Molly, joined the adventure at Crater Lake. High in the Cascades, along the flanks of Oregon's peaks, we hiked. Relative amateurs gaining experience and confidence. Crossing Devils Peak and finding the trail mostly snow covered for the next seventy miles. Dodging forest fires and powered more and more by the staples: peanut butter and candy bars.

As Webster says, "The issue hangs on unforeseen events." I never imagined I wouldn't finish because of vertigo. But the success of an adventure is not always hitting the target you envision. Fulfillment begins and builds when you first say yes. Yes to a little risk. Yes to the unknown. And yes to my good friend, Bob.

Appendix

Appendix 1: John Waldo's Twenty-Six Summers in the Cascades

    1880—July 30-September 26, south to Central Oregon's Davis Lake, north to Breitenbush Hot Springs. Climbed the South Sister September 12.
    1881—Waldo's shortest summer, just one day, July 22, Pamelia Lake.
    1882—July 20-September 2. Elk Lake, Davis Lake, Crater Lake, and Black Butte.
    1883—July 30-August 18. Mainly spent in what's now the Willamette Pass area, Davis Lake, and Crescent Lake.
    1884—No journal posts.
    1885—July 30-August 5. Probably along the North Santiam River and at Jefferson (later called Pamelia) Lake.
    1886—July 20-August 9. More than three dozen posts from Diamond Lake in the south to Mount Jefferson. Climbed the Middle Sister August 2; within 100 feet of the top of Mount Thielsen August 25 and, again, August 27; climbed Mount Bailey on the day in between.
    1887—July 7-October 8. Crater Lake to Breitenbush Hot Springs. First report of a stay at Summit Lake.
    1888—July 12-October 6. First exploration of the southern Cascades, including a foray into northern California to summit Mount Shasta Sep-

tember 26. Climbed Mount Pitt (now Mount McLoughlin). Most miles Waldo would record in a single summer.

1889—July 20-29. Headwaters of the North Umpqua to Crescent and Waldo Lake, a short, tight trip. (Perhaps to win back favor with wife Clara after the nearly three-month trip of the previous summer!)

1890—July 12-September 4. Mainly Waldo, Odell, and Crescent Lakes.

1891—July 24-October 16. First—and only—recorded trip to Mount Hood. Traveled north to Eagle Creek July 26. Latest recorded trip into autumn—October 16 on the Santiam Pass.

1892—August 11-September 27. Mainly Odell Lake, specifically Otter Point.

1893—August 2-7. Mainly in the Breitenbush area north of Mount Jefferson.

1894—July 21-September 15. Mainly the Odell Lake, and Diamond Peak areas.

1895—July 16-September 22. Mainly Waldo Lake and Odell Lake.

1896—August 6-September 27. Mainly Odell Lake.

1897—August 2-5. Journal remembers 1886 trip and includes quotations.

1898—September 6-September 29. Waldo's only all-September trip, mainly at Inscription Camp.

1899—No journal reports.

1900—August 13-18. North Santiam, South Santiam.

1901—July 10-September 4. McKenzie Pass and Elk Lake, not the one in Central Oregon but a smaller lake northeast of Detroit near the North Santiam Pass.

1902—August 2-20. McKenzie Pass, mainly Belknap Springs.

1903—August 30-September 9. Hensleys Meadow.

1904—August 6-13. Area north of Mount Jefferson, including Clackamas Hot Springs.

1905—August 9-September 6. Almost all of it spent at Pamelia Lake, west of Mount Jefferson.

1906—August 16-September 4. North Santiam.

1907—August 10-14. Pamelia Lake, Mount Jefferson.

Note: While Waldo's journal covered a span of twenty-eight years, no entries were found for 1884 and 1899.

Appendix 2: My 2011 Oregon PCT hike, day by day.

PART I

Day on trail	Day of wk.	Date	PCT Miles Start *	PCT Miles Finish *	Miles Day	Miles Total	Location Start	Location Finish	Elevation Start	Finish
1	F	7/22	1703.2	1715.2	12	12	Ore-Cal border	Long John Saddle	6100	5900
2	Sa	7/23	1715.2	1730.2	15	27	Long John Saddle	Callahans	5900	4350
3	Su	7/24	1730.2	1752	21.8	48.8	Callahans	Little Hyatt Res.	4350	4650
4	M	7/25	1752	1766.2	14.2	63	Little Hyatt Res.	Griffin Pass	4650	5650
5	Tu	7/26	1766.2	1788.2	22	85	Griffin Pass	Freye Lake	5650	6200
6	W	7/27	1788.2	1801.4	13.2	98.2	Freye Lake	Deer Lake	6200	6150
7	Th	7/28	1801.4	1820.4	19	117.2	Deer Lake	Jack Spring	6150	6200
8	F	7/29	1820.4	1833.6	13.2	130.4	Jack Spring	Mazama Village	6200	7100
9	Sa	7/30	1833.6	1846.8	13.2	143.6	Mazama Village	Grouse Hill	7100	5900
10	Su	7/31	1846.8	1864.4	17.6	161.2	Grouse Hill	Thielsen Creek	5900	6950
11	M	8/1	1864.4	1880.8	16.4	177.6	Thielsen Creek	Tolo Camp	6950	6200
12	Tu	8/2	1880.8	1899.6	18.8	196.4	Tolo Camp	Summit Lake	6200	5600
13	W	8/3	1899.6	1920.8	21.2	217.6	Summit Lake	Upper Rosary Lk.	5600	5850
14	Th	8/4	1920.8	1943.6	22.8	240.4	Upper Rosary Lk.	Jezebel Lake	5850	5650
15	F	8/5	1943.6	1962	18.4	258.8	Jezebel Lake	Elk Lake	5650	5250

PART II

Day on trail	Day of wk.	Date	PCT Miles Start *	PCT Miles Finish *	Miles Day	Miles Total	Location Start	Location Finish	Elevation Start	Finish
16	Sa	8/27	1962	1967.8	5.8	264.6	Elk Lake	Sisters Mirror Lake	5250	6000
17	Su	8/28	1967.8	1991.6	23.8	288.4	Sisters Mirror Lk	Lava Camp	6000	5300
18	M	8/29	1991.6	2012.6	21	309.4	Lava Camp	Above Hwy 20	5300	5300
19	Tu	8/30	2012.6	2032.8	20.2	329.6	Above Hwy 20	Shale Lake	5300	5900
20	W	8/31	2032.8	2056.4	23.6	353.2	Shale Lake	Olallie Lake	5900	4950
21	Th	9/1	2056.4	2077.4	21	374.2	Olallie Lake	Warm Springs Riv.	4950	3300
22	F	9/2	2077.4	2102.5	25.1	399.3	Warm Springs Riv.	Above Hwy. 26	3300	4350
23	Sa	9/3	2102.5	2110.8	8.3	407.6	Above Hwy. 26	Timberline Lodge	4350	5950
24	Su	9/4	2110.8	2126.8	16	423.6	Timberline Lodge	Polallie Picnic Area	5950	2900
25	M	9/5	2126.8	2138.8	12	435.6	Polallie/Rainy Lake	Eagle Creek	2900	3300
26	Tu	9/6	2138.8	2150.2	11.4	447	Eagle Creek	Bridge of Gods	3300	200

* — Miles from Mexican border

Appendix 3: What I took with me.

Backpack—ULA Ohm ultra-light.

Footwear—For hiking: Merrell Moab Ventilators, extra wide, mid-cut boots, SmartWool socks, light liners. For camp: Traded flip flops for Crocs on Part II.

Trekking poles—REI Traverse aluminum.

Tent and sleep-related stuff—Six Moon Designs Lunar Solo tent, four-by-six foot piece of Tyvek house wrap for ground cloth, Therm-a-Rest Z-Lite accordion foam sleeping mat, Mountain Hardwear Phantom 32 down sleeping bag, Exped air pillow.

Water—100-ounce CamelBak bladder, Katadyn Hiker Pro water filter, 16-ounce plastic water bottle for emergency backup.

Food—Utensils: Rubber collapsible cup, plastic fork, plastic spoon. Breakfast: Svenhard's danish variety pack. Lunch: Summer sausage and string cheese for first few days, muffins with chocolate almond spread or peanut butter and jelly, chips in small crush-proof tubs. Dinner: Mountain House freeze-dried meals for two, eaten by one. Snacks: Beef and teriyaki jerky, Clif Bars, trail mix, almonds, Lifesaver Gummies, Good & Plenty candy.

Clothes—For hiking: Columbia wide-brimmed sun hat with neck flap, Nike dri-fit short-sleeve T-shirt, REI ExOfficio Air Strip Lite Long-Sleeve shirt, Columbia six-pocket detachable pants, Under Armor Boxer Jock underwear (thigh length), REI nylon gaiters. For sleeping: Patagonia long johns (upper and lower), running shorts for warm nights and swimming, fresh socks, long-sleeve nylon Eugene Marathon shirt (2011). For cold: Light Patagonia sleeveless vest for Part I, Patagonia down jacket for Part II, Nike stocking cap. For wet: REI poncho. Miscellaneous: bandana.

Toiletries—Miniature tooth brush, travel-sized toothpaste, miniature hand sanitizers, Body Glide, Anti Monkey Butt, Tums, pills (too many), toilet paper (not enough).

Feet care—Duct tape, Leukotape, Second Skin, moleskin.

Skin care—DEET, sunblock, lip balm, mosquito-net hat.

Emergency—Compass, whistle, single-blade Swiss Army knife, two Bic lighters, matches, half-inch adhesive tape, EpiPen, ten-foot nylon cord, Ultralight/Watertight Medical Kit, tweezers, four safety pins, surgical blade, Black Diamond headlamp with two extra batteries, space blanket.

Maps—Hard Copy: Erik the Black's *Pacific Crest Trails Atlas: Volume*

4 Oregon and a National Geographic 1:31,680-scale contour map that was printed on 8½-x-11-inch sheets, with PCT trail and other notes of interest by California hiker trail-named "Halfmile." iPhone: TopoMaps downloads of sections we would hike.

Communication—iPhone 4, half the 2011 Athlon's Pac-12 College Football Preview magazine, cigarette-pack-sized notebook. On Part II added Spot Connect satellite location/communication device and Pioneer satellite radio with headphones for Oregon football game we ended up watching on TV at Timberline Lodge.

Appendix 4: By the numbers

Months of preparation—12. Number of hikes in preparation—27. Average mile per hike—9.4. Vertical feet climbed on those hikes—22,500. Pack weight on PCT trip—28 to 38 pounds. Length of Oregon's Pacific Crest Trail, in miles—452. Total miles hiked—447. Days on the trail—26. Overcast or foggy days—2. Amount of rain, in hours—1. Highest estimated temperature, in Fahrenheit degrees—85. Lowest—35. Estimated steps taken—1,012,075. Average speed we hiked, in miles per hour: 2. Estimated hours spent hiking—224. Equivalent, in terms of 40-hour work weeks—5.6. Average number of hours spent hiking per day—9.3. Time on trail spent reading, in minutes—17. Average miles hiked per day—17.2. Per full day—18.6. Most miles in a single day—25.1. (Warm Springs River to just above Highway 26.) Fewest miles—5.8. (Evening hike from Elk Lake to begin Part II.) Estimated number of thru hikers seen—33. Other section hikers like us—24. Of those 57 hikers, the number from Oregon, excluding ourselves—10. From other states—38. From foreign countries—9. Weight lost during my PCT training and actual hike, in pounds—27. Average elevation, in feet—5,120. Most elevation gained in a single stretch, in feet—2,650. (Warm Springs to Timberline Lodge.) Most elevation lost—3,100. (Eagle Creek to Bridge of the Gods.) Resupply stops—5. Estimated percent of trail with snow on it—10. Number of photos taken (Glenn and I combined)—1,002. Number of modifications made to my hiking boots, excluding failed jam-tub additions—7. (Cut holes in them; wrapped with four kinds of duct tape; shoe shop put leather patches on; replaced leather patches with nylon patches.) Svenhard's danishes eaten—60. Hot dogs eaten—0.

Appendix 5: The best, worst, least, and most. (Epilogue not included.)

Most beautiful views—1. Eagle Creek. 2. Along west side of The Three Sisters. 3. Three Fingered Jack and Mount Jefferson.

Least beautiful view—Just west of Interstate 5 in Southern Oregon.

Easiest stretches to hike—1. Olallie Lake to Warm Springs River. 2. Eagle Creek. 3. Griffin Pass to Brown Mountain.

Most difficult stretches to hike, because of snow—1. Shale Mountain and Lucifer, just before Devils Peak. 2. Just south and north of Crater Lake. 3. Mount Thielsen and just north of it.

Most difficult stretches to hike, without snow—1. Blow-down at Minto Pass. 2. Lava on Brown Mountain. 3. Lava switchbacks at Opie Dilldock Pass.

Funniest line—"And the least likely? That's simple. Elmer Fudd over there." (At Odell Lake's Shelter Cove, fishing guide Mike Jones on which one of us was least likely to be a doctor: Glenn, of course.)

Fewest other hikers seen—Zero in the sixty-mile stretch from Crater Lake to Summit Lake.

Best meal—Timberline Lodge's all-you-can-eat brunch.

Worst meal—Grouse Hill's watery freeze-dried scrambled eggs.

Three best camp sites—1. Thielsen Creek. 2. Upper Rosary Lake. 3. Eagle Creek.

Three worst camp sites—1. Polallie Campground. 2. Freye Lake. 3. Jack Spring.

Worst moment—Saying goodbye to Glenn in Parkdale before continuing on by myself.

Best moments—1. Celebratory dinner with Sally, Ann, Cisco and Roadrunner at Elk Lake to conclude Part I. 2. Reaching the Columbia River. 3. The first step north from the Oregon-California border.

Appendix 6: *The Register-Guard's* "Base Camp" Web site

www.registerguard.com/follow-bob

Includes video slideshow; blog postings and Tweets from the trail; columns I wrote before and after the 2011 PCT adventure; and more.

Bibliography

Allan, Stuart; Buckley, Aileen R.; Meacham, James; Loy, William, editors. *Atlas of Oregon.* Eugene, Oregon: University of Oregon Press, 2001.

Asorson, "Erik the Black." *Pacific Crest Trail Atlas: Oregon.* Sugarloaf, California: BlackWoods Press, 2009.

Bell, Jon. *On Mount Hood.* Seattle: Sasquatch Books, 2011.

Carruth, Gorton. *What Happened When: An Essential Collection of Facts & Dates from 986 to Today.* New York: Harper & Row, 1989.

Cody, Robin. *Voyage of a Summer Sun: Canoeing the Columbia River.* New York: Knopf, 1995.

Conley, Cort; Dimock, Brad; Welch, Vince. *The Doing of the Thing: The Brief Brilliant Whitewater Career of Buzz Holmstrom.* Flagstone, Arizona: Fretwater Press, 1998.

Hall, Don Alan. *On Top of Oregon.* Corvallis, Oregon: Golden West Press, 1975.

Hatton, Raymond R. *Oregon's Sisters Country.* Bend: Geographical Books, 1996.

Hazzard, Joseph. *Pacific Crest Trails.* Seattle: Superior Publishers, 1946.

Hughes, Rees; Lewis, Corey Lee, editors. *The Pacific Crest Trailside Reader; Oregon & Washington.* Seattle: The Mountaineers Books, 2011.

McArthur, Lewis A., and Lewis L., editors. *Oregon Geographic Names*, 7th ed. Portland: Oregon Historical Society Press, 2003.

McDonnel, Jackie. *Yogi's PCT Handbook.* Shawnee Missions, Kansas:

Yogi's Books, 2009.
Miller, David. *AWOL on the Appalachian Trail.* Las Vegas: Amazon Encore, 2010.
Morine, David E. *Two Coots in a Canoe.* Guilford, Connecticut: Globe Pequot Press, 2009.
Patterson, Kevin. *The Water in Between.* New York: Anchor Books, 1999.
Peattie, Roderick, ed. *The Cascades.* New York: Vanguard Press, 1949.
Schaffer, Jeffry P., and Selters, Andy. *Pacific Crest Trail: Oregon & Washington.* Berkeley, California: Wilderness Press, 2004.
Sullivan, William L. *Listening for Coyote.* Corvallis, Oregon: Oregon State University Press,1998.
Vonhof, John. *Fixing Your Feet: Prevention and Treatments for Athletes.* Berkeley, California: Wilderness Press, 1997.
Walth, Brent. *Fire at Eden's Gate.* Portland: Oregon Historical Society Press, 1994.
White, Dan. *The Cactus Eaters.* New York: Harper Perennial, 2008.
Williams, Gerald, editor. *Judge John Breckenridge Waldo: Diaries and Letters from the High Cascades of Oregon, 1880-1907.* Umpqua National Forest Publication #R-6-Umpqua-001-1985, 1986.

Acknowledgments

BEHIND EVERY Pacific Crest Trail hiker is a holy host of Trail Angels. And so it is for every writer. My deepest appreciation for those who helped us make the hike—and the book—possible.

To:

♦ My father, Warren, who, as I inscribed in a book I gave him shortly before he died, "... taught me to love the trees and mountains."

♦ My mother, Marolyn, whose life has been a constant lesson in the things of the trail: bouncing back, carrying on, and taking time to stop and smell the Indian paintbrush.

♦ Laura Buhl, whose 1999 solo completion of the PCT planted the seed of possibility in me.

♦ Gerald W. Williams, who, as a sociologist and social historian with the Umpqua and Willamette National Forests, compiled *Judge John Breckenridge Waldo: Diaries and Letters from the High Cascades of Oregon 1880-1907*.

♦ Bobbie Snead, who not only wrote the book on John Waldo, *Judge John B. Waldo: Oregon's John Muir*, but patiently answered my e-mailed questions during the writing of the book.

♦ Steve Coady, historian and retired U.S. Forest Service information receptionist, who helped me better understand John Waldo and the landscape he traveled.

• Douglas Card, among Oregon's finest historians, for perspective on Waldo and the times.

• Gary Kirk, a Eugene climber/hiker who helped me accurately describe an incident on Mount Jefferson in which he was involved.

• Craig Mayne, whose lessons learned on his own Oregon PCT journey helped me immensely. And who let me test his backpack to the top of Spencer Butte—with a hundred golf balls in the main pouch.

• Bob Keefer, a *Register-Guard* colleague whose son was doing the entire Mexico-to-Canada enchilada and who offered a wealth of advice.

• Keefer's son, Noah Strycker, who discussed strategy with me at Quizno's before he left to attempt the entire PCT. He reached Canada September 18, 2011.

• Ron ("Snowplow") and Julie ("Rubber Legs") Cluster of Eugene, PCT vets who offered an array of pre-trip advice.

• Paul and Pauline Petersen, Glenn's folks, who gave up a Saturday to be our back-to-the-trail taxi drivers so we could begin Part II at Elk Lake.

• Micky Hulse, who spearheaded *The Register-Guard's* blog site for the trip and, for his efforts, won a 2011 Northwest Sigma Delta Chi first-place award.

• *Register-Guard* editors Dave Baker, Christian Wihtol, and Jeff Wright, who believed in my idea for the hike and allowed me the chance to share the trip with readers.

• The folks at the Eugene REI store, who listened, offered advice, and answered even the stupidest of questions without laughing.

• The four people who helped prepare my bad foot for the trip: Dr. James Buie, Dr. Donald Jones, orthopedic specialist Kathy Sherwood, and physical therapist Brian Gesik.

• Dr. Kraig Jacobsen, my allergist and mastocytosis expert, who cared enough to give me his cell-phone number and "call-anytime" permission.

• Dean Rea and Lou Rea, who proved once again to be stellar copy editors. (Any litter still left on the trail belongs entirely to me.)

• Dan Roberts, Paul Neville, and Theresa O'Brien, who read my original draft and helped me get back on the trail after I'd wandered off.

• Deena Welch and Marolyn Tarrant, who edited the near-final draft.

• Carrie Petersen and Molly Petersen, whose PCT presence with me was far too short, but will always remain part of the trip.

- The Aussies, Ben and Kate, PCT veterans who took the time over three days to welcome a couple of newbies to the trail.
- The folks at Callahans Mountain Lodge, who gave Glenn and me all the respect they gave their formally attired wedding guests.
- Mike Jones, a fishing guide at Odell Lake's Shelter Cove, who duct-taped my boots and, more importantly, splashed much-needed humor on our summer afternoon.
- The good folks at Big Lake Youth Camp, who provided a great afternoon of rest, replenishment, and a blessed shower.
- MaryEllen Fitzgerald, a special-uses permit administrator with Mt. Hood National Forest, for delivering the alternative route when the Dollar Lake Fire closed the PCT.
- Beachside Writers Workshop students, who infuse me with inspiration each time we meet in our beloved Oregon coast hub of Yachats or on the McKenzie River.
- Dale Bradley, who touched me deeply with a song he wrote, "Generations," based on my book, *A Father for All Seasons*—a song that inspired me as I wrote *Cascade Summer*.
- Mark Isham, whose music for *A River Runs Through It,* did the same.
- Tom Penix, a great designer and an even greater friend, who worked meticulously for months to create the book's wonderful cover and interior maps.
- The CIA, which, in 2004, funded a company called Keyhole, Inc. to create a software program that later would become Google Earth, which allowed me to follow the trail from the sky as I researched and wrote the book. How cool is that?

And, finally, to the five people whose sacrifices made the difference between success and failure:

- Roadrunner (Baerbel Steffestun) and Cisco (Rich Combs), whose willingness to lead us through the snow—and to adopt me for three days—saved our journey.
- Sally Welch and Ann Petersen, who not only read and edited the manuscript—in Ann's case, twice—but were with Glenn and me at trail's start, Eagle Creek, in 1974; with us at trail's end in 2011; and have been with us every step of life's hike in between.
- And, finally, to my partner in climb, Glenn Petersen: navigator, leader, joke-taker, foot-fixer, quiet inspirer, and, above all, friend.

From mosquito-bitten head to blistered toes, I am grateful to you all.

Book club guide

Ralph Waldo Emerson was right. Every experience leaves us differently than it found us, even reading a book. In that spirit, here's a list of questions whose intent isn't to belabor my story but to illuminate your own:

- 1. "In the woods," says Emerson, "is perpetual youth." Do you agree with this quote the author used? If so, what is it about the wilderness that brings out such youth? What evidence was there that Bob and Glenn pined for that sense of youth? And did they find it?
- 2. Welch writes that the hardest times for him were getting ready in the morning and having to fetch water at the end of a day's hike. If you were to attempt a similar hike, what might you find the hardest thing? What would you hate to give up? What item would you *have* to bring?
- 3. When Glenn gets sick, Bob worries about what to do. Did he make the best choice? Place yourself in his boots. Also assume cell coverage was unavailable. What would you have done?
- 4. Among the gobs of advice that the two gathered prior to their leaving was this: "Hike your own hike." What do you think that means? What, if any, application can be made to our broader lives?
- 5. Early on in the book, the author suggests his biggest fear is "the fear of failure." How would you define fear of failure? How can such fear

stymie us in life? How can we overcome it?

◆ 6. Mountains. Snow. Fire. Weariness. Blisters. Illness. The trail was full of obstacles. Choose one of those five challenges and use it as a metaphor for your own life. What lesson or lessons might you take away from the Oregon Boys' hiking experience?

◆ 7. Given your choice, when would you rather be hiking in the Cascades: today or in Waldo's era of the late 1800s and early 1900s? Why?

◆ 8. Why bother telling the stories of long-gone people like John Waldo? What's the value in understanding the past? What lesson, if any, did you learn from Waldo?

◆ 9. Early in the journey, Bob has an interaction with Roadrunner at a Mazama Village that changes his perspective. Discuss that interaction. What did he learn about himself from it? How did it change the trip for him?

◆ 10. Glenn's decision to take his daughters to Diamond Lake—and have Bob team up with Cisco and Roadrunner—proved pivotal. But some might see his decision as a defeat. Was it? Why or why not?

◆ 11. In some ways, this is a book about friendship, not only between two men who were already close but also between those two men and some of the strangers they met. How was the Oregon Boys' friendship tested? How did they benefit from their friendship? The friendship of others?

◆ 12. Welch alludes to the pull of his father on a number of occasions, most dramatically in Bob's quest to find Comma Lake on the ten-year anniversary of his dad's death. What is the tie that seems to bind men and their fathers? Is the daughter-father relationship different? If so, how?

◆ 13. Initially, Waldo was not credited with being the protector of the Cascades that he ultimately proved to be. And yet he never clamored to set the record straight. Why do you think he did so little to toot his own horn? Was his attitude consistent with what you see in our culture today?

◆ 14. Waldo wrote of how, beyond the Cascades, there were "other beauties around me: a beautiful sweet wife, a wise little daughter, and a home of light." Is there a danger in becoming too tightly bound to nature and the outdoors? If so, what is that danger, how do you avoid it, and why should you avoid it?

◆ 15. An adventure, remember, doesn't necessarily need to be physical.

As Glenn pointed out with his Webster reference, an adventure is "a bold undertaking in which hazards are to be met and the issue hangs on unforeseen events." What adventure have you pined to undertake? What's keeping you from doing so?

To contact the author:
web site: bobwelch.net
email: bobwelch23@gmail.com

Made in the USA
Columbia, SC
20 June 2023